Praise for *Cultural Intelligence: A Blueprint for 21st-Century Leadership*

"In *Cultural Intelligence: A Blueprint for 21st-Century Leadership*, Dr. Harden positions cultural intelligence as an essential leadership skill for driving innovation and success. Through case studies and a practical, actionable framework, the book guides leaders in developing skills to lead multicultural teams effectively. Dr. Harden demonstrates how cultural intelligence delivers benefits from improved teamwork to new market opportunities while providing straightforward strategies for embedding CQ into organizational culture. This must-read equips leaders with the tools and confidence to foster inclusive, high-performing teams in today's global landscape."
—**Douglas Pflug**, author of *Ironwill 360° Leadership: Moving Forward – 12 Emerging Trends for Forward-Thinking Leaders*

"*Cultural Intelligence: A Blueprint for 21st-Century Leadership* redefines how leaders approach diversity, equity, and inclusion by turning theory into actionable solutions. With reflective prompts, real-world case studies, and adaptable strategies, this book offers a hands-on framework for fostering cultural intelligence and creating inclusive environments. Packed with tools and resources, it challenges readers to think deeply, act intentionally, and lead with purpose, making it an indispensable guide for organizations committed to meaningful and lasting transformation."
—**Nancy Marmolejo**, CEO, TalentAndGenius.com

"Dr. Harden's *Cultural Intelligence: A Blueprint for 21st-Century Leadership* masterfully presents a comprehensive framework for developing cultural intelligence (CQ) through cognitive, emotional, and physical dimensions. With its well-structured chapters featuring theoretical foundations, case studies, and practical exercises, this timely work addresses critical leadership gaps in today's workplace. Drawing from solid data and real-world applications, Dr. Harden provides an essential toolkit for leaders seeking to build inclusive cultures and enhance organizational effectiveness, making it an indispensable resource for modern leadership development."

—**Carmen D'Arcangelo, Founder, The Justice Together Project**

"This transformative book on cultural intelligence delivers essential insights for modern leadership, offering clear and actionable strategies for thriving in diverse environments. Dr. Harden's emphasis on emotional engagement, psychological safety, and paradoxical thinking presents a compelling framework that balances traditional leadership approaches with inclusive methods. Her focus on leading with compassion rather than control, coupled with practical tools for self-reflection and cross-cultural understanding, makes this book an invaluable resource for leaders seeking to create a positive impact across various professional settings, from classrooms to courtrooms."

—**Craig Sims, Attorney, Schroeter Goldmark & Bender (Seattle)**

"Dr. Harden masterfully teaches leaders what cultural intelligence is and how to develop their CQ to become the best kind of leaders, those that others want to emulate and staff willingly follow. Through vignettes addressing common cross-cultural workplace tensions across industries, leaders gain practical strategies while learning to appreciate and utilize diverse perspectives within their workforce. This book provides the essential blueprint for leaders across the globe seeking ways to improve their businesses."

—**Caprice D. Hollins, Psy.D., Co-Founder of Cultures Connecting, LLC**

CULTURAL INTELLIGENCE

A Blueprint for 21st-Century Leadership

Dr. Kimberly Harden

ALLYSHIP
Publishing, LLC

Copyright © 2025 Kimberly Harden

All rights reserved.

No part of this publication may be reproduced

This publication is designed to provide accurate and authoritative information regarding the subject matter covered. It is sold with the understanding that the publisher is not rendering professional services. If legal

The web addresses referenced in this book were live and correct at the time of the book's publication but may be subject to change.

Library of Congress Cataloging-in-Publication Data

Cultural Intelligence: A Blueprint for 21st-Century Leadership / Kimberly Harden

ISBN: 979-8-9914940-0-7 (paperback)

ISBN: 979-8-9914940-1-4 (ebook)

Library of Congress Control Number: 2024918634

Printed in the United States of America

To Barbara Crook,
whose boundless generosity and compassion embody the
essence of cultural intelligence. Your leadership is a constant
source of inspiration, illuminating the path forward.

"The measure of intelligence is the ability to change."
— Albert Einstein

Contents

Foreword	XI
Preface	XIII
How to Use This Book	XVII
Introduction	XXI
Part 1: Unveiling the Power of Cultural Intelligence: Its Significance and Relevance	1
1. CQ Foundations	3
2. Cultural Values: Dimensions and Differences	39
3. The Strategic Advantage of CQ	67
4. The Culturally Intelligent Leader's Mindset	97
Part 2: Navigating the Dimensions of Cultural Intelligence: A Deep Dive	123
5. Developing Cognitive CQ Discernment	125
6. Cultivating Emotional CQ Across Cultures	161
7. Physical CQ: Developing Behavioral Agility Across Cultures	195
Part 3: Harnessing Cultural Intelligence: Strategies for Inclusive Leadership and Sustainable Success	215
8. The Growth Journey: Strategies for Developing CQ Leadership	217
9. The Power of CQ in the Workplace	241
10. Sustaining Organizational Commitment to CQ	277

Conclusion: Heed the Call	299
Acknowledgments	301
Appendix	305
References	345
About the Author	373

Foreword

As CEO of Maxwell Leadership and with over 25 years of experience in leading and developing teams around the world, I've had a unique opportunity to observe how important culture is for the success of any business. Dr. Kimberly Harden's book *Cultural Intelligence: A Blueprint for 21st-Century Leadership* arrives at a pivotal moment.

A common temptation for leaders is to prioritize technical skills and industry knowledge above other areas. I've come to learn that more is needed in today's interconnected world, which is what I love most about this book! Dr. Harden reminds us of our critical need for cultural intelligence (CQ)—a competency that extends beyond traditional diversity and inclusion efforts. The personal experiences and insights Dr. Harden shares make a compelling case for CQ as a necessary skill for any leader aiming to excel in our globalized society.

Information is widely accessible today. On the other hand, practical applications to help you implement the knowledge you gain are scarce. Dr. Harden goes beyond theory and hypotheticals to provide actionable strategies and real-world examples that leaders can immediately practice in their organizations. Whether you're at the helm of a small team or a multinational corporation, the principles and practices outlined in this book will equip you to navigate cultural complexities, foster innovation, and create truly inclusive environments where everyone can contribute their unique strengths.

As a leader who has guided companies through various challenges, I can attest to the transformative power of culturally intelligent leadership. This book will help you navigate the complexities of your organization and the world in which you do business. It's not just about building better businesses—it's about creating a more understanding and harmonious world. A world where we complete one another rather than compete with one another. A world where we lift each other up rather than tear each other down. I believe it's possible if we all do our part.

Many businesses are facing increasing pressure to reconcile internal cultural conflicts. Technology is growing rapidly. Society is shifting. The need for adapting and integrating diverse cultural perspectives is more critical than ever. This book is a comprehensive guide for navigating these challenges, offering leaders a road map to cultivate a resilient and adaptive organizational culture. By fostering an environment that values diverse experiences and viewpoints, leaders can harness the full potential of their teams and drive their organizations toward unprecedented growth and innovation. It is with great confidence that I recommend this book to any leader who is ready to grow personally, professionally, and organizationally.

Mark Cole
Owner & CEO of Maxwell Leadership

Preface

As a Leadership and Culture consultant and a former professor of Communication Studies, I have observed our world's growing cultural complexity and interconnectedness. Navigating this terrain, whether in classrooms or in boardrooms, is no longer a choice—it's a necessity. This shift demands new competencies that foster unity, understanding, and adaptability. Chief among these is cultural intelligence: the ability to navigate and connect across different cultural contexts. Cultural intelligence is not limited to understanding race or gender; it includes the intersectionalities of identity—ethnicity, socioeconomic background, abilities, and more. In today's globalized world, having this competency is essential.

Moments of exclusion or bias, like one I experienced during my career, vividly illustrate the critical need for cultural intelligence in leadership. During a team meeting at a healthcare organization where I worked, I shared my insights on a project, only to be interrupted by a senior leader who said, "Who do you think you are, Michelle Obama?!"

The room fell silent, and I felt a mix of shock, anger, and humiliation. The comment was not only disrespectful but also carried racist and sexist undertones that reflected an underlying resistance to my presence and contributions as a Black woman. It was clear to me that if this senior leader treated me, his colleague, in this way, then patients and families from historically marginalized communities probably faced similar or worse treatment.

This experience was a turning point. It sharpened my understanding of the critical role cultural intelligence plays in fostering inclusive leadership. It also sparked a broader conversation in the organization, which led the CEO to reinforce the importance of creating an environment where everyone's perspectives are valued. The senior leader was required to apologize to me and attend cultural sensitivity training.

This incident underscored a truth I had long understood: Creating inclusive workplaces requires more than good intentions. It requires action, accountability, and the tools to bridge cultural gaps. Witnessing these challenges firsthand inspired me to found Harden Consulting Group, LLC, where I help organizations develop cultural intelligence and build cohesive, high-performing teams.

Cultural intelligence is the foundation for creating workplaces where innovation thrives. It's about moving beyond surface-level diversity initiatives to embrace the unique strengths, perspectives, and experiences that every individual brings to the table. By focusing on the collective knowledge and wisdom, organizations can create environments that drive creativity, productivity, and growth.

That journey is not without its challenges. But the costs of neglecting cultural intelligence are immense: Businesses lose innovation, collaboration weakens, and employees become disengaged. Educational institutions that fail to address disparities in dropout rates among marginalized groups limit societal progress and leadership diversity. But there is hope! By developing cultural intelligence, we can create workplaces and communities where everyone can flourish.

This journey requires commitment, humility, and a willingness to engage in self-reflection. We must incorporate lessons for both the mind and the heart. True growth happens when we lead with intentional strategy and compassion.

With this book, I aim to guide you on a journey of cultural enrichment by equipping you with practical tools and insights to bridge divides and foster transformation. You'll learn how to cultivate self-awareness, lead teams through change, and build organizational cultures rooted in equity and belonging.

Together, we can create a world where cultural intelligence isn't just a concept but also a lived reality. Join me as we explore the principles and practices that will inspire meaningful change—for ourselves, our teams, and our organizations.

How to Use This Book

This book is a comprehensive roadmap for developing and leveraging cultural intelligence in professional settings. It offers a blend of theoretical knowledge and practical applications designed to meet the needs of diverse readers. Wherever you find yourself on the spectrum of cultural leadership — novice or expert, local or global — there's something here to advance your skills. The insights and strategies presented are tailored to help you navigate the complexities of our multicultural business landscape with confidence and competence.

This book can be used in various ways, depending on your needs and preferences:

- As a self-study guide for individual leaders seeking to enhance their CQ and leadership effectiveness

- As a resource for leadership development programs or workshops in organizations

- As a basis for discussion and shared learning in a book group or peer learning circle

Organization

The book is divided into three main parts, followed by an appendix of key resources:

Part 1 (chapters 1–4) unveils the power of cultural intelligence, exploring its significance and relevance in today's world.

Part 2 (chapters 5–7) takes a deep dive into the dimensions of cultural intelligence, providing a thorough understanding of how it applies in the cognitive, emotional, and physical realms.

Part 3 (chapters 8–10) focuses on harnessing cultural intelligence for sustainable success and inclusive leadership; it offers practical strategies and techniques for developing and implementing CQ in yourself, your team members, and your organization.

The Appendix provides additional tools, resources, and references to empower your CQ journey and support ongoing learning and development.

Case Studies

Each chapter includes a case study that illustrates the concepts and strategies discussed in the chapter. These case studies can be approached in different ways, delineated below.

1. Read the chapter first, then read the case study, and finally, reflect on the questions provided. This approach allows you to gain a solid understanding of the concepts before applying them in a real-world scenario.

2. Start with the case study and questions; then go back and read the chapter for more background and explanation. This approach may be more engaging for those who prefer to learn through concrete examples and problem-solving.

3. Use the case studies and questions as a starting point for discussion in a book group or leadership development program.

Regardless of your approach, the key is to engage with the material, reflect on your own experiences and challenges, and commit to ongoing learning and practice.

For group learning and seamless organizational implementation, visit www.hardenconsultinggroup.com for a complete facilitator's guide. This resource offers structured activities, dynamic discussion frameworks, and practical tools to help leaders and trainers foster transformative learning experiences that build cultural intelligence.

Introduction
The Imperative of Cultural Intelligence

Hello, and welcome to *Cultural Intelligence: A Blueprint for 21st-Century Leadership*!

In today's complex and interconnected world, cultural intelligence (CQ) has become a critical skill for leaders and organizations. Although diversity, equity, and inclusion (DEI) are essential to CQ, CQ goes beyond traditional DEI efforts. Whereas DEI focuses on creating fair representation, treatment, and opportunities for all, CQ equips us with the mindset and skills to effectively navigate and leverage diversity to come up with answers that are unique and advantageous.

Put simply, CQ is the capability to appreciate, adapt to, and leverage cultural differences for more effective interactions and relationships across diverse contexts. It equips us with the awareness, skills, and agility to navigate the complexities of our multicultural world with sensitivity and savvy.

But let's be honest: Developing cultural fluency can be challenging, especially with so many voices and perspectives competing for our attention. That's where this book comes in. It's here to provide practical, actionable strategies and tools to help you successfully develop cultural intelligence in any workplace environment, thereby giving you the confidence to navigate cultural complexities more easily.

Why CQ Matters

Consider these scenarios:

1. A company launches a new product with a marketing campaign that resonates in one market but fails to gain traction in others. What went wrong? —The company didn't adapt its approach to different cultural preferences and norms.

2. A manager leading a diverse team finds that her communication style leaves some team members feeling unheard and undervalued. By developing her CQ, she learns to adjust her approach, leading to improved collaboration and engagement.

3. An organization introduces a new policy without considering how it might affect employees with different backgrounds, abilities, or life experiences. As a result, the policy creates barriers and inequities. By applying a CQ lens, the organization can create more inclusive practices that work for everyone.

These examples illustrate why CQ is crucial in today's landscape. Without CQ, organizations face risks such as miscommunication and conflict among teams, difficulty attracting and retaining top talent from different backgrounds, missed opportunities in new markets, and reputational damage from cultural missteps.

Conversely, culturally intelligent organizations reap significant benefits:

- Improved collaboration and innovation
- Higher employee engagement and retention
- Enhanced ability to navigate complex global environments
- Stronger customer relationships and brand reputation

Becoming a Culturally Intelligent Leader

Developing CQ starts with self-awareness. Leaders must examine their own biases and assumptions and how these influence their behavior and decision-making. Doing so requires humility, curiosity, and a willingness to step outside one's comfort zone.

Next, leaders need to actively seek out diverse perspectives and experiences. This might involve engaging with communities different from their own, participating in cross-cultural training programs, or conversing with colleagues and involved parties from various backgrounds. The key is to listen with empathy and an open mind.

As leaders gain cultural understanding, they must apply it to adapt their leadership style and practices. Imagine yourself as a social scientist, decoding different communication styles (direct vs. indirect), understanding both individualistic and collectivist mindsets across cultures, and making adjustments as needed. It's like being a chameleon, blending in seamlessly and making everyone feel valued.

Organizational Implications

Developing CQ requires systemic change at the organizational level. Leaders must examine their organizations' policies, practices, and culture to identify and address any barriers to inclusion. This might involve reassessing recruitment and hiring processes, providing learning and development opportunities, and/or creating employee resource groups to support and empower diverse communities.

Leaders must also model CQ and hold others accountable for creating an inclusive environment. This requires ongoing commitment, not just one-off initiatives.

Metrics matter, too. By tracking representation, equity, and inclusion data, organizations can pinpoint areas for improvement and measure progress.

The Business Case for CQ

Investing in CQ is the right thing to do, and it's good for business. Companies with inclusive cultures tend to outperform peers in innovation, profitability, and customer satisfaction, meaning they're better positioned to thrive.

The Path Forward

Developing CQ is an ongoing journey. It requires continued learning, practice, and commitment. Key principles of CQ include:

- Embracing humility and curiosity
- Seeking out diverse perspectives
- Practicing empathy and active listening
- Adapting leadership approaches to different contexts
- Fostering an inclusive culture through systemic change
- Measuring progress and accountability

To support you on this journey, this book provides a comprehensive framework and practical tools for developing and applying cultural intelligence. Whether you're an executive, manager, team leader, or individual contributor, you'll find valuable insights and strategies to enhance your CQ and leadership effectiveness. As we embark on this exploration of cultural intelligence together, remember that the journey toward CQ is both personal and organizational. It's about transforming not just how we think and act as individuals, but how our entire organizations operate and thrive in a multicultural landscape.

Part 1

Unveiling the Power of Cultural Intelligence:

Its Significance and Relevance

Chapter 1
CQ Foundations
Understanding the Basics

In today's rapidly evolving and interconnected world, navigating cultural differences has become essential for success. As globalization continues to bring people from diverse backgrounds together, we face the challenge of effectively communicating, collaborating, and building relationships across cultural boundaries. This is where cultural intelligence, or CQ, comes into play. CQ is the capability to function effectively in culturally diverse situations, and it encompasses a set of skills and attributes that enable individuals and organizations to adapt to and thrive in multicultural environments.

Cultural intelligence is not just about understanding and appreciating different customs, traditions, and ways of life; it's also about developing the mindset and skill set to bridge cultural gaps and create meaningful connections. It involves recognizing our own cultural biases and assumptions, seeking to understand and empathize with others' perspectives, and adapting our behavior to build trust and rapport. By cultivating CQ, we can break down barriers, foster inclusive environments, and unlock the full potential of diversity.

In a world where businesses operate across borders, politicians serve diverse constituencies, and social movements transcend geographic boundaries, CQ has become a critical competency for success. Leaders with high CQ can see beyond surface-level differences and tap into the rich tapestry of human experience, harnessing the power of diversity to innovate, solve problems, and create value.

Developing cultural intelligence is not a one-time event but a lifelong journey of learning, growth, and self-reflection. In this chapter, we will explore the core elements of cultural intelligence and provide practical strategies for developing and applying CQ in various contexts.

Before we delve deeper into CQ, it's important to understand how it relates to other cultural concepts such as cultural awareness, cultural sensitivity, and cultural competence. Although these terms are often used interchangeably, they represent distinct stages in the journey toward cultural intelligence. Cultural awareness acknowledges differences, cultural sensitivity respects these differences, and cultural competence appreciates and adapts to these differences. Cultural intelligence, however, goes a step further by enabling individuals to effectively function in diverse cultural contexts. A detailed illustration of these concepts and their relationships can be found in the Appendix (see Figure 1). Whether you are a business leader or an engaged citizen, this book will equip you with the tools and insights you need to succeed in today's globalized world.

Accelerating Need for CQ in a Globalized World

Business, political, and social landscapes are becoming more diverse daily, with people from different backgrounds, generations, and ideologies interacting more frequently. This diversity brings both challenges and opportunities. On one hand, it can lead to misunderstandings, conflicts, and polarization if not managed effectively. On the other hand, it offers a gold mine of ideas, perspectives, and solutions that can drive innovation and progress.

So what's the key to navigating the challenges and opportunities of our diverse world? Developing your cultural intelligence capabilities! It's about building trust, empathy, and understanding in a world where these qualities are becoming both increasingly rare and valuable.

Let's first explore the business, political, and social imperatives that underscore the critical role of CQ in today's world. Then we will delve into the various aspects of cultural intelligence, including its definition, models, and the three key dimensions: cognitive, emotional, and physical. By understanding these imperatives and developing your CQ capabilities, you'll be well on your way to succeeding in an increasingly complex and interconnected global landscape.

Business Imperatives

Globalization has combined markets, workforces, and consumer behaviors into a complex network. Companies that effectively adapt their products, services, and messaging to local contexts gain a competitive advantage. Companies need to recognize cultural nuances to navigate uncertainties and take advantage of opportunities presented by this interdependence. Companies that can adapt their products or messaging to local contexts gain a competitive edge; those that don't can quickly become irrelevant.

Let me give you an example. Nimble "glocalization" strategies effectively balance efficient standard processes and tailored regional variants, enabling multinational corporations to cater to new demographics while expanding market share (Schilke et al., 2009). Platform infrastructure efficiency enables companies to offer tailored product flavors aligned with cultural preferences—it's like an intricate global–local dance that brings success in both markets and hearts!

CQ is also crucial for driving innovation and creativity through diverse perspectives and problem-solving approaches. Culturally intelligent talent recruitment, as is seen in diaspora hiring and international ambassador programs, enables organizations to access diverse language competencies and unique perspectives that foster creativity and innovation (Lanvin & Evans, 2018). Inclusive leadership, which cultivates trusted relationships across cultural intersections within and outside organizations, is essential for sustainable growth fueled by solidarity.

However, cultural misunderstandings and insensitivity can lead to significant risks and costs in business contexts. Companies must develop advanced scenario-planning capabilities that account for geodemographic impacts on supply chains to ensure organizational resilience during times of crisis. Multicultural advisory councils can provide early warning of political risks or (for instance) pandemic-related concerns in localized areas, helping companies navigate uncertainties and mitigate potential losses.

Political Imperatives

As societies become more divided, politicians must possess the skills and empathy to navigate differing priorities without compromising social cohesion. Adaptive policymaking that ameliorates local concerns while uniting communities across differences is crucial for promoting stability and progress.

CQ is also vital for promoting diplomatic relations and international cooperation on global challenges. Leaders with high CQ can build bridges across cultural and ideological divides to foster understanding and collaboration on issues such as climate change, poverty, and public health. Embracing diverse perspectives and finding common ground, culturally intelligent leadership has the potential to drive meaningful progress on the world's most pressing problems.

Moreover, restorative justice interventions, which emphasize collective healing rather than solely penalization, offer a powerful example of culturally intelligent policymaking (Daly, 2017). By providing skill training and transitional housing programs, these approaches promote rehabilitation and reintegration, thereby contributing to a more equitable and compassionate justice system.

Social Imperatives

In the social sphere, CQ is essential for building communities that welcome everyone for the different qualities they bring. To promote justice that is real and lasting, we have to understand that different people have different backgrounds and perspectives, and we must find a balance between fitting in with society and celebrating cultural diversity. Social movements and initiatives that embrace CQ can drive powerful change and reduce systemic inequalities. Fostering cross-cultural dialogue, understanding, and empathy can break down barriers and promote social justice. Solidarity networks that unite people across differences and provide support during times of crisis demonstrate the transformative potential of culturally intelligent social action.

Social media empowers us—it enables us to have an effect in real-time. Social media platforms provide tools for crowdsourced volunteering to support communities in need, whether by organizing childcare, elder assistance, or food deliveries during emergencies. Solidarity networks unite people regardless of differences; they join and strengthen us.

Do not overlook restorative justice programs that facilitate open dialogue between law enforcement and nonviolent offenders, offering a powerful example of culturally intelligent social intervention (Daly, 2017). These conversations focus on human needs and challenge institutional biases; they lay the groundwork for meaningful change and foster a more equitable and compassionate society. We can build the basis for real change through such conversations and active listening.

As our world becomes increasingly dynamic and interconnected, embracing CQ is not just a choice but a necessity. By coming together, confronting the mistakes of the past, and working toward a future where everyone can flourish without fear, we can harness the power of CQ to build a more just and inclusive world. The journey toward CQ begins with understanding its core elements and how they manifest in our daily lives and interactions. So: What is this cultural intelligence, exactly?

From Awareness to Intelligence

Let's start with a bit of history.

German psychologist Kurt Lewin pioneered cultural sensitivity training after World War II. At that time, his workshop for teachers and social workers to alleviate racial and religious prejudice began in earnest. Lewin's mission was not to simply become aware of different cultures but to actively put judgment aside by learning about experiences or stories that had historically been left out, potentially resulting in biases that cause unintentional harm; Lewin focused his energies on resolving social conflicts as well as on aiding minority and disadvantaged groups (Burnes, 2004).

Thanks to civil rights legislation, cultural awareness education picked up steam during the 1960s, over a decade after Lewin's death (Anand & Winters, 2008). Cultural awareness means being aware that differences exist among identity groups, even if we do not fully comprehend their impacts or how to respond (Rew et al., 2003). Unfortunately, cultural awareness education was criticized: Some saw it as too politically correct, and others did not believe that any tangible change would result from it.

The concept of cultural competence first took root in the U.S. during the 1980s, beginning with attempts to provide better care for minority children with mental health concerns (Cross, 1989) and then evolving into theories of intercultural nursing (Leininger, 1994). Cultural competence involves constantly increasing our knowledge of different cultures—their histories, values, communication styles, and power dynamics (Jirwe et al., 2009). Professionals who demonstrate cultural competence incorporate what they have learned into their actions and behaviors with marginalized individuals without expecting them to conform to the majority or mainstream culture. Instead, their goal is to provide intentional support by attuning to situations and creating equitable policies (Jirwe et al., 2009).

P. Christopher Earley and Soon Ang, business school professors, coined the phrase *cultural intelligence* to refer to a set of skills that empower diverse groups by combining paradoxical thinking with ethical adaptation and situational responsiveness. In other words, having CQ enables a person to navigate complex cultural dynamics.

Cultural intelligence builds upon concepts like awareness, sensitivity, and competence to create something even more significant: something that helps you move from simply "getting it" to making wise decisions in various cultural contexts (Earley & Ang, 2003). Now imagine being led by someone with cultural intelligence—someone who can manage multiple competing demands while gracefully and effectively handling even tricky ambiguities and simultaneously creating an inclusive and psychologically safe space. That's the kind of leader you can trust!

Defining CQ

Navigating complexity efficiently is critical for leaders today, in both a technical and a cultural context. Earley and Ang (2003) defined cultural CQ as "a person's capacity for adapting successfully to unfamiliar cultural settings" (p. 9).

Over time, CQ has been defined in various ways. According to Ang and Van Dyne (2008), CQ refers to "an individual's ability to function effectively in situations characterized by cultural diversity" (p. xv). According to Brooks Peterson (2018), CQ involves knowledge about cultures, self-awareness, awareness of others, and specific behaviors. Nosratabadi et al. (2020) defined CQ as "soft skills used by leaders working across cultures in communicating effectively in these environments" (para. 1).

Now let me provide my definition:

Cultural intelligence is all about appreciating, adapting, and capitalizing upon cultural differences to promote positive interactions and build cross-cultural relationships.

CQ raises our collective consciousness by making us more aware of each other for the benefit of all. Leaders with high CQ have a distinct advantage when it comes to navigating complexity, uniting people, and driving meaningful change. This benefit, in turn, has a direct impact on the bottom line.

Companies that prioritize CQ are better equipped to tap into new markets, attract and retain top talent from diverse backgrounds, and foster innovation by drawing on different ideas and perspectives. And when employees feel valued and included, they're more engaged, productive, and likely to stick around—all of which translates to a healthier, more productive organization. Given all this, CQ is a nonnegotiable for leaders and organizations looking to succeed in today's global economy. As we have already seen, it's not just a nice-to-have—it's a must-have.

By investing in CQ development, leaders will be able to navigate the complexities of a diverse workforce, build stronger relationships with clients and partners from different cultural backgrounds, and create a more agile and resilient organization that can adapt to change and thrive in the face of uncertainty.

Moreover, the benefits of cultural intelligence extend far beyond the balance sheet. Leaders with high CQ are more empathetic, compassionate, and effective communicators. They can bridge divides, build trust, and create a sense of belonging for all. By bringing diverse perspectives to the table and creating an environment where everyone feels heard and valued, they foster collaboration, creativity, and innovation.

The Cultural Intelligence Models

Cultural intelligence is about effectively handling diverse cultural situations. To better grasp it, researchers have identified key components of this competency. While various frameworks have emerged, this book relies on Earley and Ang's (2003) three-factor framework due to its comprehensive yet accessible approach to understanding and developing cultural intelligence. The framework divides CQ into:

1. Cognitive CQ: This involves cultural knowledge and understanding.

2. Emotional CQ: This covers empathy, confidence, and motivation, which are crucial for managing conflicts and building relationships across cultures.

3. Physical CQ: This involves adapting body language, greetings, or speech to fit various cultural norms—a crucial factor in managing conflict situations and fostering effective communication.

By focusing on these three core components, this book aims to provide a straightforward, practical approach to developing cultural intelligence. This simplified model allows for a more streamlined discussion of CQ while still capturing its essential elements, making it easier for readers to grasp and apply these concepts in their personal and professional lives.

CQ isn't just about knowing facts. It's also about forging genuine connections and understanding across groups. By cultivating CQ as part of leadership training, leaders can develop stronger relationships while closing gaps between people. Let's examine each factor—cognitive, emotional, and physical CQ—more deeply to understand its role. A visual summary of these three dimensions and their interplay can be found in the Appendix (see Figure 2).

Cognitive CQ: A Strategic Decision-Making Superpower

At its core, CQ is about understanding different worldviews, histories, and motivations and being culturally savvy enough to recognize how they affect perceptions, priorities, and communication styles. It's not about conforming—it's about embracing diversity of thought and making decisions that show respect for all perspectives and ways of being.

Imagine a company expanding into a new market that has a different cultural background. A leader with high cognitive CQ would take the time to research and understand the local customs, values, and communication preferences. They might discover that in this culture, building personal relationships is crucial for business success and that confrontation is avoided. With this knowledge, the leader can adapt their approach, build trust with local partners, and make strategic decisions that resonate with the target audience.

Dr. Wanda Evans-Brewer, founder and CEO of WandaLand Naturals, demonstrated cognitive CQ when she moved to Ghana and aligned herself with male elders. Understanding that Ghanaian society is highly patriarchal, Dr. Brewer recognized the importance of having the respect, approval, and protection of male allies who appreciate her goal of supporting the community by hiring local women who will, in turn, use the funds to support their families. By adapting her approach to the cultural context, Dr. Brewer effectively navigated the social hierarchy and built strong relationships that would help her achieve her business objectives while benefiting the community.

CQ helps leaders to become master synthesizers of information. Then they can quickly spot sensitivities or needs that others might miss. The resulting inclusivity is powerful. When leaders incorporate diverse information and perspectives into their decision-making, they avoid blind spots that might alienate communities or result in missed niche growth opportunities. Inclusivity brings people together and breaks down divisions to create strategies that work for everyone involved.

For instance, Bedrock Management Services, a real estate investment and development company owned by NBA team owner Dan Gilbert, launched a campaign with the slogan "See Detroit Like We Do" (Winowiecki, 2017). However, the banner featured a predominantly white crowd, which was a far cry from the reality of Detroit's demographics, with the city's population being approximately 80% Black. After receiving negative press, Dan Gilbert acknowledged that his organization "screwed up badly," called the campaign slogan "dumb," and removed the banner (Allen, 2017). A leader with high cognitive CQ would have been attuned to the potential impact of this ad on Black residents and would have taken steps to ensure accurate representation. They might have organized focus groups or conducted surveys to gather input from a diverse cross-section of Detroiters and used those insights to develop an ad campaign that genuinely reflects the city's population. By adopting a culturally intelligent leadership approach, Bedrock Management Services could have avoided alienating a large portion of its target audience and instead conveyed a message of inclusivity and understanding.

As adaptive leaders, we must consider cultural impacts before making strategic decisions. Stress testing various scenarios with reactions from diverse groups and perspectives helps us anticipate conflicting perceptions or risks and develop policies that align with different cultural values for optimum resonance. We must carefully consider cultural nuances beyond surface traits to craft outstanding go-to-market strategies, localization efforts, and contingency preparations. Doing this enables us to gain greater insight into diverse populations while ensuring our solutions are responsive to everyone's needs (rather than staying with the status quo) and inviting communities to help shape the ideas that affect them.

Culturally intelligent leaders also take proactive steps to ensure equitable decision-making by embedding cultural aptitude into their institutions, safeguarding inclusive deliberation, and preventing bias from creeping into their protocols. When they prioritize CQ, they create experiences tailored to each customer's needs and preferences while strengthening grassroots co-creation as an additional layer of legitimacy for different communities.

Think about it this way: Just as diverse people bring different ideas and perspectives to a table, leaders with high cognitive CQ can tap into multiple possibilities. By considering other people's experiences and viewpoints, they can avoid making assumptions and identify new opportunities through collaboration.

How can leaders foster an empathetic worldview? Recognizing cultural resonance and social responsibility is essential. Leaders can create an environment that encourages growth and creativity by showing respect for others while being empathetic regarding diversity.

CQ doesn't refer solely to one's intelligence; rather, it includes understanding and appreciating the collective potential of an organization with various people from diverse backgrounds. Leaders who acknowledge different viewpoints can gain a broader perspective on future developments and make more informed decisions. This journey demands continuous learning, curiosity, and empathy—but the benefits are well worth the effort.

Harnessing Cognitive CQ to Optimize and Decode

In today's fast-paced marketplace, successful marketing campaigns must go beyond simply targeting demographics. Instead, they must draw on cultural attunement to fully comprehend human motivation. This means entering collectivist communities and understanding what drives their values rather than just appealing to superficial considerations. By doing so, marketers can foster lasting loyalty and create deeper bonds with people.

Finding the right balance when communicating your message is crucial. Some cultures appreciate subtle, poetic messages with room for interpretation, while others require clear and direct instructions. Striking the perfect balance between nuance and clarity ensures that everyone involved will understand and receive your messages.

And let's not forget the power of visual cues in effective marketing! Carefully selected imagery, color symbolism, and presenter choices can make all the difference in avoiding potential disconnect or offense. It's truly fascinating how much meaning can be communicated through visuals and how culturally specific some of those meanings are. For example, the color white is associated with purity and innocence in Western cultures, but in some East Asian cultures, particularly China, Korea, and Vietnam, white is commonly associated with death, mourning, and funerals. However, this association is not universal across all Eastern cultures. In Japan, white is often associated with purity, innocence, and cleanliness, similar to Western cultural associations.

Leaders with high cognitive CQ are attuned to these cultural nuances and can adapt their visual messaging accordingly. They understand that what works in one culture may not work in another, and they're willing to research and understand the cultural context of their target audience. By taking a culturally intelligent approach to visual messaging, brands can create campaigns that resonate with diverse audiences and avoid unintentional offense or misunderstanding. This helps them build stronger relationships with customers and sets them apart as a brand that truly understands and respects cultural differences.

Personalization is also of utmost importance in global marketing; your core proposition must authentically and genuinely reflect cultural outlooks across regions. That means teaming up with grassroots community advocates and international influencers to create campaigns that diverse audiences will appreciate. This way, you'll respond intelligently to cultural shifts and form meaningful bonds that endure over time.

The bottom line is that diversity should be seen not as something to overcome but as an incredible opportunity. When you recognize and appreciate consumers' diverse natures, you'll be able to communicate more easily with them, build trust with them, and achieve competitive growth.

But that is only half the story. If you're aiming for actual effectiveness, grassroots immersion must also play a part. Showing that you care on that level will set you apart from those who offer only superficial hospitality. By patiently investing in interpersonal rapport, you can build reserves of goodwill that can serve you when inevitable disruptions come your way.

Cognitive flexibility is the secret weapon for comprehensively understanding cultural environments. It helps you design engagement strategies to fit various settings and leadership styles. Going beyond assumptions is the only way to unlock potential alliances across multiple cultures and contexts.

Master negotiators adept at managing cognitive complexity know when to be direct and when to embrace ambiguity. They can plan carefully to build confidence, even in an uncertain situation, while remaining open-minded enough for spontaneous discovery or serendipity. These masterful individuals unlock exponential value by code-switching across cultures and uncovering hidden opportunities at the intersections of diverse alliances.

Successful partnerships that overcome differences flourish when their foundation is cultural understanding. Seeking common ground, nurturing good faith, and going beyond mere transactions are hallmark activities for effective partnerships, and cognitive CQ provides the glue that holds strategic relationships together while connecting us all as humans.

Influencing Organizational Culture Through Cognitive CQ

Today's organizations are dispersed across various regions, and they have diverse teams of people from multiple backgrounds. To keep things running smoothly, we need leaders who can bring everyone together without forcing everyone to conform. The goal isn't homogenization—it's about cultivating a culture that embraces diversity while giving equal credit to every contributor.

At their core, these innovative leaders know they must rely on more than theoretical frameworks to understand various cultures. They dive in headfirst, immersing themselves in satellite operations while watching, learning, and understanding each environment's dynamics. They act like cultural detectives investigating the historical influences, family structures, power relationships, and influence dynamics that determine people's perspectives. This enables them to identify factors causing disconnects or collaboration issues between teams. And it isn't all numbers and statistics; successful leaders understand cultural nuances that data alone can't capture.

Cultural adepts know how to adapt. They know it's all about relevance and commitment rather than resisting change. But the awe-inspiring thing is how they avoid cultural missteps that could alienate critical hubs around the globe. They understand the value of cognitive discernment and that diversity brings innovation and creativity, and they champion belonging, coordination, and cultural contributions as intrinsic assets. All this adds up to a workplace where every employee feels respected, included, and empowered.

Remember: It isn't enough to view things through one cultural lens; the key to successful multicultural leadership lies in harnessing diversity's collective power and channeling it effectively through excellent management practices. That is when magic occurs!

Recommendations for Building Cognitive CQ

Cognitive CQ isn't something we are born with—it is acquired through intentional experiences and reflection. But how can you increase yours? Let's break it down.

1. Make an effort to immerse yourself in cross-cultural settings. Travel, or in some other way make connections between people from diverse backgrounds—you will learn so much!

2. Study essential frameworks like Hofstede's Cultural Dimensions, Trompenaars' Seven Dimensions of Culture, the Lewis Model of Cultural Types, Schwartz's Theory of Basic Values, and the GLOBE Framework of Cultural Dimensions (see Chapter 2 and the Appendix). Once you gain mastery, you'll be able to decipher cultural differences more readily; once it clicks, it becomes like possessing X-ray vision that enables you to appreciate all the cultural nuances around you.

3. Discover different cultures by reading books and watching films that explore them from multiple viewpoints. It will help deepen your understanding of other people—not to mention being an enjoyable way of expanding movie night options!

4. Take time to seek feedback from people from various cultures. This can be like having your own coach who helps you understand how your actions and words may be perceived differently in different cultural environments. Consider it an opportunity for growth and self-improvement!

5. Reflect upon your cultural experiences and interactions. Take some time to stop and think about how cultural differences influence your understanding and behavior. This will be like hitting "Pause" to gain

clarity into any assumptions or biases you might hold about others or yourself.

6. Be wary of making assumptions based on logic alone. Don't be afraid to question your beliefs and open your mind to new perspectives—mental gymnastics help broaden cultural horizons while inhibiting an exclusive mindset.

By honing your cognitive CQ skills, you will establish a firm basis for thinking more broadly and making culturally sensitive choices. Cognitive CQ will be discussed in greater detail in Chapter 5.

Emotional CQ: Understanding Its Impact on Relationships

Navigating the complex, ever-evolving landscape of diverse environments is no simple task, so understanding emotions and culture becomes vital to leaders looking to succeed in today's global environment. Emotional CQ can serve as an invaluable guide in doing just this. Emotional CQ goes far beyond being just another dimension of leadership; it serves as a special lens that helps leaders decode emotional subtleties that influence team dynamics, motivation, and organizational culture. Given that emotions underpin effective leadership practices, honing your emotional CQ should be considered not just any additional skill, though it is definitely that: It should be an imperative.

Let's embark on an expedition to uncover the immense influence of emotional CQ on leadership and team dynamics. Prepare to delve deep into three vital areas—motivation, team cohesion, and organizational culture—to explore how emotions mesh with cultural nuances to form the basis for effective leadership across diverse and multicultural settings.

Unlocking Motivational Potential Through Emotional Intelligence

As leaders in diverse organizations, our most crucial task is to guide progress by inspiring excellence. Developing our emotional CQ to navigate a multicultural reality means understanding subtle cultural nuances embedded in emotions so that we can build cohesion and purpose among disparate populations. We must go beyond traditional carrot-and-stick approaches when motivating our teams. We must recognize cultural norms that value duty, shared visions, and encouragement of one another as part of a collective effort.

Conversely, individualists who value autonomy, rewards, and skill-building shouldn't be forgotten; each person may find inspiration differently. For example, in a team with members from both individualistic and collectivistic cultures, a leader with high emotional CQ might tailor their recognition and rewards system to accommodate both preferences. They might offer individual bonuses for outstanding performance while acknowledging the team's collective efforts and emphasizing how each member's contributions have helped the group succeed.

But we must also be wary of another factor. Exuberance may excite people from some cultures, but it might become overwhelming for those who prefer a more subdued style. Leaders must find that balance! Imagine a leader who is used to giving enthusiastic high-fives and loud praise for a job well done. Although this approach might work well in a culture that values overt displays of emotion, it could make team members from more reserved cultures feel uncomfortable or disrespected.

For example, though individuals from African cultures are often described as more expressive and emotionally open, it's crucial to recognize that Africa is a vast continent with numerous countries and diverse ethnic groups, each with its own unique cultural norms and values. Emotional expressiveness can vary depending on the context, such as personal relationships, professional settings, or public spaces. As leaders navigating a multicultural reality, we must approach cultural differences with nuance, curiosity, and a willingness to learn about the specific individuals and contexts we encounter. A leader with high emotional CQ would pick up on these cues and adjust their style accordingly, perhaps opting for a subtler yet sincere form of recognition.

Developing emotional CQ means taking the time to learn about different cultural norms and values and being willing to adapt our leadership style. Take the example of H&M, a well-known clothing retailer, which faced severe backlash in 2018 after featuring a Black child model wearing a hoodie with the phrase "coolest monkey in the jungle" on its UK website (Hardy, 2018). The use of the term "monkey" in reference to a Black person is a highly offensive and racist trope with a long and painful history. A leader with strong cognitive CQ would have immediately recognized the potential for harm and taken action to prevent it. They would have engaged a diverse team, including members of the Black community, to gain insights into how the imagery and language might be perceived. By considering these different perspectives, the leader could have made a more culturally appropriate choice, such as selecting a different model or altering the hoodie's design, to avoid reinforcing hurtful stereotypes and offending customers.

Leaders with high emotional CQ can build stronger relationships with diverse parties, from customers and partners to investors and regulators. They can anticipate and mitigate cultural misunderstandings or conflicts and find creative solutions that bridge divides and create value for all. As leaders, we must regularly identify and address any unnoticed biases in our teams or organizations. Performance feedback must align with cultural preferences without unintentionally discouraging team members; any ethnocentric criteria that might impede minority groups from reaching their full potential should also be removed as quickly as possible, thereby making room for wonderful things to happen. The satisfying result is an inclusive environment where everyone feels included.

Consideration of different emotions and cultures can also foster equity and a sense of belonging. Bringing this attitude on board is like unleashing an superpower that's been restrained for far too long. By adopting an inclusive approach, we can maximize multidimensional capabilities and reach greatness together.

Developing emotional CQ is not a one-time task but a lifelong journey. It requires us to step outside our comfort zones, to listen with empathy and curiosity, and to learn and grow continuously. It's a commitment, but for leaders who are dedicated to thriving in a multicultural reality, it is an essential skill that can make all the difference.

So as we strive to inspire excellence in our increasingly diverse organizations, let us remember the power of emotional CQ. By understanding and embracing the cultural nuances of emotion, we can create a more inclusive, collaborative, and successful workplace for all.

Fortifying Team Synergy with Emotional CQ

As remote and multicultural team structures become the new normal, leaders must maintain productivity through practical leadership skills that transform diversity from a potential source of discord into a source of harmony.

Emotional CQ is the key. This concept is about understanding different communication styles, motivational needs, conflict resolution preferences, and even comfort levels regarding vulnerability. When leaders know how to navigate these differences successfully, friction between team members turns into synergy and collaboration.

But that is only part of it. Emotionally adroit leaders can recognize verbal and nonverbal cultural signals to understand the deeper meaning behind spoken words, the one that goes beyond their literal interpretation. That skill helps prevent all sorts of miscommunication. Someone appearing quiet during a meeting could be deep in thought rather than disengaged; showing deference toward authority might indicate respect rather than a lack of interest.

And now let's talk about praise. If it is to be effective, it must be offered appropriately. Different people value collective or individualistic recognition differently, and great leaders understand this and give credit where credit is due—in this way, they motivate and engage all team members equally. In addition, celebrating milestones together builds loyalty while keeping team motivation high and creating little parties within teams that bring people closer.

Differing opinions will come up on any team; that's simply life. However, great leaders don't shrink from these difficult moments. Instead, they act compassionately while giving everyone a voice. Rebuilding emotional bonds that may have been ruptured takes time, patience, and vulnerability, but in the end, it is well worth it—those debates become opportunities for reconciliation that foster creativity while keeping teams together through all types of storms.

Emotional CQ is the keystone of leadership that brings it all together. It requires leaders who know how to create cohesion across diverse organizations. And team-oriented organizations that embrace variability are the ones that bring true innovation. Through empathy, equity, and genuine respect for human dignity, emotionally intelligent leaders unlock the potential of their teams to realize greatness that lasts over time.

Shaping a Progressive Work Culture Through Emotional CQ

As organizational leaders, we have a growing global responsibility to foster workplace diversity. It's not just about recruiting diverse talent—it's about creating an environment where everyone feels respected, valued, and empowered to share their unique perspectives without compromising their authenticity. This requires exceptional emotional CQ, or the empathy and situational skills necessary to comprehend emotional dynamics within teams while dismantling subtle systemic barriers and creating a sense of belonging for everyone.

So, how can we become emotionally perceptive executives? The first step is to observe small behaviors and signals that indicate microinequities in our workplaces. We can watch employee interactions, review performance evaluations, and pay attention to informal social events or discussions. If discrepancies or disproportionate engagement levels among certain demographic groups arise, we must explore their causes. These could include biases in talent development processes, obstacles to achieving work-life balance, or assumptions that exclude specific individuals without realizing it. For instance, a company might inadvertently exclude working parents by scheduling important meetings outside regular business hours. A leader with emotional CQ would recognize this issue and work to find more inclusive scheduling solutions.

As leaders, we need to adapt our responses to the situation at hand. Embracing restorative justice principles means members of minority groups have a safe space to share their experiences openly, which helps us better comprehend their viewpoints. However, we should also acknowledge when private assistance may be necessary to preserve individuals' dignity and prevent them from losing face. When it comes to creating inclusive cultures, no single solution fits all situations. I can't stress this enough. Co-creating solutions with those affected is vital to creating workplace equity; unilateral decisions made without considering situational knowledge cannot achieve that end. Through cultural and emotional discernment, leaders can establish an equitable workplace culture that goes beyond rules and policies.

Emotional CQ strengthens our sense of belonging through policies, symbols, and environments that unconditionally celebrate diversity. When leaders compassionately decode dynamic landscapes across demographic differences with nuanced understanding, they foster cultural progression within their organizations. This progression moves beyond reactive measures and creates an environment where diversity is actively embraced and leveraged as an asset. Just as cross-cultural emotional fluency and literacy are vital for creating global peace, culturally sensitive leaders are essential for paving the way to organizational equity and unity through diversity.

Remember, as leaders, our journey toward inclusivity is an ongoing one. It's a challenging but rewarding path—one that requires constant self-reflection, learning, and growth. But with empathy, adaptability, and a commitment to understanding and celebrating our differences, we can shape a progressive work culture that empowers everyone.

Recommendations for Building Emotional CQ

Developing emotional CQ requires experiencing, reflecting on our feelings about, and immersing ourselves in different cultures. Here are some practical steps for doing these things.

1. Immerse yourself in cross-cultural environments and pay close attention to emotional cues; become a detective of emotions.

2. Reflect on how you react and adapt emotionally as part of this self-awareness exercise; this will enable you to navigate cultural differences more effortlessly.

3. Use the insights into the intricacies of culture and communication styles by studying different cultural frameworks and models. It's like cracking open the secret codes of different societies!

4. Do not hesitate to seek feedback from people familiar with the culture you are exploring. Their expertise can provide invaluable in-

sights and help you to refine your interpretative abilities.

5. Before taking action, carefully evaluate your interpretations and assumptions to reduce the chance of making awkward gaffes or embarrassing faux pas!

6. Accept diversity not as a mere initiative but with genuine passion and create an inclusive and vibrant environment that starts with solid leadership.

Being adaptable, empathic, and insightful are core competencies required of the kind of leaders who create vibrant organizations bursting with diversity. Emotional CQ will be discussed in greater detail in Chapter 6.

Physical CQ: Manifestations in Cultural Interactions

Physical CQ is a critical tool for leaders who wish to succeed in our multicultural environment. It involves finely tuning nonverbal behaviors to connect with people from diverse backgrounds. Expanding your physical CQ will unlock doors to better communication, stronger relationships, and an appealing image, all crucial aspects of effective leadership in various environments.

Physical CQ in Effective Communication

Being an effective leader requires more than technical qualifications; it involves understanding human dynamics rooted in diversity and having the physical CQ to decode cultural codes that influence communication styles.

Imagine yourself at an international gathering. From introductions and gift exchanges to conversations, there are all these etiquette rituals you need to keep track of. Did you know that professional attire varies wildly across industries and religions? Even our choice of colors and accessories sends subtle signals—it's almost like speaking in coded messages that only leaders gifted in physical CQ understand. For example, in some Middle Eastern cultures, it's customary for men to wear long robes called thobes or dishdashas in professional settings. These garments are not only comfortable in the hot climate but also serve as a symbol of respect and modesty. Imagine the cultural faux pas you could make by wearing shorts and a T-shirt to a business meeting! A leader with high physical CQ would take the time to research and understand these cultural norms, ensuring they dress appropriately and show respect for their international colleagues.

But dressing the part is only half of it: Behavior is also crucial. We should mirror our group by adapting our posture and orientation while also being sensitive to everyone's comfort levels. Let's also be mindful that language is not only about words but also about body gestures. Different cultures have differing expectations regarding nonverbal communication cues such as vocal animation, posture and gestures, facial expressions, eye contact, and touch. Some cultures value restraint; others may expect more exuberant interaction.

For example, in Japan, maintaining eye contact for too long can be seen as aggressive or disrespectful, whereas in some Arab cultures it's considered a sign of trustworthiness and sincerity. A leader with high physical CQ would be aware of these differences and adjust their eye contact accordingly to build rapport and avoid misunderstandings.

Some cultures don't approve of touching between genders—not even handshakes. Imagine this scenario in a multinational tech company: During a team meeting, Sarah, a friendly American project manager, extends her hand to greet Akira, a newly transferred software engineer from Japan. Akira hesitates and awkwardly bows instead, leaving Sarah confused and slightly offended. She interprets his behavior as standoffish or even sexist. In reality, Akira's reaction stems from Japanese cultural norms, where bowing is the standard greeting, and physical contact, especially between genders in professional settings, is often avoided. This misunderstanding creates tension within the team, affecting collaboration and productivity.

A leader with high physical CQ would recognize this cultural difference and take proactive steps. They might:

1. Privately explain to Sarah the cultural context behind Akira's greeting.

2. Educate the entire team about various cultural greeting norms.

3. Implement a policy of asking team members about their preferred greeting styles.

4. Encourage open discussions about cultural differences to foster understanding and prevent misinterpretations.

By addressing this situation thoughtfully, the leader can transform a potential source of conflict into an opportunity for increased cultural awareness and team cohesion.

Understanding cultural nuances is essential for building strong connections. Such understanding is like a key that unlocks communication flows that would otherwise remain restricted. Going beyond mere translation and connecting on a sociocultural level is the key to creating shared goodwill that transcends transactions alone. We foster exchange and pluralism by being open and receptive to other cultures. At first, this may take some practice; eventually, however, these cultural considerations become second nature—you'll feel just as at home as diplomats at an international table!

Building Relationships Through Physical CQ

Physical CQ can be likened to dancing. Leaders with high physical CQ understand their cultural rhythm, moving gracefully and precisely. Imagine leaders with this level of awareness navigating cultural expressions smoothly while making sure their gestures align harmoniously with diverse cultural norms.

Physical CQ goes beyond gestures. It involves understanding the significance of personal space and understanding that intrusion into another's personal space may cause discomfort. For example, in Latin American cultures, people tend to stand closer together when conversing, whereas in Northern European cultures, people prefer more personal space. Adept leaders who excel in this dimension recognize the discomfort that can result from these variances.

As we all know, gift-giving can be tricky. Leaders with high physical CQ understand the nuances of giving presents with great skill, knowing their significance to the culture. Physical CQ, in this context, refers to the ability to navigate the tangible, nonverbal aspects of cultural interactions, including the exchange of physical objects like gifts. For instance, in China, giving a clock as a gift is considered taboo because the Chinese word for "clock" sounds similar to the word for "death." A thoughtful present can transcend language barriers to convey an essential message of goodwill across language barriers; culturally intelligent leaders understand which gifts might not resonate well culturally and work to ensure that their offerings convey the intended message.

Let's also remember social invitations. Whether at a business meeting or an informal gathering, leaders with high physical CQ understand that an invitation can take many forms, varying from straightforward and explicit approaches to indirect or nuanced ones. Consequently, these leaders adapt to these variations to ensure that their invitations are accepted warmly.

We aim to become leaders who can tap into cultural understanding. Building relationships through physical CQ means adapting to different cultures with ease, not just by mastering nonverbal cues but also by understanding the cultural history that shapes each interaction. Leaders who embrace physical

CQ can act like architects of connections, creating trust bridges across diverse terrains of global business. What could be better?

Now that we've explored how physical CQ can help build these strong cross-cultural relationships, let's dive into some practical recommendations for developing this essential skill.

Recommendations for Building Physical CQ

Building physical CQ may initially seem daunting, but it can be done with deliberate practice, focused observation, and cultural immersion. Here are some practical steps you can follow.

1. Identify and Acquire Culturally Appropriate Nonverbal Behaviors

    Pay close attention to body language, use of personal space, touch behaviors, and other nonverbal signals that vary between cultures, take note of any discrepancies from what you were taught during your upbringing.

2. Immerse Yourself in Different Cultural Settings

    Seek opportunities to immerse yourself in unfamiliar cultural environments through travel, events, restaurants, and neighborhoods. Watch how people greet each other, exchange gifts, and engage in conversation.

3. Practice Adaptive Code-Switching

    When meeting people from other cultures, intentionally adapt your nonverbal behaviors, such as gestures, proximity, and eye contact, to their cultural norms. Think of it as adjusting your body language for different environments!

4. Discover Cultural Dimensions Frameworks

Explore various aspects of cultural differences by analyzing comprehensive data and insights from cross-cultural research. Consider elements such as values, social norms, decision-making processes, and relationship dynamics across different societies. This holistic approach to understanding cultural nuances can provide valuable insights into how diverse cultures operate and interact.

5. Search for External Feedback

Please don't be shy about seeking external feedback from trusted advisers who are familiar with the cultures you interact with; they may provide valuable insight on areas in which your nonverbal communication needs to be recalibrated or, where misalignments exist.

6. Push Yourself

Break out of your comfort zone and put yourself into diverse environments that challenge you to adapt. Think of it as an exciting adventure—like attending an international conference that welcomes diverse cultures.

Remember, developing your physical CQ is an ongoing journey. Welcome the learning process with an open mind and be willing to adjust along the way. Soon, you'll become an expert at cross-cultural interactions! Physical CQ will be discussed in greater detail in Chapter 7.

Case Study: Masterpiece in the Making: Finding Common Ground at MoCA

Walt, the vice president of finance at Coastal Commercial Bank, recently took on the role of board chair at the city's Museum of Contemporary Art (MoCA). With an MBA focused on quantitative analysis, Walt is known for his data-driven approach to decision-making. Savannah, MoCA's CEO, comes from an arts education background and strongly believes in the museum's mission to engage the community and showcase thought-provoking art.

During a recent board meeting, Walt pushed Savannah to set more metric-driven goals around visitors and donations to ensure the museum's financial sustainability, rather than focusing on qualitative ones that emphasize cultural resonance. "We need to focus on increasing our visitor numbers and securing more high-value donations," Walt insisted. "These are the key performance indicators that will ensure the museum's financial sustainability."

Though she understood the importance of financial stability, Savannah stressed that the museum's success should not be measured solely by numbers but also by its impact on the community and its contribution to the city's cultural fabric. Savannah, visibly frustrated, responded, "Walt, I understand the importance of financial metrics, but we can't lose sight of our mission to engage the community and showcase thought-provoking art. Our success isn't just about numbers; it's about our impact on people's lives and the cultural fabric of our city."

As the discussion heated up, board members exchanged uneasy glances. It became clear that Walt and Savannah's differing perspectives created tension and hindered effective collaboration. As the debate grew tense, both Walt and Savannah realized they needed to find a way to bridge their perspectives and work together to create a balanced approach that would ensure the museum's long-term success.

Case Study Questions

1. Given their vastly different perspectives, how could both Walt and Savannah adjust their leadership approaches to collaborate more effectively with each other? What specific steps could each of them take to bridge their differences and find common ground?

2. How could Walt's tendency to prioritize quantitative metrics over Savannah's emphasis on cultural resonance present collaborative challenges?

3. How can Walt shift his perspective to find a balance between financial sustainability and expanding the museum's cultural significance?

4. What steps can Walt take to develop his cultural intelligence and better understand the value of qualitative goals in the arts and culture sector?

5. How might Walt and Savannah work together to create a balanced set of goals that satisfies both financial and cultural objectives?

Case Study Resolution

When creating inclusive cultures, no single solution fits all situations. After the board meeting, Walt and Savannah agreed to have open and honest conversations to help them understand each other's perspectives better. Savannah shared examples of how engaging the community and showcasing compelling art had increased visitor numbers, media attention, and donor interest in the past. She also highlighted that the museum's cultural impact had attracted new corporate sponsors and grants.

Walt, in turn, recognized the value of the museum's cultural objectives and worked with Savannah to create a financial plan that allocated resources to support community engagement and artistic innovation. He also suggested leveraging the museum's cultural impact to attract new donors and create innovative fundraising campaigns.

Through their collaboration, Walt and Savannah developed a shared vision for the museum that balanced cultural and financial objectives. They set key performance indicators that measured the museum's financial health and cultural impact and worked together to communicate this vision and share updates with the board, staff, and community.

By demonstrating culturally intelligent leadership, Walt and Savannah found common ground and created a stronger, more sustainable future for the Museum of Contemporary Art. Their partnership served as a model for how leaders with diverse backgrounds and perspectives can work together to create meaningful change and impact.

Advancing Your Leadership Journey

Reflection Questions

1. What are some of your cultural biases and assumptions, and how might they affect your interactions with people from different cultural backgrounds? What steps can you take to mitigate the impact of these biases and assumptions on your development of cultural intelligence?

2. Reflect on a time when you experienced a cultural misunderstanding or faced a challenge in a cross-cultural situation. What did you learn from that experience, and how can you apply those lessons to future interactions?

3. What aspect of cultural intelligence—cognitive, emotional, or physical—would you identify as most important for leaders to develop? Why? Provide an example of a situation where developing this aspect of cultural intelligence would enhance your leadership effectiveness.

4. Identify a specific culture you would like to learn more about and outline a plan for immersing yourself in that culture through travel, study, and/or local experiences.

5. What strategies seem most immediately feasible for embedding cultural intelligence practices into your organization's leadership and employee levels? What potential challenges might you encounter when implementing these strategies, and how could you overcome them?

Practical Application Activity

Commit to expanding your cultural intelligence.

- Conduct a Cultural Intelligence Inventory

1. Over the next month, document daily cross-cultural encounters and interactions, noting where you excel or struggle across dimensions of CQ. In particular document:

a. Cognitive CQ – interactions demonstrating nuanced cultural understanding or gaps.

b. Emotional CQ – your emotional reactions and regulation in various contexts.

c. Physical CQ – instances in which individuals change their gestures and behaviors in response to external stimuli or feel disconnected.

2. Additionally, consider studying another culture significantly different from your own:

a. Read an authoritative book that covers its history and cultural values.

b. Attend a local community event or shared meal to gain firsthand exposure and experience.

c. If you have spent time abroad, write down any observations, reactions, or assumptions of yours that were challenged during your time abroad.

3. After one month, distill all your documented experiences into key insights about your strengths, blind spots, and goals for improving your cultural intelligence. Share this assessment with a peer or mentor as an accountability measure.

As we wrap up this foundational overview of cultural intelligence, let's crystallize some key insights.

Key Takeaways

1. CQ has become a critical competency for success in business, politics, and social spheres. Developing CQ enables individuals and organizations to navigate diverse cultural contexts effectively, build strong relationships, and drive positive change.

2. CQ goes beyond cultural awareness and competence: It is the capability to adapt successfully to unfamiliar cultural settings by leveraging cognitive, emotional, and physical dimensions. Leaders with high CQ can integrate diverse perspectives, manage cross-cultural emotions, and align their behavior with cultural norms.

3. Cognitive CQ enables strategic decision-making by considering multiple viewpoints and avoiding cultural assumptions. Emotional CQ fosters motivation, strengthens relationships, and promotes inclusive cultures. Physical CQ facilitates rapport-building through adaptive nonverbal communication and respect for cultural norms.

4. Developing CQ is a lifelong journey requiring continuous learning, self-reflection, and growth. By embracing cultural intelligence as a core competency, individuals and organizations can position themselves for success in an increasingly diverse and interconnected world.

When we understand and develop these core elements of cultural intelligence, we lay the foundation for effectively navigating cultural value dimensions and differences, which we'll explore in the next chapter. Get ready to surprise yourself with your new insights!

Chapter 2

Cultural Values: Dimensions and Differences

As the world becomes more interdependent, leaders like you must navigate increasingly complex cultural forces. This challenge can feel like sorting through and assembling multiple puzzle pieces from countless societies, national values, ethnic traditions, generational differences, and identity group experiences.

Culture is an integrated set of beliefs, rituals, symbols, and norms that shape different social groups. It acts like an invisible force guiding everyday routines and communication among us, leaving outsiders seeking to understand its complexities. But it does not have to be a mystery to us: By applying cultural intelligence principles and engaging in open dialogue, we can better navigate this intricate cultural web and foster mutual understanding.

Developing cultural intelligence is so worth it on many levels, including but not limited to your organization's financial bottom line. Later in this chapter, we will look at how fostering cultural intelligence is a win–win proposition with many different kinds of benefits. It's never too late to learn and grow in this crucial area of leadership. With your new, deeper understanding of culture's dynamics, you'll be empowered to build bridges, unlock new opportunities, and bring out the best in yourself and your diverse teams.

Cultural intelligence means being open-minded when navigating different cultural systems, rather than making quick judgments based on our biases. It means that we have to put ourselves in other people's shoes and understand their cultural outlook—even if it differs drastically from our own. At its core, successful international engagement hinges on building bridges between cultures and creating mutual understanding.

Culture's Building Blocks

Culture is passed from generation to generation. It gives rise to distinct social groups—each with its own secret language—and provides us with our shared cognitive framework. A number of different conceptual frameworks have been designed to categorize cultural systems and identify areas where they vary; some cultures prioritize social harmony, while others place greater importance on direct communication or rigid schedules. Although these frameworks don't always accurately portray cultural logic, they help us gain insight into this topic.

Subverting the conventional iceberg metaphor, I prefer depicting culture as a tree to emphasize its organic, interdependent, and living essence. My Roots of Culture Model highlights the deep foundational aspects of culture while showing its capacity for branching into different co-cultures. This arboreal analogy perfectly captures the dynamic nature and growth of culture over time. A detailed visual representation of this model and its components can be found in the Appendix (see Figure 3).

Being new to any culture can be confusing and disorienting to someone who is not from the group; it's like entering an entirely unfamiliar universe with its own unspoken rules or, on a more intimate scale, like trying to understand a puzzle without all its pieces. Luckily, the frameworks that some experts have developed can help us to more thoroughly understand cultural forces such as our shared needs for security, identity, and growth, and anthropologists have identified economic cycles, governance procedures, and relationship patterns that can be recognized across cultures; these are extremely helpful lenses through which we can decode all these differences between societies.

At this point, though, do let me add one warning: These frameworks may be helpful, but we must use them carefully to avoid putting people into boxes or making assumptions based on culture alone. Let us not use cultural diversity as an excuse for exclusionary policies—cultural diversity is complex and should not be understood as one culture being superior to another. Please use these frameworks with consideration and be mindful of cultural diversity all around us when using them; they should *never* be used to exclude or stereotype people.

That said, there is still value in trying to understand cultural differences. Two famous anthropologists, Clifford Geertz and Geert Hofstede, have conducted remarkable research in this area: Geertz examined political systems, communication norms, and religious assumptions that shape daily lives, and Hofstede analyzed global survey data to uncover systematic differences across cultural dimensions, such as power distance, uncertainty avoidance, and individualism versus collectivism.

Let's delve deeper into these cultural mapping schemas, which can serve as road maps as we try to navigate this vast and diverse world.

Examining Cultural Forces Through Systemic Spheres

Clifford Geertz (1973) offered several helpful categories that enable us to understand why different groups behave the way they do. His framework is focused on uncovering the hidden cultural forces that shape behavior and social institutions, so it offers valuable insights into the various spheres that shape cultural influence. By examining these spheres, we can better understand the underlying factors that contribute to developing and maintaining cultural norms, values, and practices. Let's look at Geertz's definitions of cultural influence spheres.

Political systems include governance models, decision-making policies, the norms of power hierarchies, and the principles according to which conflicts are revolved. These systems establish the rules and guidelines for exercising authority and ensuring fairness within a given culture. They are crucial in determining who holds power, how decisions are made, and how disputes are resolved.

Economic forces, including production, distribution, trade, and commercial activities, also follow cultural paths. How a culture understands ownership and what the factors are that motivate entrepreneurial activity can vary significantly across societies. Understanding these economic forces is essential for navigating the complexities of global business and fostering sustainable growth.

Social ecosystems, which include relationships, family and community dynamics, and expectations based on factors such as gender, age, and caste, give us insight into how groups form and maintain strong ties. These ecosystems also encompass acceptable norms and status-signaling rituals, which can vary widely across cultures.

Communicative modes, such as dialects, accents, vocabularies, idioms, and slang, are another critical aspect of cultural influence. How thoughts are exchanged and meaning is created can differ significantly among individuals and groups. When exploring these communicative modes, it is important to consider how truth is established and the purpose behind articulation.

Epistemological foundations, which pertain to how knowledge is acquired and validated, define the sensemaking journey within a given culture. Educational practices and assumptions about fact versus fiction can vary greatly, and cultures may clash when confronted with issues such as data privacy and ethical research norms.

Finally, **belief systems**, including orientations toward purpose, supernatural and metaphysical concepts, and theological ideologies, shape a culture's understanding of reality and guide individual actions. These webs of thoughts, values, and convictions give rise to assumptions about humanity's place in the universe and the nature of moral principles.

By examining these spheres of cultural influence, leaders can better understand the factors that shape cultural norms and practices. This knowledge is essential for navigating the complexities of cross-cultural communication, helping to create inclusive environments, and driving positive change in our increasingly interconnected world.

Hofstede's Cultural Dimensions

And now let me introduce Geert Hofstede. This cross-cultural psychologist's empirical research quantified cultural differences with astounding precision. Imagine: He conducted surveys with over 100,000 participants from 50 different nations, all working for IBM—a truly extensive multinational effort!

Let's dig deeper. Hofstede's Cultural Dimensions Framework provides incredible insights into how national cultures vary across countries, so let's examine his six core dimensions. A visual representation of this framework can be found in the Appendix (see Figure 4).

Hofstede's Cultural Dimensions Framework

1. *Power distance* measures the extent to which less powerful members of a society accept and expect that power is distributed unequally. Hierarchy is clearly established and accepted in high power distance cultures, whereas low power distance cultures strive for equal distribution of power and demand justification for inequalities. High power distance cultures, such as that of Malaysia, for instance, have leaders commanding subordinates who respect formal authority. In contrast, in low power distance Nordic cultures, for example, everyone gets an equal say, organizational pyramids are flatter, and everybody has equal rights—which creates an entirely different playing experience!

2. *Uncertainty avoidance* refers to a culture's tolerance of unpredictability and ambiguity. High uncertainty avoidance societies such as Portugal often prioritize playing it safe with structured procedures, expert consultation, and gradual change. In contrast, in Singapore, people embrace uncertainty head-on while improvising along the way—they might be considered risk-takers!

3. *Individualism vs. collectivism* measures how much cultures emphasize personal choice and recognition as opposed to communal obligations. Individualistic cultures like Australia typically emphasize personal autonomy. In Colombia, in contrast, team goals and working together are central elements.

4. *"Masculine" vs. "feminine"* qualities does not refer to gender bias but rather to how a culture emphasizes traits traditionally associated with masculinity (e.g., competitiveness, assertiveness) versus femininity (e.g., modesty, work-life balance). Japan, for instance, tends to value dominance and assertiveness—traits traditionally associated with masculinity—whereas Denmark prioritizes collaboration and empathy, relying more on cooperation, traits traditionally associated with femininity.

5. *Long-term vs. short-term orientation* is another critical dimension, covering cultures' focus on the future, ease of adaptation, traditions, and instant gratification. Countries like China and South Korea value persistent long-term goals. In contrast, countries like Kenya and the U.K. value seizing the moment and immediate gratification more highly.

6. *Indulgence vs. restraint* measures different cultures' willingness to enjoy the pleasures of leisure versus promoting strict self-discipline. Latin American countries such as El Salvador and Ecuador lean toward indulgence; Singapore in Asia exhibits more restrained behavior than its Latin American counterparts. It's fascinating to observe how work cultures fluctuate between rigidity and laxness accordingly.

Hofstede's early critics claimed that his framework was too simplistic. But later researchers verified the statistical relationships between Hofstede's dimensions and essential things such as leadership, innovation, and social indicators, so Hofstede was onto something important here; he paved the way for quantifying cultural differences or, as I call it, this cultural intelligence foundation.

Beyond Hofstede: Complementary Cultural Models

Hofstede was unquestionably the go-to expert when it came to understanding different cultures; his system for quantifying cultural differences between nations was revolutionary in its day. But other frameworks have been proposed as well.

The Global Leadership and Organizational Behavior Effectiveness (GLOBE) research program, initiated in 1994, was an ambitious project that brought together 160 scholars to study societal culture, organizational culture, and attributes of effective leadership across 62 cultures (House et al., 2004). This long-term program surveyed 17,000 middle managers from diverse societies to identify what made different cultures tick.

The project's primary goal was to conceptualize, operationalize, test, and validate a cross-level integrated theory of the relationship between culture and societal, organizational, and leadership effectiveness. To achieve this, the GLOBE Project expanded on Hofstede's ideas to create a comprehensive framework for understanding cultural differences. It developed nine cultural dimensions, providing a more nuanced approach to analyzing cultural variations and their impact on leadership and organizational behavior. A visual representation of this framework can be found in the Appendix (see Figure 5).

The Nine Dimensions of the GLOBE Framework are:

1. **Power Distance** measures how a society views and accepts power inequalities and hierarchical structures.

2. **Uncertainty Avoidance** assesses how comfortable a society is with ambiguity and unpredictability.

3. **Institutional Collectivism** evaluates the degree to which societal institutions encourage collective action and resource sharing.

4. **In-group Collectivism** measures individuals' loyalty and dedication to their immediate groups or families.

5. **Gender Egalitarianism** examines a society's efforts to minimize gender-based discrimination and promote equality.

6. **Assertiveness** evaluates how much a society values assertive, confrontational, and aggressive behaviors in social interactions.

7. **Future Orientation** assesses a society's focus on long-term planning and delayed gratification.

8. **Performance Orientation** measures the extent to which a society values and rewards excellence and continuous improvement.

9. **Humane Orientation** evaluates how much a society encourages and rewards kindness, altruism, and generosity.

The GLOBE Project went beyond Hofstede's research by exploring different value sets and practices that shape cultural mentalities. Its findings revealed fascinating disparities between cultural values and practices, particularly in areas like gender equality. Many cultures espouse gender equality in principle, but their practices often diverge significantly from this ideal.

The team measured these cultural dimensions and studied various leadership styles and their connection to cultural orientations. They discovered that cultures that prioritize performance tend to favor charismatic leaders, whereas those emphasizing teamwork and collaboration respond better to team-oriented leadership styles. These interconnections demonstrate the nuanced relationship between cultural values and practical leadership approaches.

The GLOBE Project's significance lies in its enormous global sample, its generation of ideas and concepts that go beyond Hofstede's original framework, and its distinction between values and practices. Its robust model adds depth and color to our understanding of national and organizational cultures, offering valuable insights for developing global leaders and for navigating cross-cultural business environments.

Trompenaars' Seven Dimensions of Culture Model, developed by Fons Trompenaars and Charles Hampden-Turner (1997), takes an unconventional approach to understanding cultural differences. Rather than using statistical scores as units of analysis, it examines reconciliation dilemmas. It uses them to dive deeper into cultural conflicts—for instance, by contrasting rules with relationships or analysis with holistic intuitions. The Appendix provides a comprehensive illustration of this model and its key dimensions (see Figure 6).

This model identifies seven fundamental dimensions of culture:

1. **Universalism vs. Particularism:** This dimension contrasts cultures that prioritize rules and standards (universalist) with those that emphasize relationships and exceptional circumstances (particularist).

2. **Individualism vs. Communitarianism:** Similar to Hofstede's dimension, this one refers to whether a culture prioritizes individual needs and achievements or group harmony and collective goals.

3. **Specific vs. Diffuse:** This dimension examines how deeply people get involved with others' lives. Specific cultures keep work and personal lives separate, whereas diffuse cultures see overlap between these spheres.

4. **Neutral vs. Emotional:** This dimension explores whether cultures encourage the open expression of emotions or value more controlled and reserved behavior.

5. **Achievement vs. Ascription:** This dimension examines whether status is accorded based on individual achievements or on factors like age, class, gender, or education.

6. **Sequential vs. Synchronic:** This dimension refers to how cultures perceive and manage time—either as a linear sequence of events or as a synchronous, circular process.

7. **Internal vs. External Control:** This final dimension examines whether cultures believe they can control their environment (internal) or are more fatalistic and adaptive to external circumstances (external).

What sets the Trompenaars model apart is its focus on reconciling these seemingly opposing values. Rather than viewing cultural differences as fixed points on a spectrum, Trompenaars argues that effective cross-cultural leadership involves integrating and harmonizing these apparent contradictions.

For example, in the universalism vs. particularism dimension, a leader might find ways to uphold general rules while allowing flexibility in special circumstances. This approach acknowledges that most cultures value both principles to some degree, and that the key to effective leadership lies in balancing and integrating these values rather than choosing one over the other. The model also emphasizes the importance of context in cultural interactions. It suggests that cultural preferences can shift depending on the specific situation, further highlighting the complexity of cross-cultural dynamics.

By providing this nuanced view of cultural differences, the Trompenaars model offers valuable insights for leaders who are navigating diverse global environments. It encourages a more flexible and integrative approach to cross-cultural leadership by moving beyond simple categorizations to a deeper understanding of how cultural values interact and can be reconciled in practice.

The Lewis Model of Cultural Types, developed by Richard Lewis in 1996, provides insights into human behavior and personality across cultures. It categorizes cultures into three main types: Linear-active, Multi-active, and Reactive. These categories correlate with the Thinking, Feeling, and Action dimensions and offer a comprehensive framework for understanding cultural differences. A detailed visual representation of this model can be found in the Appendix (see Figure 7).

The **Thinking Dimension**, represented by Linear-active cultures, is characterized by a logical, structured approach. These cultures tend to be task-oriented; they value planning, punctuality, and direct communication. They often separate personal and professional life, prioritize facts and logic, and display limited body language. Examples of Linear-active cultures include Germany, Switzerland, and the United States.

The **Feeling Dimension**, correlated with Multi-active cultures, emphasizes emotional expressiveness and social relationships. These cultures are people-oriented, expressive in their communication, and flexible in their approach to time and plans. They often blend personal and professional life, value diplomacy over direct truth-telling, and are comfortable with interruptions and multitasking. Examples include Italy, Spain, and many Latin American countries.

The **Action Dimension**, associated with Reactive cultures, focuses on reflection and harmony in interactions. These cultures prioritize listening over speaking, value indirect communication, and emphasize patience and respect in relationships. They tend to hide their feelings, avoid confrontation, and take a long-term view of goals and relationships. Examples of Reactive cultures include Japan, China, and many East Asian countries.

The Lewis Model's strength lies in its taking a comprehensive view of these dimensions rather than looking solely at isolated traits. It recognizes that although individuals and cultures may have dominant tendencies, they can also exhibit traits from other dimensions depending on the context.

Understanding these cultural tendencies can give leaders significant insights into strengths, blind spots, and developmental needs across diverse teams. This awareness can help leaders navigate cross-cultural interactions more effectively by tailoring their communication style, feedback approach, and motivation strategies to resonate with different cultural orientations.

For example, when working with Linear-active team members, a leader might focus on clear, logical explanations and structured plans. With multi-active team members, they might emphasize relationship-building and allow for more flexibility in schedules. For Reactive team members, they might prioritize listening and indirect communication, giving time for reflection before decision-making.

The Lewis Model provides valuable insights into cultural tendencies, but it's important to remember that these are generalizations. Individual personalities and experiences can lead to variations within cultures. The model serves as a guide for understanding and adapting to cultural differences but should be applied with flexibility and openness to individual nuances.

Ultimately, the Lewis Model complements other cultural dimensions discussed earlier, providing a nuanced perspective on the interplay between cultural influences and behavioral tendencies. By applying this model, leaders can enhance their cultural intelligence and create more inclusive, effective cross-cultural work environments.

Next, let's examine the Schwartz Theory of Basic Values (Schwartz, 1999, 2012), which offers a comprehensive perspective on cultural values based on extensive surveys conducted in 80 countries. Schwartz identified ten core values recognized across cultures, organized into four higher-order value categories. This model explores the relationships between values, practices, and individual choices to provide a nuanced understanding of cultural priorities. A visual representation of this framework can be found in the Appendix (see Figure 8).

The ten fundamental values identified by Schwartz are:

1. **Self-Direction:** Independent thought and action

2. **Stimulation:** Excitement, novelty, and challenge in life

3. **Hedonism:** Pleasure and self-indulgence

4. **Achievement:** Personal success through demonstrating competence

5. **Power:** Social status, prestige, and control over people and resources

6. **Security:** Safety, harmony, and stability of society and relationships

7. **Conformity:** Restraint of actions likely to upset or harm others

8. **Tradition:** Respect and commitment to cultural or religious customs

9. **Benevolence:** Preserving and enhancing the welfare of one's in-group

10. **Universalism:** Understanding, appreciation, and protection for all people and nature

These values are organized into four higher-order categories:

1. **Openness to Change:** Self-Direction, Stimulation, Hedonism

2. **Self-Enhancement:** Achievement, Power

3. **Conservation:** Security, Conformity, Tradition

4. **Self-Transcendence:** Benevolence, Universalism

The arrangement of these categories reveals inherent tensions between competing values, highlighting the dynamic nature of value systems and explaining why certain values may be prioritized over others in different cultural contexts or individual situations.

Openness to Change vs. Conservation: This pairing illustrates the conflict between values that emphasize independence, readiness for change, and self-direction (Openness to Change) and those that stress self-restriction, preservation of traditional practices, and protection of stability (Conservation).

Self-Enhancement vs. Self-Transcendence: This pairing captures the opposition between values that prioritize the pursuit of one's interests and personal success (Self-Enhancement) and those that emphasize concern for the welfare and interests of others (Self-Transcendence).

In addition to these individual-level value categories, Schwartz's framework includes three cultural-level dimensions:

1. **Embeddedness vs. Autonomy:** This dimension contrasts cultures that view people as embedded in collectivity with those that see people as autonomous entities.

2. **Hierarchy vs. Egalitarianism:** This dimension addresses how societies ensure responsible behavior that preserves the social fabric through unequal distribution of power and resources or through voluntary cooperation for everyone's welfare.

3. **Mastery vs. Harmony:** This dimension explores humankind's relation to the natural and social world, contrasting active self-assertion to master the environment with acceptance and fitting in with the world.

By examining these various dimensions and values, Schwartz's model provides a nuanced understanding of how cultural values shape societal priorities, behaviors, and institutions. It illuminates the underlying drivers of cultural differences and offers insights into potential areas of conflict or compatibility between different value orientations.

For leaders operating in cross-cultural environments, grasping these value categories and cultural dimensions is essential. It enables them to tailor their leadership styles, communication methods, and organizational practices to the prevailing values of various cultural contexts. Identifying potential conflicts between differing value orientations is crucial for managing diverse teams and resolving disputes stemming from conflicting cultural priorities.

As we noted about the Lewis Model, Schwartz's model provides a broad perspective on cultural values; but it's important to realize and acknowledge that individuals within any culture can differ significantly in their personal values. The model serves as a foundational framework for grasping cultural tendencies, but it must be used with an awareness of individual variations and of the intricate, evolving nature of cultural values in our globally interconnected world.

Examining Cultural Models Critically

Cultural frameworks provide us with glasses through which to perceive societal differences more clearly. Still, we must remain aware of the risks of oversimplification, stereotyping, and adherence to dominant paradigms.

Quantifying culture on a national scale can obscure our vision of the vibrant diversity in nations. Immigrant subcultures often have values that differ from those of their host country, and generational shifts are continually altering identities in ways we cannot predict; failing to notice those would be like looking at a rainbow and missing the fact that it is made up of so many colors! So let's pay attention to intersectional exclusion.

Here's something that's worth remembering: Early conceptual models were highly biased toward Western paradigms and disregarded less individualistic societies as "deficient." Talk about ethnocentric thinking! Unfortunately, this bias perpetuated harm by reinforcing systemic inequities that are still present in institutions. Let's focus on decolonizing our methodology—it matters!

But let us also add some layers to this discussion. Culture does not completely define us. Gender, sexual orientation, religious affiliation, and global diasporas are some of the other factors that play a part in how we identify ourselves. Intersectionality reminds us to elevate marginalized groups without tokenizing them. Human psychology is far more nuanced and varied than can be captured with cultural stereotypes alone; each individual brings different experiences and influences into their unique human way of being, so let's treat each other as whole, dignified people rather than labeling people based on cultural background.

Applying CQ

We've now looked at several different models of CQ. Our goal is to apply them to how we work and interact. Let's take a look at how cultural intelligence affects global organizational leadership.

CQ can be defined as your "culture reading" ability; it's what enables you to comprehend the inner dynamics and subtle nuances of various cultural contexts. More than just theoretical knowledge, this is about personal growth and self-awareness. CQ emphasizes metacognition and reflection—meaning that before engaging others, cross-cultural leaders need to reflect upon their assumptions and biases to gain understanding of diverse viewpoints.

Not just a simple tool, communication is also a powerful catalyst in building bridges across cultural differences. Tailoring your communication style to match others' cultural beginning points is key in avoiding miscommunication and developing stronger bonds. This includes being aware of verbal and nonverbal cues that might cause offense or misinterpretations, and it can significantly contribute to trust-building and creating inclusive environments.

As leaders and teams collaborate, they harness the power of diversity. This fosters innovation and generates shared value. When you integrate different thinking styles, breakthroughs can develop quickly, letting you push limits further while supporting systemic transformation.

Decoding the Leadership Impact of Cultural Dimensions

Now that we've seen some of the things we need to keep in mind when looking at these frameworks, let's dive in and discover more about the implications of Hofstede's dimensions for leadership.

1. **Power distance:** This refers to how communication is approached across cultures. High power distance cultures focus on clear, direct messaging from leaders to subordinates: Two-way dialogue and consultation are encouraged in lower power distance environments. Adjust your leadership style accordingly. Forcing consensus in high power distance cultures, for example, may not be effective.

2. **Uncertainty avoidance:** Change management is a formidable challenge, but accounting for different cultural perspectives toward uncertainty can help. When diving into modernization initiatives, cultures with strong uncertainty aversion prefer structured road maps and careful planning, whereas low uncertainty avoidance environments embrace agile sprints and iterative learning. You must determine each culture's risk tolerance and adjust your approach accordingly.

3. **Individualism vs. collectivism:** When evaluating performance, instead of focusing solely on individual productivity, consider collaborative outputs from collectivistic cultures. And when rewarding your team, consider profit

shares for collectivistic cultures and individual bonuses for individualistic ones.

4. **"Masculine" vs. "feminine" qualities:** In "masculine" cultures, leaders are expected to be assertive, decisive, and focused on material success; in feminine cultures, they are expected to be more consensus-oriented, intuitive, and focused on quality of life. Leaders who understand these differences will adapt their styles to meet their teams' expectations.

5. **Long-term vs. short-term orientation:** Long-term-oriented cultures encourage persistence, and short-term-oriented cultures tend to strive for quick wins. As a leader, you will want to tailor the delivery of value to the local cultural sense of urgency rather than attempting to implement sweeping redesigns all at once.

6. **Indulgence vs. restraint:** Leaders should cater to the cultural values of enjoyment or discipline when setting productivity norms and expectations. Team events can provide the perfect balance, from structured, disciplined efforts to creative collaborations.

Understanding and embracing these cultural dimensions is not just about knowledge—it's about adaptability. It's about rising above one-size-fits-all policies in our leadership and aligning our communication mediums, giving developmental feedback, and offering workforce incentives to create resonance. It's about altering our pace and social environments to meet the predominant cultural codes. This artful approach is what brings the magic of cultural intelligence alive!

Applying CQ Across Industries and Sectors

Although cultural models like Hofstede's were initially developed for large corporations, they have also proved invaluable across other fields of work. From healthcare, academia, and diplomacy to humanitarian work and public policy, the approach to understanding and embracing diversity has taken hold and had a significant impact.

Healthcare leaders must ensure that their staff can demonstrate empathy and understanding toward migrants who are unfamiliar with medical jargon. We're talking about respecting cultural standards regarding touch, eye contact, and such issues as whether the provider is of the same gender. It's also important to consider religious-based diets. Customer-centric hospitals pride themselves on offering tailored care that goes beyond an institutional approach.

University leaders have the crucial task of creating welcoming classrooms that cater to international students who might need to become more familiar with educational norms in a foreign country. This is not just about effective communication; it's also about considering diverse perspectives and unspoken assumptions about critical thinking. We want to address these issues head-on. And let's remember first-generation students. Administrators need to ensure that student support services are adaptable enough to alleviate any unique difficulties these students might be experiencing because of family obligations, financial constraints, or other unique issues.

In the same way, **diplomats** must use their cultural intelligence to navigate tricky diplomatic situations and challenging circumstances. Diplomats should know how to effectively manage conflicts while empathetically understanding historical grievances and avoiding any misunderstandings that might result from projecting their own personal cultural biases onto others. In an era filled with tensions, the resilience provided by such an approach becomes even more necessary.

Nonprofit-sector professionals understand that strengthening local communities is of the utmost importance. That means working closely with partners on solutions that meet community needs and mitigate any existing or emerging obstacles—for instance, by providing funding support structures that meet intersectional needs rather than catering only to block segments of demographic groups.

CQ also plays an integral role in **technology**. Take mobile app design, for example. Tech firms must consider emotional and sociocultural dimensions when developing apps to ensure they resonate with people from various cultures and generations. Software engineers need to seek input from a range of diverse user communities, while consumer insight teams must also gather local advice to ensure their ideas meet cultural expectations.

Finally, **public administrators** are responsible for striking the ideal balance between efficiency and collective care. They should consider every constituent's needs when making infrastructure upgrades that benefit everyone equally rather than only specific neighborhoods. They must also consider socioeconomic class differences, diversity issues, and other significant cultural aspects that influence community life.

Navigating Turbulence With Discernment

Let's face it: We're at a crossroads, and it's high time we address the unequal access of historically marginalized communities. We're talking about unfair policing, sneaky microaggressions, and unequal healthcare services. We must roll up our sleeves and work together to build a society that's equal, fair, and free from all those shenanigans that contribute to disparities. But in all the chaos, there is good news too: We can counter the sensationalist rumors fueling prejudice and division by spotlighting everyday intercultural harmony and celebrating shared characteristics to create events where everybody's welcome (except for extremists—they need to stay home!).

Diverse teams lead to a broader market reach. They also contribute to better decision-making, enhanced problem-solving, and more effective conflict resolution by bringing various viewpoints and experiences to the table. Moreover, organizations that prioritize the values of diversity and inclusion are seen as more ethical, progressive, and socially responsible. This emphasis, in turn, leads to improved employee performance as individuals feel valued, respected, and motivated to contribute and do their best. Greater retention is another advantage, as employees are more likely to stay with organizations that foster a sense of belonging and provide equal opportunities for growth and advancement.

Let me be upfront: The journey of developing cultural intelligence is ongoing. It requires a lifetime commitment to open-mindedness, continuous learning, and adaptation of our approaches to different cultural contexts. There is no single "right" or "wrong" way, but rather a need to navigate the complexities of each situation with sensitivity and understanding. But in embracing this lifelong journey, we can cultivate a motivational vision that appeals to our consciences and awakens a sense of interconnectivity that breaks down barriers and unifies us as one community. This journey starts with us.

Case Study: The Quest for Inclusive Support at AutismConnect

Sonia, the founder of the nonprofit organization AutismConnect, had a vision of creating a supportive and inclusive community for individuals on the autism spectrum and their families. But despite her best efforts, Sonia realized that the organization's programs and services were not reaching the diverse range of people in the autistic community, particularly those from marginalized backgrounds.

During a community outreach event, Sonia met Lila, a single mother of an autistic teenage boy. Lila shared her struggles in accessing AutismConnect's resources arising from language barriers and cultural differences. "I appreciate what you're trying to do," Lila said, "but your programs don't really understand my family's unique needs and challenges."

Sonia realized that AutismConnect needed to bridge the gap between its intentions and the reality of the diverse autistic community it aimed to serve. She recognized that the organization's leadership, which was predominantly white and middle-class, might hold assumptions that differed from the experiences of the marginalized communities the organization wanted to support.

Case Study Questions

1. What steps can Sonia and her team take to create a safe and welcoming space where individuals and families from diverse backgrounds can share their experiences and needs?

2. How can AutismConnect ensure that its community listening sessions capture the full range of experiences and challenges faced by the diverse autistic community?

3. What strategies can Sonia's organization employ to co-design culturally sensitive and responsive programs and services with community members and invested leaders?

4. How can AutismConnect navigate the challenges that may arise when incorporating diverse cultural perspectives and values into its existing organizational structure and practices?

5. What metrics can Sonia's nonprofit use to measure the impact of its inclusive approach on the lives of individuals and families in the diverse autistic community it serves?

Case Study Resolution

To address the gap between AutismConnect's intentions and the reality of the diverse autistic community that was the organization's target audience, Sonia initiated a series of community listening sessions, inviting individuals and families from various cultural backgrounds to share their stories, needs, and aspirations. These sessions revealed a complex tapestry of experiences, ranging from the lack of culturally sensitive support services to the stigma and discrimination faced by autistic individuals in specific communities.

Armed with these insights, Sonia and her team collaborated with community leaders to co-design programs and services that incorporated the cultural wisdom and values of the diverse autistic community. They established a community advisory board composed of individuals with autism, family members, and community leaders from diverse backgrounds. The board had the authority to review and approve budgets, programs, and strategic plans, ensuring that the organization's efforts were genuinely inclusive and responsive to the needs of all those served. This power-sharing structure fostered trust, accountability, and a deep sense of partnership between AutismConnect and the communities the organization supported.

During these sessions, Sonia and her team listened with open hearts and minds as individuals and families shared their stories, challenges, and hopes for the future. They heard from parents like Lila, who faced language and cultural barriers in accessing support services. To address this hurdle, AutismConnect hired multilingual staff members and interpreters to help bridge the language gap and ensure all families could access the support they needed. The organization also partnered with local cultural associations to gain a deeper understanding of different communities' unique challenges and perspectives.

AutismConnect partnered with community leaders and organizations to co-design various culturally sensitive programs and services. It offered multilingual support groups, vocational training programs that respected cultural norms and practices, and social events that celebrated the richness and diversity of the autistic community.

As they navigated the challenges of incorporating diverse cultural perspectives into their organization, Sonia and her team remained committed to open communication, flexibility, and a willingness to learn and adapt. The community advisory board played a crucial role in guiding the organization's efforts, in that way ensuring that decision-making power was shared with the communities served and that resources were allocated to prioritize equity and inclusion.

Over time, AutismConnect became a beacon of hope and inclusion for the diverse autistic community in Seattle and beyond. The group measured its impact not only by the number of individuals and families served but also by the meaningful relationships and trust built with the supported communities. By embracing CQ and inclusive practices, Sonia and her team demonstrated the transformative power of listening, self-reflection, collaboration, and a genuine commitment to equity and justice.

Advancing Your Leadership Journey

Reflection Questions

1. Reflect on a time when you experienced a cultural misunderstanding or conflict in your personal or professional life. How might the cultural dimensions and models discussed in this chapter help you better understand and navigate similar situations in the future?

2. Consider the various cultural models presented in this chapter (i.e., Hofstede, Project GLOBE, Trompenaars, Lewis, Schwartz). Which model has a particular appeal for you, and why? How might you apply insights from this model to enhance your cross-cultural leadership effectiveness?

3. In what ways might your cultural background and experiences influence your leadership style and approach? How can you leverage your cultural self-awareness to build stronger, more inclusive teams and organizations?

4. This chapter emphasizes the importance of intersectionality and of recognizing identity's complex, multidimensional nature. How can leaders create a culture that celebrates and leverages diversity across multiple dimensions (e.g., ethnicity, gender, age, ability, socioeconomic status)?

5. Developing cultural intelligence is an ongoing process that requires a commitment to lifelong learning and growth. What steps can you take to enhance your CQ and to model cultural intelligence for others in your organization or community?

Practical Application Activity

Commit to developing cultural discernment.

- Conduct a cultural analysis of your organization.

1. Assess your organization's cultural orientation using various metrics, including power distance, uncertainty avoidance, and individualism/collectivism balance. Provide evidence that supports your assessment.

2. Name at least three subcultures that exist according to factors like roles, generations, or location, and identify the values or practices that define each subculture.

3. Conduct interviews with 3–4 individuals from various subcultures about their perspectives on the organizational culture. What insights or differences exist among the viewpoints?

4. Evaluate current leadership approaches. Where are they aligned or misaligned with cultural dimensions, and which changes could improve cultural intelligence?

5. Create 3–4 recommendations designed to assist leaders with adapting their communication style, motivational tactics, and approach to managing change so that they resonate more strongly across cultural groups.

6. Share your analysis and recommendations with peers/leadership to gain additional perspectives.

Now that we've discussed cultural dimensions and differences, let's review our key takeaways.

Key Takeaways

1. Culture is a complex web of beliefs, rituals, symbols, and norms that shape the behaviors and interactions of various groups. Understanding the intricacies of different cultural traits, such as power distance, individualism, and uncertainty avoidance, is crucial for effectively navigating diverse cultural landscapes.

2. Although cultural models provide valuable insights, it is essential to recognize the unique complexities of individual identities shaped by factors such as ethnicity, age, and diaspora status. Avoiding oversimplification and stereotyping is a critical piece of developing genuine cultural intelligence.

3. Leaders with high CQ can tailor their communication styles, motivate teams, and foster ethical cultures that ring true in local contexts. By adapting their approach to cultural norms and values, they build trust, promote innovation, and generate shared value across diverse cultures.

4. Developing CQ is an ongoing journey that requires leaders to confront their biases, challenge assumptions, and seek out diverse perspectives. By

engaging in continuous learning and self-reflection, leaders can effectively decode complex cultural forces operating in their teams and organizations to drive success in their respective fields.

Chapter 3

The Strategic Advantage of CQ

As we have already seen, our increasingly interconnected world means that we must be able to navigate cultural differences if we are to succeed. Cultural intelligence, the ability to function well in diverse global environments, has emerged as a critical competency for leaders, organizations, and teams seeking to adapt to and thrive in multicultural environments. And to embark on that path of CQ, we must first embrace three essential elements: self-reflection, a heightened sense of awareness of our surroundings, and a genuine appreciation for the multitude of perspectives that enrich our world.

CQ as a Strategic Leadership Capability

Culturally intelligent governance offers a path forward that involves finding a balance between acknowledging competing demands, cultural patterns, and decentralized community participation and giving agency back to local populations through decentralized participation. Without it, chaos could quickly reign supreme!

Let us take note of some wisdom from the African philosophy of Ubuntu. This philosophy emphasizes community interdependence and helps leaders avoid falling into false overconfidence when making predictions (Lutz, 2009). In our culturally sensitive governance, we should employ a more nuanced approach, upholding time-tested knowledge while welcoming innovation (Hofstede, 2001) and continually learning from the emerging voices of marginalized communities. This way, with our core values as a stable base, we can navigate turbulent waters while mitigating risky tendencies.

Understanding this, culturally intelligent leaders lead by example, modeling inclusive behaviors that ensure all hierarchy levels can participate and have their voices heard (Hirak et al., 2012). Teams that feel psychologically safe are generally more innovative, make better decisions, and are highly motivated (Frazier et al., 2017). Psychological safety must be achieved, and barriers anticipated before they even arise—this constitutes being proactive!

Emotionally engaging one's teams and involved parties is equally essential, with the leader acting as the glue that binds everything together. Culturally intelligent leaders understand when to diplomatically resist pressures to conform while simultaneously realizing inclusion (Wasserman et al., 2008). The goal is to be compassionate while serving others rather than seeking control.

Paradoxical Thinking for Discrimination

CQ means using broad discernment to make informed decisions while considering individual needs in complex situations. Great leaders are masterful balancers: They know how to avoid public embarrassment during conflicts by adopting "face-saving" tactics (Ting-Toomey & Oetzel, 2001) while encouraging open cultural dialogues and providing space for uncertainty with flexible policies. This is paradoxical thinking at its best.

And these discerning leaders don't stop there! They are able to anticipate societal shifts through careful observation and analysis of cultural trends. They're also adept at using data-driven approaches to detect subtle clues and microaggressions, in efforts to ensure that their innovation always aligns with cultural values. These leaders act like cultural forecasters, always striving to stay one step ahead in understanding and responding to cultural dynamics.

Participatory Infrastructure Creation for Inclusion

Let's think about how to optimize diverse participation. Culturally intelligent leaders avoid decision-making processes that benefit only a select few at the expense of others by actively recruiting various advisory councils (Kankanhalli et al., 2019) that provide critical guidance and bring deep community knowledge to the table. These leaders ensure that decisions are made collaboratively, with the interests and perspectives of all affected parties taken into consideration, rather than allowing a select group of individuals to dominate the process. Furthermore, to ensure no insensitive behavior goes undetected, they have an anonymous grievance reporting process in place. Think of this like a beacon sending distress signals saying "Hey, something seems off, and I could really use your assistance!"

But these leaders don't stop at diversity awareness. They use predictive models and sophisticated scenario planning techniques to understand how policies might affect minority groups before implementing them, and they ensure that everyone receives equal advancement opportunities (Lindgren & Bandhold, 2009). Furthermore, leaders regularly conduct cultural audits—like an inclusivity checkup!

Effective leadership requires that leaders respond to signals indicating that changes are needed with cultural intelligence, by developing an open learning mindset that strikes a balance between preserving tradition and being flexible enough to adapt to emerging needs (Hofstede, 2001) playing an integral role. To maximize their cultural understanding and growth, leaders must actively participate in mutual learning experiences, engaging in open, two-way conversations with individuals from diverse backgrounds, where both parties share their perspectives, experiences, and knowledge. By listening attentively and sharing their own insights, leaders can gain a deeper appreciation for different cultural contexts and adapt their leadership style accordingly. Additionally, seeking mentors who have experience with navigating cultural differences can provide valuable guidance and support. Participating in global competency training programs can help leaders develop the skills and knowledge they need to lead effectively in diverse environments. Such practices help leaders quickly understand and adapt to new cultural contexts while preventing them from feeling overwhelmed by the complexities of cross-cultural leadership.

Culturally intelligent leaders must seamlessly navigate cultural intersections by adapting their communication style, comfort norms, and etiquette to evolving environments (Molinsky, 2013). This approach helps eliminate disruptive dissonance and efficiently fosters cooperative energies. Culturally intelligent leadership requires paradoxical discernment and the flexibility to learn from different cultures. It also involves encouraging participation from all levels of the organization, not just top-down decision-making. These are essential skills for leaders who wish to thrive amid continual change. Progress rests upon our collective ability to adapt wisely.

The ROI on CQ Initiatives

One thing I find genuinely captivating about the development of CQ capabilities is CQ's impact on financial performance. Let me share some interesting research with you. Duke University conducted a five-year study of 180 midsize, publicly held American firms, and what they found was astounding! Managers who demonstrated high cultural metacognition (or a deep awareness and understanding of various cultures) managed to boost annual revenues by 15% more than industry averages while expanding market share 30% faster than their competitors who lacked this cultural discernment (Earley & Mosakowski, 2004). Talk about an edge! These findings demonstrate the significant competitive advantage that cultural intelligence can provide to organizations.

Another study, conducted by INSEAD, a top business school, explored senior executives of global organizations who demonstrated behavioral CQ through immersion programs, international rotations, virtual team experiences, and similar activities. As a result of engaging in such activities, these executives saw 19% higher revenue growth rates over three consecutive years than their industry peers and an astonishing 17% greater profit margin over three straight years (Earley & Mosakowski, 2004).

To further illustrate the impact of CQ, a Harvard meta-analysis containing findings from 56 studies across 22 industries assessed firms with CQ capabilities. The results were astonishing: Over seven years, these firms had a market value growth rate of more than 100% greater than their tangible capital controls! This impact was particularly evident in the technology, pharmaceutical, and financial multinational sectors, which experienced significantly higher benefits than other industries (Earley & Mosakowski, 2004).

CQ doesn't mean just playing a numbers game; it profoundly affects key outcomes like talent retention, innovation, governance, and reputation. An organization excelling in CQ often enjoys higher workforce engagement rates, greater customer targeting capabilities, ethical supply chains, and positive community reviews and endorsements. These factors contribute significantly to an organization's overall success and public perception (Livermore, 2015).

So it's clear: CQ is not simply about adapting well in diverse environments—it also directly improves organizational outcomes such as growth, sustainability, and competitive market resilience. Without CQ at their senior levels, organizations lacking discernment prowess may fall further behind their industry peers.

Diagnosing and Measuring Intercultural Capability Gaps: The CQS, IDI, and COI Tools

Instrumental tools are essential for increasing CQ and COI over time. They enable us to discover blind spots and track progress systematically. Professors Linn Van Dyne, Soon Ang, and Christine Koh (2008) created the Cultural Intelligence Scale (CQS) as a comprehensive assessment tool for all dimensions of cultural intelligence across cognitive, emotional, and physical domains. Leaders can leverage CQS for individual or team benchmarking capabilities and tailored coaching or continuous remeasurement against growth targets over time.

Complementing this, the Intercultural Development Inventory (IDI) measures mindset orientation by providing quantitative metrics of adaptability and inclusiveness, along with important qualitative insights to support them. The IDI scale evaluates adaptable and inclusive intercultural mindsets, positioning individuals along a spectrum encompassing "monocultural mindsets," transitional worldviews, and intercultural mindsets (Hammer, 2011; Paige et al., 2003). (See the Appendix for a link to the IDI evaluation tool.)

Additionally, Thomas International has made its Cultural Orientations Indicator (COI) assessment available online (Carper, 2014). This assessment tool enables you to understand your cultural tendencies better regarding how they compare with national, regional, and organizational culture patterns, thereby giving you a glimpse into your own thoughts and feelings. (See the Appendix for a link to the COI assessment tool.)

These tools facilitate introspection as well as structured development planning, in that way providing a view of your cultural capability levels from outside and prompting inner reflection. Use these tools regularly to monitor any incremental shifts in cultural perspectives throughout your leadership journey.

Enabling Cultural Growth

Let's delve into cultural development and discover ways to increase our CQ over time. I would like to provide you with some strategies that will significantly assist with this journey, on both the individual and the organizational level.

Individually, you can start by tracking incidents from your intercultural interactions. Discussing competing narratives during coaching or affinity group sessions is another great way to deepen your understanding. And don't forget about cultural assessments—they can really open your eyes! But it doesn't stop there. Building authentic cross-cultural relationships, consuming minority-focused media, attending heritage events outside your culture, volunteering with immigrant/refugee groups, and/or volunteering *as* an immigrant/refugee group member will help broaden your perspectives and deepen your empathy (Livermore, 2015). Soon enough, you will uncover more of your own hidden assumptions and become increasingly adept at navigating diverse settings as you recognize that this is an ongoing journey of growth and self-discovery.

Developing CQ requires more than simply amassing knowledge; it involves undergoing transformative learning that changes your mindset and fosters intercultural confidence. According to MacNab and Worthley (2012), high CQ directly correlates with increased general self-efficacy. In other words, believing in your abilities to navigate unfamiliar cultural scenarios leads to further growth. Cross-cultural management education comes into play here, as it challenges your assumptions and biases through cultural metaphors and communication symmetries, thereby breaking down mental barriers (Eisenberg et al., 2013). It's like working out your brain in a way that expands your awareness and shifts your perspective.

On an organizational level, there are various methods for fostering CQ.

1. Cultural Agility: Cultural agility is a crucial aspect of cultural intelligence development. An established cultural curriculum will be necessary for cultivating personal self-efficacy and to prepare yourself for unfamiliar environments. Motivational mastery and mental model remodeling techniques can unlock your full potential and expand your behavioral repertoires. These resources and techniques can be found through various channels, such as academic institutions, online courses, professional development programs, and, of course, books and scholarly articles.

2. Inclusivity: When it comes to elevating our organizations, inclusivity in leadership development programs is essential. Imagine immersive global leadership programs, mentorships that bridge differences, and speaker series dedicated to historically marginalized voices: These initiatives can have a tremendous impact. And let's remember coaching: Each session should perfectly fit the individual's growth needs!

3. Audits: Now let's investigate what might be holding us back and closely examine our existing systems, such as how we manage performance, select people for specific roles, and identify talent. Audits provide a great way to ensure that all people, and especially those from marginalized groups, are given equal chances. They are potent checks of an organization's diversity, fairness, and inclusivity.

4. Creativity: Let's think of creative ways to motivate and reward people for broadening their perspectives. We could design fun assessments to measure our learning, offer virtual high-fives when people courageously speak up even when it's uncomfortable to do so, or promote open and honest dialogue about what's happening in our organization.

5. Connecting Within and Across Identities: Add some spice and depth by being welcoming of various religious and cultural needs. We could create groups for employees who share similar identities, organize exchanges with colleagues from around the globe, and even offer opportunities for service trips where we can learn while helping globally.

6. Systemic Policies: I also encourage you not to overlook engagement-boosting policies such as religious and cultural accommodations, employee resource groups that celebrate intersectional identities, global exchange programs, and sabbaticals for service abroad.

By integrating these individual and organizational strategies, we can forge a path to sustainable growth; we can challenge assumptions and break down barriers to open channels of equitable advancement.

These strategies are crucial for progress, but leaders must also fully adapt their own mindsets to embrace inclusive leadership. Honing a specific set of skills and capabilities will allow leaders to tackle various challenges with agility and smarts. These proficiencies are essential components of a culturally intelligent leader's mindset and can significantly affect their ability to navigate diverse cultural landscapes effectively. Trust me, it's a game changer! Let's dive into what it takes to become an inclusive and effective leader.

Developing Cultural Fluency: A Leader's Journey

First, we must acknowledge some significant barriers that prevent global leadership capabilities from being effectively integrated—barriers that must be tackled head-on. From individual limitations to systemic inequities, these hurdles require our full consideration if we are to foster genuine adoption of CQ. Hearts and structures must change together for this effort to advance.

To prioritize and invest in CQ development, we must address rational concerns about embracing and fostering CQ. We need to examine who might be most affected by these changes and identify common conflicts that need reconciling to find pathways that align with our values. It's important to recognize that the impacts of CQ initiatives may not be evenly distributed across all levels of an organization. As leaders, we are responsible for championing this change and leading by example, demonstrating our commitment to cultural intelligence and inclusive excellence while ensuring fairness in its implementation.

It all begins with us: Leaders must honestly examine the blind spots that impede inclusive excellence and growth across differences. Such issues as ethnocentrism, biases, discomfort with vulnerability, and limited understanding are likely holding us back from fully expanding across differences. So let's do some inner work and discover where improvements need to be made—this will create ripple effects throughout all of our interpersonal relationships and institutions.

Understanding Barriers to Cultural Intelligence

Ethnocentrism

Ethnocentrism is a stubborn bias that keeps us from appreciating other cultures. It arises when we view our culture as superior and look down upon those not belonging to it. Such prejudiced viewpoints can lead to unfair evaluations of foreign practices that do not align with our society's cultural norms; basically, they're a refusal to see things from another point of view.

Leaders with an ethnocentric mentality often view different approaches as ineffective or inferior without considering that they may be just as successful, if not more so, in their own context (Schaetti et al., 2008). For instance, Western leaders who rate high in institutional ethnocentrism might struggle to appreciate how building personal trust before doing business is essential in Asian cultures (Sims & Schraeder, 2004).

Ethnocentric decision-makers tend to undervalue the power of collectivist approaches and instead favor individualistic leadership styles (Gelfand et al., 2006). They view consensus-building as ineffective and overlook the benefits associated with broad participation. They fail to recognize that different cultural paradigms can be effective in different contexts, and therefore, rather than respecting diverse perspectives, they force others into conformity with their own majority viewpoint.

To become influential global leaders who honor local cultures, we have to have an open and empathetic mindset. We need to adapt our leadership styles and understand the values and needs of different societies (Gelfand et al., 2006). Overcoming ethnocentrism may not be easy, but it is an essential part of our journey toward becoming truly culturally intelligent leaders.

Cognitive Bias

As Fuller et al. (2020) noted, "To identify bias, we must first know what it is and the relationship between our biases and our identities, understand the basic neuroscience of why it happens, know some common terminology, and learn when we are most susceptible to bias traps" (p. 10). When it comes to cultivating CQ, certain individual-level assumptions may impede our growth—something we do not want! Let's examine some of those assumptions now.

Confirmation bias refers to our tendency to seek, interpret, and remember information that reinforces our existing assumptions and beliefs (Nickerson, 1998). It can be like selective hearing in that instead of asking broad questions and trying to understand different viewpoints, it causes us to tend to stick with what we already know, meaning we perpetuate the blind spots that keep us from understanding outsiders.

Conformity bias involves uncritically following dominant conventions and norms without seriously questioning them (Cialdini & Goldstein,

2004)—just following along without considering alternative viewpoints. To break free of conformity blindness, we must critically reflect on the group conventions that shape our CQ.

Negativity bias means placing too much weight on the way in which certain information or material is culturally unfamiliar or unappealing to us (Rozin & Royzman, 2001). People often perceive differences as deficiencies that need correcting rather than understanding their underlying causes or considering alternative solutions. But by moving our focus away from dislikable differences and appreciating diverse perspectives, we can become cross-culturally adept.

These biases can make us narrow-minded and restrict our exposure to different countries and contexts (Schaetti et al., 2008). However, don't despair: Metacognition provides hope! By becoming aware of our mental models through coaching conversations, perspective-taking scenarios, or deep introspection, we can begin to break free from our biases and reach a more equitable understanding (Nisbett & Miyamoto, 2005).

Vulnerability and Comfort Zones

Many leaders can become unnerved by unfamiliar cross-cultural situations, seemingly lacking the necessary courage to take interpersonal risks and test out new behaviors beyond their comfort zones (Brislin et al., 2006). According to renowned researcher Brené Brown (2018), when venturing into new interactions, you may feel uncertain, powerless, and emotionally exposed. But when we make a point of trying to avoid that vulnerable feeling, we forgo the invaluable opportunities for experiential learning that would otherwise exist.

Our reluctance to embrace trial and error can get in the way, over time, of our developing intercultural communication skills (Gudykunst, 1998). Perhaps we need to be more confident in testing out different forms of speaking and behaving across cultures, even though it seems daunting. We do need to recognize the complexity of cross-cultural contexts. They can often prove challenging as we attempt to interpret different responses; it is usually easier to return to what we know and what feels comfortable. However, we can become more thoughtful and culturally competent by persisting through discomfort with positive intent and taking all errors as learning opportunities (Hofstede, 1993). All that is necessary to succeed here is adopting a learner mindset, accepting mistakes as learning experiences, reflecting upon them afterward, and building resilience against awkward encounters.

Here's the rub: To experience genuine transformational learning, we have to summon the courage to take social risks and push past our comfort zones (Illeris, 2014). Dr. Steve Robbins (2003) tells us that breakthroughs occur when we move past initial resistance phases and strive to understand each other. Unfortunately, our desire for control over interactions can stop us from being vulnerable in those interactions. We often fear to admit our own ignorance; yet it is precisely by accepting the fact that our knowledge is limited that we can develop cultural empathy and better judgment. Workplaces that foster psychological safety provide ideal environments for individuals to feel safe to express differing viewpoints and take risks without fear of reprisal (Edmondson, 2019). Noticing and celebrating even small acts of vulnerability can facilitate engagement across our differences.

Here is the bottom line: Leaders who want to adapt and succeed in intercultural situations must exercise courageous patience when engaging in unfamiliar exchanges, even when they initially feel vulnerable or uncertain. Part of being an adaptive leader means giving up privilege and becoming a cultural novice. Doing this allows us to build meaningful connections across borders while pushing ourselves beyond our comfort zones. The discomfort itself is valuable and lets us know that we are going someplace new, breaking a boundary. Continue pushing those boundaries—the rewards are worth it!

Deepening Cultural Understanding

Leaders can make surface-level adjustments in different situations, but without serious self-reflection, we might never really address our deeper mindsets (Sue et al., 2019). In other words, we change how we act on the outside but do not dig into our beliefs. This approach seriously limits our cultural sensitivity. Derald Wing Sue (2016) emphasizes that to be truly culturally competent, individuals must go beyond changing their actions and transform their thought processes. This involves challenging our own assumptions and biases, and actively working to understand and appreciate different cultural perspectives.

For example, consider a leader who greets people using different languages or dresses in traditional outfits when visiting other branches. But that's all just on the surface. If that is all they do, it is like putting on a show without changing anything deep down—trying to be politically correct without making any meaningful change (Jefferson, 2023).

One issue that comes up when leaders return from global experiences is that they fail to incorporate what they have learned into their leadership styles (Caligiuri & Tarique, 2012). Instead, they tend to compartmentalize the experiences and thus miss the chance to build multicultural repertoires. Temporary adaptation won't suffice; leaders have to step up and challenge the assimilationist expectations in dominant environments while pushing for systemic change.

In other words, developing CQ is not just about exposure. It requires us to challenge our assumptions and be open to critical self-reflection during immersive activities (Chao et al., 2017). Journaling about critical incidents or counternarratives in affinity groups and seeking ongoing coaching are some of the essential ways we can push ourselves to become more open and culturally intelligent. We cannot rely solely on exposure; we must actively identify and address our blind spots, with vulnerability and courage.

Organizations are also responsible for addressing systemic barriers—including unequal access, burdensome adaptation expectations, and an absence of diversity among leadership—that impede cultural growth among nondominant groups. Let us create an inclusive and supportive environment that embraces cultural growth.

Individuals and organizations seeking to fully embrace cultural intelligence should strive to eliminate the assumptions and barriers that hinder progress (Hajro et al., 2017). I am talking here about systemic issues that limit openness or create inequalities—they act like walls that block CQ from flourishing!

Let's break this down further: Lack of equitable access, assimilationist expectations, homogenous leadership structures, and limited engagement initiatives have all contributed to our current state (Hajro et al., 2017). For us to get to a place where we have organizations and institutions that flourish and promote cultural intelligence, we require responsible leaders who recognize these obstacles and take proactive steps to remove them, not simply checking boxes off diversity quotas but creating an environment where everyone can thrive while contributing their unique perspectives (Sue et al., 2019).

One way that organizations can foster cultural agility is by providing equal opportunities for growth. We cannot tolerate situations in which only certain groups receive global experiences, language training, and high-visibility assignments (Castilla, 2008). Now is the time to level the playing field and ensure that all qualified individuals have equal advancement opportunities, without allowing our workplace cultures to place extra and undue burdens on marginalized teams (Bourke & Dillon, 2016a). We need leaders willing to adjust their expectations and lead by example. Progress in CQ requires us to look deeply and uncover all the obstacles within organizations that hinder minority participants (Castilla, 2008).

Organizational Challenges in Developing CQ

As organizations work to cultivate CQ in their teams, they often face significant challenges. These barriers are not just individual shortcomings but are typically entrenched in the organizational structures, policies, and cultures. Facing these issues is critical for any organization aiming to fully leverage and benefit from cultural intelligence.

Three primary challenges often pose significant obstacles to CQ development: inequitable access to growth opportunities, assimilation pressures that suppress diverse perspectives, and a lack of diverse representation in leadership roles. Tackling each of these areas demands thoughtful analysis and specific strategies. By delving into these challenges, we can better understand how to shape organizational environments that truly support the development of CQ across all employees, irrespective of their background or role within the organization.

Lack of Equitable Access as a Barrier to CQ

One often overlooked challenge is the systemic barriers that marginalized groups face in accessing opportunities to develop their own CQ. Biased systems create unequal access to opportunities for growth and development, restricting the chances for members of marginalized communities to build global leadership capabilities over time. This is a serious problem, as research indicates that race, ethnicity, gender, and socioeconomic status all play roles in perpetuating these inequities (Castilla, 2008; Cook & Glass, 2013; McDonald et al., 2009).

Existing organizational structures and practices may inadvertently limit the exposure and experiences necessary for members of marginalized groups to enhance their CQ. This lack of access to learning opportunities can perpetuate a cycle of exclusion and hinder personal and professional growth.

As leaders, we must recognize and work to dismantle these barriers. By creating inclusive environments that provide equal access to CQ development resources and experiences, we can empower individuals from all backgrounds to build their CQ and contribute their unique perspectives to our organizations.

Consider this: Women and racial minorities often find it more difficult than their white male counterparts to gain the kind of international job placements and local lateral moves that provide exposure and growth opportunities. One reason could be their exclusion from informal networks where decision-makers reside (Castilla, 2011; Kulik, 2014). This lack of access compounds the issue, as creating a diverse leadership force requires mechanisms that ensure equitable screening processes and representation.

First-generation college students, particularly historically marginalized students, face hurdles in accessing faculty advising or alumni connections (Eagan et al., 2014). Such relationships are necessary for them to access the mentorship and coaching that are crucial for developing cultural fluency and successfully navigating global environments. We must not allow access to these essential resources to depend solely on privilege: That erects a barrier at the very beginning of these students' college careers that can limit all their future opportunities for growth and development.

Given all these obstacles, we must act. Employers should prioritize correcting the policies, practices, and cultural messaging that hinder historically marginalized groups from accessing equal developmental opportunities. Each of us is integral in breaking down barriers and creating an inclusive workplace where all can safely, and with support, navigate global environments.

The Assimilationist Pressures That Restrict CQ Growth

In a misguided attempt to boost cultural intelligence, organizations may place unreasonable expectations of assimilation on historically marginalized groups, and in that way impede their progress rather than encouraging it. This approach fails to incorporate the unique perspectives and experiences that these individuals bring to the table, and it can ultimately hinder the development of a genuinely inclusive and culturally intelligent workforce. Such demands for conformity are typically placed only on minorities, by the majority, and these demands limit reciprocal and pluralistic evolution—leaving nonconformists or newcomers entirely responsible for their own integration rather than creating bilateral engagement (Hajro et al., 2017; Sue et al., 2019).

Messages such as "our way is the proper way" are prevalent, reinforcing the belief that those whose workplace behaviors or leadership styles deviate from institutional norms should be the ones to change by conforming to the workplace norms and leadership styles imposed from above. This dynamic leads to the unspoken understanding that mainstream practices are superior and should remain unchanged.

Unfortunately, without reciprocal adaptation, nondominant groups may face pressures to subsume their authentic cultural identities and navigate the politics of respectability, where the issue of which traits are acceptable for viability as a leader comes into play (Jefferson, 2023). Finding an optimal balance between professional assimilation and heritage preservation becomes vital; without it, the members of nondominant groups risk straining their mental health through the splintering of their identity and the restriction of their cultural insights (Showunmi et al., 2016).

Leadership Diversity and Representation

Homogenous leadership models set assimilationist expectations, signaling that conformity with dominant paradigms is essential for authority (Cook & Glass, 2013). Tokenized visibility doesn't create genuine pluralism. Lack of deep minority representation at senior levels restricts cognitive flexibility and diverse decision-making. By emphasizing one-way adaptation, where only minority groups adjust, we undermine cultural learning. Sustainable progress requires collective evolution toward norms that honor diverse expressions, with all groups participating in cultural adaptation.

Diverse and inclusive leadership, then, goes beyond simply checking off boxes; it requires understanding that a lack of diversity at the top restricts the growth of emerging leaders while diminishing our capacity to recognize and appreciate different perspectives.

When we see only one type of leader, it can be hard for individuals from marginalized groups to picture themselves in similar positions. During their research, Cook and Glass (2013) discovered that role models who break from stereotypes provide much-needed inspiration (Leslie, 2019). Cook and Glass found that representation and diversity have a vital impact on marginalized groups. They also noted that it is especially problematic when decision-makers fail to recognize the importance of these groups' participation and the motivation such representation provides for others to pursue leadership roles. To put it plainly, exposure brings about expectation. Having diverse role models in leadership demonstrates to marginalized individuals that such positions are attainable for them.

Representation is only part of the equation, though; what matters even more is how leaders think. Without diverse leadership, organizations tend to rely on traditional approaches that may be ill-suited for our multicultural society (Chin, 2013). Therefore, leaders who can bring new perspectives, tackle race-based issues head-on, empower women, and understand marginalized groups' unique struggles are needed more than ever.

Let's turn our focus for a minute to diversity recruitment. Hiring diverse talent is great! But are we creating an inclusive environment where everyone feels valued and heard? Dobbin and Kalev (2016) noted that ongoing inclusion efforts are essential to recruitment efforts, because people must feel supported and empowered enough to bring all aspects of themselves to work.

It's essential to celebrate milestones in our journey toward cultural inclusion, even as we remain aware of the work that still needs to be accomplished. For example, we can acknowledge the progress we've made by increasing diversity in our organizations. At the same time, we must push forward and challenge any structural biases that continue to hinder the advancement of marginalized groups. Change is necessary, and the pursuit of CQ and inclusion should be seen not just as a nice gesture but as a critical component of our organization's success and values.

Moving Beyond Limited Engagement

Some organizations rely on limited engagement initiatives that do not drive systemic evolution. You know those one-off workshops that raise awareness but don't lead to lasting change? For effective, lasting change to happen, we require ongoing immersion experiences, accountability mechanisms, and support systems that foster sustainable growth.

My best-selling book *The Allyship Challenge: How to Move Beyond Performative Allyship and Become a Genuine Accomplice* (Harden, 2021) defines this limited support as "performative allyship." This is what occurs when organizations make public gestures solely to improve their reputation without actually taking risks or redistributing power for real change, for instance by including affinity group panels at meetings without providing any funds to employee resource groups, or by leaving minority voices out of strategy roles while building out recruiting bureaucracy—such efforts are not enough!

Organizational figureheads also need to avoid making public declarations about justice and equity that conceal a lack of data or avoid addressing patterns of cultural hostility patterns in the workplace. We require courageous conversations and tangible solutions instead of empty statements.

To truly make a potent difference, we must have the courage to confront brutal truths and reinvent our systems. Beyond mission statements and marketing, real change comes when those involved fairly redistribute access, decision rights, and leadership potential. To achieve real change, we must embrace productive discomfort without protecting egos—silence and spin tactics don't suffice. As leaders, we need to create environments that foster CQ growth for all members of our organizations.

Remember, cultural intelligence is not a destination but an ongoing process of learning, adapting, and growing. Embrace the journey, stay curious, and keep pushing the boundaries of your cultural comfort zones. The rewards of enhanced global leadership, stronger relationships, and more effective cross-cultural collaboration are well worth the effort.

The Bottom Line: How CQ Drives Business Performance

Scholars and practitioners both recognize CQ as an essential capability for leadership to create positive results in today's global and interdependent business environment. Increased CQ allows your organization to communicate sensitively, form trust-based relationships, retain top talent, adapt to local preferences, drive improved financial performance, and ultimately make your business global-ready (Ang et al., 2007). An increased CQ empowers your organization—it gives your business magical global-readiness!

Reducing risk by including cultural awareness as part of strategy and operations (Yan & Luo, 2001) is of utmost importance for multinational corporations and businesses looking to enter new territories, as 70% of international ventures fail because of cultural mismatches (Yan & Luo, 2001). Having a low cultural quotient poses real threats; major Western retailers like Home Depot, Kingfisher, and Target have failed to appropriately adapt their branding and positioning and have experienced tremendous losses and store closures resulting from cultural mismatches (Rankin, 2014).

Conversely, managers with CQ are far better equipped to build relationships and expand business opportunities (de la Garza Carranza & Egri, 2010). Over

90% of business leaders from 68 nations view multicultural leadership development as a central management goal (Palmer, 2006), underscoring CQ's necessity. Furthermore, higher CQ has been linked with better profit margins, sales growth, and overall performance across international markets (Moon, 2013), so increasing your CQ can really pay dividends!

But CQ brings much more than quantitative metrics into workplaces. CQ helps establish trust-based relationships between partners and customers that can preclude major crises (Johnson et al., 2006). Furthermore, it promotes inclusive work cultures with lower turnover and greater stability (Ang et al., 2007). CQ allows you to build an organizational reputation while still having plenty of fun!

Studies indicate that CQ indirectly correlates with innovation, growth, resilience, and other key performance indicators. One analysis of 56 research papers discovered that CQ positively affected cross-border leadership negotiations, collaboration, and virtual interactions (Ott & Michailova, 2018). Cultural intelligence in teams is paramount for their success when they are operating across diverse settings.

CQ programs have also significantly enhanced coordination, task performance, and work adjustments among diverse teams (Chen & Lin, 2013). Culturally intelligent leaders give organizations a competitive edge: Studies reveal that companies led by executives with superior CQ experience faster revenue growth, higher profitability, and greater market value than their less culturally sensitive competitors (Earley & Mosakowski, 2004). Top corporations recognize this truth.

Culturally intelligent organizations excel in talent retention, knowledge transfer, product innovation, operational efficiency, and reputation management (Livermore, 2015). CQ helps organizations retain talented employees while producing marketable innovations with market appeal; cultivating it leads to market expansion, leadership agility, and organizational resilience

(Livermore, 2015). As Robin Sharma (2008) rightly noted, "People do business with people who make them feel good. Human beings are creatures of emotion. We want to be with those who make us feel happy and special and cared for and safe" (p. 177).

For these reasons, CQ must be prioritized in any organization's global growth strategy. From building partnerships to avoiding embarrassing cultural gaffes, cultural intelligence is vital to understanding the experiences of diverse communities while driving sustainable innovation.

Case Study: Bridging the Gap at Sunrise Hospitality

Maggie, a senior director at Sunrise Hospitality, a leading hotel chain, hired an instructional designer to create five-minute continuing education modules for her multigenerational sales team. She believed these short, focused lessons would provide maximum efficiency and fit into her staff's busy schedules. However, an anonymous survey revealed a generational divide in learning preferences and sales performance.

During a team meeting, Maggie's colleague, Robert, a seasoned sales representative in his late fifties, expressed his frustration, saying, "Maggie, I've been in this industry for over three decades, and I don't see the value in these quick, superficial lessons. I have a wealth of experience, and I don't believe that spending more time on in-depth training would benefit me and those of my caliber."

Maggie realized that her one-size-fits-all approach had failed to consider the diverse learning needs and generational differences of her team. She noticed that although the younger sales representatives were eager to participate in the short modules and consistently outperformed their older colleagues, the seasoned staff members were resistant to the new training format, which led to a growing mentality of Us versus Them.

Case Study Questions

1. How can Maggie demonstrate CQ by recognizing and valuing her multi-generational sales team's diverse perspectives and experiences?

2. What steps can Maggie take to develop her CQ and better understand the different generations' learning preferences and work styles?

3. How can Maggie use her CQ to create a training program that is inclusive and responsive to the needs of all generations on her team while also addressing the concerns of seasoned staff members like Robert?

4. What strategies can Maggie employ to foster a culture of CQ in her team and promote mutual respect, empathy, and collaboration across generations?

5. How can Maggie leverage her CQ to bridge the generation gap and create a sense of unity and shared purpose among her diverse sales team while also acknowledging the unique contributions and wisdom of experienced team members?

Case Study Resolution

Recognizing the need to address the generational divide, Maggie realized that she had to enhance her own CQ by attending workshops and reading literature on generational differences in the workplace. She gained a deeper understanding of the unique perspectives, values, and learning preferences of each generation represented on her team.

Armed with this knowledge, Maggie organized a series of focus groups and individual meetings with her sales team to actively listen to their concerns and gather insights into their diverse needs. She demonstrated her CQ by acknowledging the value that each generation brought to the table—particularly the wealth of experience and industry knowledge that seasoned team members like Robert possessed.

To create an inclusive and responsive training program, Maggie collaborated with the instructional designer and representatives from each generation to design a blended learning approach. The program included a mix of short, targeted modules for quick skill acquisition and longer, in-depth sessions that provided opportunities for deep learning, experience sharing, and leveraging of the expertise of seasoned staff members. Maggie also introduced a reverse mentoring initiative, where younger team members shared their digital expertise with older colleagues to foster mutual learning and respect.

Maggie used her CQ to promote a culture of inclusivity and collaboration in her team. She organized Generational Wisdom workshops, where team members from different age groups shared their unique perspectives and experiences. Maggie also implemented a Cross-Generational Collaboration program, pairing younger team members with more experienced colleagues on projects to promote knowledge sharing and build stronger relationships.

To further strengthen the organization's commitment to inclusivity, Maggie introduced a Two-Minute Tuesday initiative, where team members from various departments, regardless of their age or tenure, were acknowledged during the company's monthly all-staff meetings and celebrated for their contributions. This practice helped create a sense of belonging and value for everyone in the company.

By modeling culturally intelligent leadership and valuing the contributions of all team members, regardless of age or tenure, Maggie helped break down the Us versus Them mentality and fostered a sense of unity and shared purpose.

As a result of Maggie's culturally intelligent approach, the generational divide in her sales team gradually diminished. The team members began to recognize and value the contributions of each generation, leading to improved collaboration, knowledge sharing, and sales performance. By leveraging her CQ to bridge the generation gap and create an inclusive environment that celebrated the wisdom and experience of seasoned staff members like Robert, Maggie successfully united her multigenerational team and drove the success of Sunrise Hospitality. Cultivating inclusive cultures necessitates an adaptable, context-specific approach rather than a standardized, universal formula.

Advancing Your Leadership Journey

Reflection Questions

1. As a leader, how can you use CQ to effectively navigate the complexities of an increasingly globalized world and foster innovation in your organization?

2. How can you develop your ability to balance competing demands, cultural patterns, and decentralized participation to make informed decisions while considering individual needs in complex situations?

3. How can you create a participatory infrastructure for inclusion in your organization? What steps can you take to recruit diverse advisory councils and ensure that all voices are heard in decision-making processes?

4. Research on the ROI of CQ initiatives demonstrates significant improvements in revenue growth, profitability, and market value for organizations with culturally intelligent leaders. How can you effectively communicate the value of CQ to key decision-makers and secure investment in CQ development initiatives for your organization?

5. How can you leverage tools such as the Cultural Intelligence Scale (CQS), Intercultural Development Inventory (IDI), and Cultural Orientations Indicator (COI) to assess your organization's cultural intelligence, identify areas

for improvement, and track progress over time to demonstrate the ROI of CQ initiatives?

Practical Application Activity

- Develop a CQ Business Case:

1. Identify a specific business challenge or opportunity in your organization where CQ could significantly contribute to success. This could be related to areas such as global expansion, diverse customer engagement, cross-cultural team collaboration, or inclusive innovation.

2. Conduct research to gather relevant data and insights demonstrating cultural intelligence's potential impact on the identified business challenge or opportunity. These may include:

- Industry benchmarks and best practices related to CQ and diversity and inclusion.

- Case studies of organizations that have successfully leveraged CQ to drive business outcomes.

- Internal data on employee engagement, customer satisfaction, and financial performance across different cultural segments.

3. Develop a compelling business case that articulates the strategic value of investing in CQ initiatives to address the identified challenge or opportunity. Your business case should include:

- A clear definition of the business problem or opportunity and its alignment with organizational goals and priorities.

- Key data points and insights that highlight the potential impact of CQ on business outcomes.

- Specific recommendations for CQ initiatives or interventions (e.g., leadership development programs, inclusive hiring practices, culturally responsive product design).

- Projected benefits and ROI of implementing the recommended CQ initiatives, including both quantitative (e.g., revenue growth, cost savings) and qualitative (e.g., enhanced reputation, improved employee morale) metrics.

4. Present your CQ business case to relevant organizational leaders (e.g., senior leadership, HR, Diversity & Inclusion Council) to gain buy-in and support for the proposed initiatives.

5. Based on the feedback and insights from key contributors:

- Refine your business case and develop an implementation plan for the approved CQ initiatives.

- Establish clear metrics and milestones to track the progress and impact of the implemented CQ initiatives over time. Regularly communicate updates and results to involved parties to maintain momentum and support.

- Monitor and adjust your CQ initiatives based on evolving business needs and cultural dynamics, ensuring ongoing alignment with organizational goals and priorities.

As we conclude our exploration of CQ's strategic advantage, let's reflect on the most critical insights and lessons learned.

Key Takeaways

1. CQ provides a strategic advantage for leaders and organizations seeking to thrive in diverse global environments. It enables effective navigation of cultural complexities, drives innovation, and enhances financial performance.

2. Culturally intelligent leadership requires paradoxical thinking that balances competing demands while respecting diverse cultural patterns. It involves making informed decisions that consider individual needs in complex situations, often through decentralized participation. This approach requires compassion, allowing leaders to navigate cultural complexities with both wisdom and genuine care for others' well-being.

3. Creating a participatory infrastructure that actively engages diverse voices and perspectives is essential for fostering inclusion and leveraging the benefits of CQ in organizations. This includes establishing advisory councils, promoting psychological safety, and ensuring equitable access to opportunities.

4. Developing CQ is an ongoing journey that requires a commitment to continuous learning, self-reflection, and the use of diagnostic tools such as the Cultural Intelligence Scale (CQS), Intercultural Development Inventory (IDI), and Cultural Orientations Indicator (COI) to identify areas for growth and development at both the individual and organizational levels.

Chapter 4

The Culturally Intelligent Leader's Mindset

Relying solely on traditional leadership approaches rooted in institutional precedent won't do in today's diverse organizations; we must take a different approach to thrive in this ever-evolving environment. We need leaders who can bridge cultural divides, which can ultimately lead to top cross-cultural talent joining our ranks while forging lasting partnerships within their respective communities.

At the core of any transformation are the leader's mindset and values. Let us explore the characteristics of a culturally intelligent leader further. First, a culturally intelligent leader must be an avid learner. They must embrace cultural discernment with humility while understanding that there is always more to discover in an ever-evolving complex environment. Such leaders continuously broaden their capabilities.

One essential characteristic of culturally intelligent leaders is the ability to embrace ambiguity. These leaders efficiently handle unfamiliar dynamics and manage communication gaps with patience and context. By welcoming uncertainty as part of everyday business life, culturally intelligent leaders foster creativity and innovation in organizations, which ultimately helps drive business success.

A culturally intelligent leader learns to suspend judgments. That's right! Culturally intelligent leaders refrain from jumping to conclusions or making quick evaluations when encountering cultural situations they are unfamiliar with; these leaders recognize that our gut reactions may often reflect personal projections more than objective realities. By creating an environment for learning, such leaders prevent bias from taking over and instead strive for more profound insight.

Culturally intelligent leaders excel at appreciating diversity. They view different orientations, styles, and motivations as valuable assets that drive innovation. These leaders recognize that diverse perspectives provide novel insights and solutions that would not emerge if everyone thought alike.

Now let's talk about biases: Culturally intelligent leaders take a hard, honest look inward and engage in courageous self-reflection, mindful that we all come from our own cultures that influence our perceptions and biases. By making themselves aware of potentially hidden biases and regularly consulting marginalized voices for input on policies meant to promote equality, culturally intelligent leaders ensure that their so-called impartial policies do not perpetuate unfair systems.

Culturally intelligent leaders understand the value of inclusive leadership! They strive to establish fair policies, use inclusive language, and make resources readily available while developing paths based on merit rather than privilege. Their goal is to ensure all individuals feel accepted by creating environments where everyone feels like they belong—based not who knows who, but on what each one brings to the table.

No one should forget the value of trust, either! Culturally intelligent leaders understand its centrality to the work environment and thus ensure psychological safety, encourage knowledge sharing, and foster an enabling atmosphere to promote individual expression without worry about fitting in or conforming. Furthermore, these leaders recognize and give credit where it is due, creating a sense of togetherness and overall well-being among their workforces.

This mindset should inform all your decision-making as you prioritize equity and create policies that uphold dignity for all individuals—even if that means going outside your comfort zone. With confidence and humility, you can transform the purpose of your organization to meet its diverse community better—that could change everything!

By embracing CQ, leaders can create organizations that not only attract top cross-cultural talent but also forge lasting partnerships within their respective communities. In the following section, we will explore the essential components of the culturally intelligent leader's mindset and how they contribute to effective leadership in today's multicultural landscape.

The Culturally Intelligent Leader's Mindset

To become an inclusive leader, one must develop cultural intelligence. And nurturing CQ requires a humble and mindful approach. It starts with turning inward, reflecting on one's own biases and limitations, being fully present and aware of our surroundings, and extending respect to the myriad of perspectives that color our world. But what specific proficiencies enable this kind of agile discernment? I can explain.

By conducting solid research into how to foster inclusion and identifying the qualities that promote organizational equity, and by studying the leaders who demonstrate adaptive cultural fluency on an ongoing basis, I have developed an inclusive leadership framework—The Culturally Intelligent Leader's Mindset—that contains all of these individual foundational elements for inclusive excellence. This framework provides you with the insights gained from extensive research and leader analysis, enabling you to benefit from the knowledge without having to undertake the study yourself.

The Culturally Intelligent Leader's Mindset model highlights eight essential leadership components that go beyond traditional command-and-control approaches and can assist individuals in effectively and inclusively navigating diverse cultural contexts. Because leaders face ever more complex problems as a result of rapid change, these proficiencies serve as guidance on where you need to develop further. A comprehensive illustration of these eight components and their interrelationships can be found in the Appendix (see Figure 9). Let's break it down.

1. Self-awareness: Self-awareness involves taking a step back and reflecting on your cultural programming, including uncovering the hidden assumptions that we all hold about various groups of people. Doing this opens you up for personal growth and awareness of how those assumptions might affect your leadership style.

2. Cultural Empathy: Cultural empathy involves making an honest effort to recognize and appreciate various cultural perspectives. Such endeavors should also strengthen sensitivity toward marginalized individuals' experiences, forming bridges of connection and understanding between cultures.

3. Situational Attunement: Flexibility is essential here; CQ involves adapting your communication style, work style, and leadership approach so that they resonate with people from various cultural contexts. Being culturally intelligent requires being comfortable navigating multiple cultural environments while developing trusting relationships.

4. Inclusive Decision-Making: No decision should be made without first consulting those affected by it and engaging and valuing diverse perspectives early on; doing this produces inclusive decision-making that yields better outcomes and fosters a sense of ownership and belonging in teams.

5. Psychological Safety: Imagine working in an environment where everyone feels secure, respected, and valued—this is psychological safety at work! Psychological safety involves creating a space where individuals can contribute without fear of adverse repercussions, which is the perfect breeding ground for innovation and collaboration to flourish.

6. Equitable Access: We must ensure our systems and processes don't unknowingly create barriers for marginalized groups. Auditing and identifying these obstacles is vital. By creating policies that promote accessibility and advancement for all, we can create a more level playing field.

7. Reciprocal Adaptation: When dealing with various cultures, adaptation doesn't simply involve nondominant groups adapting to the dominant ones; it requires mutual effort from all concerned. Understanding, respect, and willingness to learn from one another are necessary for successful communication between diverse communities.

8. Role Modeling: As leaders, we possess the power to influence and inspire those we lead. By showing cultural discernment and supporting others' growth, we can cause positive ripple effects of change—whether through mentoring programs, alliancing initiatives, or simply being honest about our limitations.

Now let's examine the research behind each of these capabilities (so that you know I'm not making up my facts!).

1. Self-Awareness

When it comes to effective leadership, self-awareness can be a game-changer. Self-aware leaders have the incredible power of genuinely understanding themselves—including their values, emotions, strengths, weaknesses, biases, and how these affect others (Boyatzis et al., 2011). Armed with this understanding, they make wise decisions while leading authentically; they continuously improve; and they inspire trust in their followers through extensive research.

Self-awareness significantly influences leaders' CQ and adaptability. CQ involves successfully navigating cultural diversity (Ang et al., 2007) across three domains: cognitive, emotional, and physical behavior. Self-aware leaders excel in accurately reading and interpreting cultural cues (Livermore, 2015) across all three domains.

Now let's examine how self-awareness helps create more inclusive and open teams. High self-awareness enables leaders to identify their cultural programming, biases, and blind spots (we all have them!). Acknowledging and working on these areas creates a safe space for empathy, openness, and psychological safety (Bücker, Furrer, Poutsma, & Buyen, 2014). And self-reflection? That superpower helps leaders identify opportunities for cultural expansion while motivating them to expand their cultural repertoire—an invaluable opportunity for personal and professional growth that should not be missed!

As leaders gain a better understanding of their own cultural perspectives, strengths, and areas for improvement, and as they adapt their behavior and communication style to connect with people from diverse backgrounds (Van Dyne et al., 2012), leaders become masterful at leading in cross-cultural situations (Van Dyne et al., 2012). Remember that nonjudgmental self-evaluation helps break down unconscious stereotypes that hinder inclusivity (Pless & Maak, 2004).

Extensive research has confirmed the value of self-awareness in becoming an adaptable leader, but that alone won't cut it! Adding curiosity, humility, and respect for others creates a super self-awareness that enables leaders to thrive in almost any cultural context. Any development program worth its salt needs to begin with and focus on cultivating self-awareness.

2. Cultural Empathy

Navigating diversity requires intentionally cultivating cultural empathy and situational attunement. Think of it like exercising your empathy muscles! Seeking different perspectives through open dialogue and active listening shows you genuinely care for your staff's well-being. Do not underestimate the power of connecting emotionally with marginalized groups' experiences via narratives and media to promote interpersonal sensitivity and build trusting relationships over time.

Research tells us cultural empathy is a necessary quality in effective leadership (Earley & Ang, 2003). With societies and workplaces becoming more diverse, leaders must understand and connect with people from various cultural backgrounds. Cultural empathy involves understanding their thoughts, feelings, and behaviors (Wang et al., 2003), and empathetic leaders have better relationships across cultures (Holladay & Quiñones, 2008).

Cultural empathy consists of both cognitive and affective components. On the cognitive side, culturally empathetic leaders seek out diverse viewpoints to fully comprehend various groups' realities (Johnson et al., 2006). They suspend judgment while developing emotional connections with others through open dialogues, stories, or media (Rockstuhl et al., 2011). This approach allows the leaders to broaden their cultural knowledge while increasing interpersonal sensitivity toward staff from marginalized backgrounds, and these leaders demonstrate genuine care for the well-being of the people involved by seeing situations from different vantage points (Johnson et al., 2006).

Cultural empathy and CQ are closely connected. Culturally intelligent leaders genuinely show an interest in diverse cultures while possessing empathy for differing perspectives; cultural empathy allows leaders to easily build deeper relationships across differences (Johnson et al., 2006).

Having cultural empathy enables us to lead from a place of shared humanity.

3. Situational Attunement

Being an influential, transformative leader goes beyond simply possessing the appropriate skills. A key ability of effective leaders is being attuned to different situations, which means adapting their communication style, leadership style, and actions to accord with cultural norms (Johnson et al., 2006). Finding a balance between adaptable leadership styles and staying true to themselves requires that leaders adopt an "attunement orientation," one that welcomes different worldviews (Dweck, 2008). Embracing these diverse worldviews in their workplace also means attuned leaders adopt a growth orientation (Johnson et al., 2006). For example, as an attuned leader, you might adjust the directness of your feedback to accommodate different verbal styles (Patterson et al., 2006). Alternatively, when working globally across diverse teams, you could incorporate different cultural rituals or ceremonies, as appropriate, to show you value and respect every individual's unique contribution. Customize your approach based on each situation.

Research demonstrates that culturally intelligent leaders do not expect everyone else to conform to their way of doing things; instead, they adapt to any situation (Ang et al., 2007). This means being mindful of different communication styles, for instance using indirect Asian communication respectfully (Patterson et al., 2006) and tapping into relevant cultural narratives to motivate immigrant teams. There is no one-size-fits-all solution—each team member deserves recognition for what they bring to the table.

Culturally agile leaders don't stop there: They also know how to navigate paradoxes and accept opposing cultural strategies, like finding an equilibrium between group harmony and individualism (Taras et al., 2013). Leaders can connect with their diverse teams by cultivating adaptability and openness to multiple worldviews while building an inclusive culture. At its core, being an inclusive leader requires adapting quickly to changing situations by perceptively attuning to their demands. This involves cultivating CQ through perspective-taking and developing a growth mindset (Bücker, Furrer, Poutsma, & Buyen, 2014; Dweck, 2008).

4. Inclusive Decision-Making

While embracing a growth mindset, as already noted, attuned leaders also bridge cultural gaps to ensure they use inclusive decision-making processes for complex issues.

As part of the decision-making process, we must include representation and input from all groups involved. Doing this allows diverse perspectives to converge while preventing groupthink or one-sided decision-making from arising—it's like tapping into an endless source of wisdom that helps us address complex problems more effectively.

Sometimes, quieter voices need more space to speak their mind. That is why co-design sessions focused on collective priorities and visual organization methods can create an atmosphere where all feel welcome to contribute ideas. Inclusivity should be at the core of decision-making processes to ensure that cultural needs and community preferences are considered, resulting in equitable and nuanced policies.

Now here is an important point to remember: Inclusive decision-making is more than just an optional leadership trait. Research shows that leaders who seek out and incorporate diverse perspectives make better decisions and create stronger teams (Hirak et al., 2012). By intentionally creating opportunities for people of different backgrounds and positions in an organization to have their say and contribute ideas freely, inclusive decision-makers foster an environment where problems are solved collaboratively and initiatives are developed with care and thoughtfulness. What's more, this approach corresponds strongly with the growth mindset associated with culturally intelligent leaders: Instead of relying solely on our assumptions or experiences, we seek to understand other worldviews (Hirak et al., 2012).

Don't take my word for it—studies have proven the power of inclusive decision-making. Leadership teams that engage in cultural dialogues and integrate the best concepts often develop more innovative products and services that better satisfy customer demands (Hirak et al., 2012). Plus, inclusive decision-making increases buy-in and the willingness to implement decisions, since participants feel heard and understood (Bourke & Dillon, 2016b). As an example, in high-reliability hospitals and healthcare organizations, seeking input from all the staff (from frontline nurses to technicians) has significantly enhanced patient safety and improved the quality of care (Weick & Sutcliffe, 2015).

Creating an environment where people feel free to express their genuine perspectives requires effort and finesse from leaders. Mastering open-ended questions, fully listening without judgment, and using visual brainstorming and collaboration techniques (such as mind mapping or collaborative digital boards) to ensure every voice is heard (Hirak et al., 2012) are essential practices for leaders who wish to facilitate an inclusive environment for employees and leaders alike. As organizations face ever more complex hurdles, inclusive decision-making becomes the cornerstone for harnessing collective brainpower.

5. Psychological Safety

Psychological safety is an integral part of team success. It creates an environment where teams feel safe to take risks, learn, and participate without fearing embarrassing or retaliatory repercussions (Edmondson, 2019).

Leaders who cultivate a psychologically safe atmosphere give their employees the permission and confidence to push the boundaries of innovation. This environment results in well-informed decision-making and fosters high levels of motivation and engagement among all team members. It's quite a magical experience! Leaders seeking to capitalize on diversity should encourage honest dialogue by fostering psychological safety—creating a space where minority perspectives are valued and acknowledged so that the power of diversity is unleashed to its fullest capacity.

Protecting those who dare to challenge norms is essential to unlocking innovation, so let's discuss this topic as an essential one: Providing psychological safety includes leading by example and being vulnerable, encouraging those who feel unsafe to take risks, and responding appropriately to microaggressions from the majority populations (Aramo-Immonen et al., 2016).

Research proves it: Psychologically safe environments lead to high-performing teams across industries and cultures (Duhigg, 2016). Do you know what's even more crucial than skills or intelligence? It's people! Seriously, by eliminating the fear of negative consequences, leaders can unlock the full potential of their teams—it's like opening an unlimited hidden treasure trove of skills and intelligence!

Oh, and did I mention that remarkable things happen when it's safe to speak up? According to research, when diverse perspectives are encouraged and celebrated, creativity explodes, solutions improve, and financial outcomes improve (Hirak et al., 2012). So let's open up those conversations so that everyone feels heard and valued (Singh et al., 2013). Psychological safety is indispensable for leaders seeking maximum value from diverse teams, and achieving it involves creating an inclusive environment where everyone can participate without fear of failure or rejection.

6. Equitable Access

Leaders face increasing pressure to promote diversity, equity, and inclusion in their organizations. Leaders must ensure employees have equal access to resources regardless of gender, race, disability status, or other factors. Okoro and Washington (2012) found that minority employees had a greater chance of excelling when given equal access. Unfortunately, historical biases have created barriers that must be recognized and dismantled.

If we are to move beyond individual interactions to systemic inclusion, we must ensure fair access. One way of doing this is by conducting privilege audits identifying barriers related to identity, income status, disability status, and more. With this data, we can adjust hiring practices, compensation packages, flexible work options, global mobility opportunities, and personalized development programs that provide equal advancement prospects for everyone. By being open about existing inequities, leaders can make long-overdue changes.

Equitable access is strongly linked with CQ, or the ability of leaders to work effectively in multicultural environments (Bücker et al., 2014). CQ includes cognitive, emotional, and physical dimensions. Self-aware leaders can critically consider their own biases when it comes to access and advancement; understanding cultural differences cognitively can inform more inclusive policies, and intrinsic motivation to advocate for equity compels leaders to challenge existing barriers; and finally, showing support for marginalized groups through authentic actions shows genuine dedication in supporting access promotion efforts.

Research supports equitable access as a must-have quality for leaders in the 21st century. Deloitte's 2016 global survey of over seven thousand professionals selected equitable access as THE top leadership quality, chosen by 38% (Bourke et al., 2017). Access to networks, sponsors, and high-visibility assignments also play a crucial role in employee retention and engagement (Roberson, [2006]). And employees who believe they have fair access to opportunities experience greater job satisfaction, commitment, and trust in their leaders (Nishii & Mayer, 2009). Therefore, equitable access is the cornerstone of creating inclusive environments.

Let's be honest here: Being aware is great, and it's important. However, we must take bold action to promote equality and equity. It is not like we can snap our fingers and *poof*, everything will be equal. Trust me—I would love to turn into The Flash for a little while and make things happen quickly!

However, I am human, just like you, and I know it takes genuine effort, some good old courageous action, and much tenacity to make a difference. Now is the time to audit barriers, challenge unconscious biases, and stand up for marginalized groups (leaders included!). Believe me, when you unleash some fantastic benefits of inclusion by making tangible changes, leaders like you have the power to implement the behavioral and workplace policy changes necessary to create equitable systems that will provide opportunities and rewards for all staff, including yourself!

7. Reciprocal Adaptation

Being an effective leader in today's diverse organizations can be arduous, but that does not have to be the case. *Reciprocal adaptation* is a term that is often considered very complex. Let me explain it in simple terms: Reciprocal adaptation is about adjusting your leadership style to connect with people from different cultures while respecting their unique identities (Hofstede, 2015). Finding that sweet spot where we can all keep our unique individual identities and get along swimmingly is like hitting the jackpot! It is about embracing individuality while fostering a harmonious environment (Hofstede, 2015). It's like making sure you speak everyone's language, literally and metaphorically. So picture yourself as an extraordinary leader who can bridge cultural gaps and make everyone feel valued while respecting their backgrounds and perspectives.

Now, according to experts, creating inclusive systems requires more than expecting historically marginalized groups to assimilate; we need two-way adaptation so that not only do dominant groups learn from others while giving space for minority identity expression, but everyone feels heard and valued (Mavletova, 2013).

Research demonstrates that the value of leaders who embrace reciprocal adaptation is extraordinary. They understand multiple perspectives, bridge communication barriers, and avoid alienating nondominant people (Rockstuhl et al., 2011). Plus, they demonstrate a growth mindset and encourage continuous cultural learning (Earley & Mosakowski, 2004). In other words, they encourage performative allies to become advocates and accomplices (Harden, 2021). Can you say "level up"? Reciprocal adaptation is a two-way adaptation that creates an inclusive environment where all members feel valued and free to express their authentic selves without restriction or shame.

8. Role Modeling

Role modeling is one of the most essential and influential aspects of effective leadership (Brown & Trevino, 2014). Employees observe and pick up on attitudes, behaviors, and ways of thinking from leaders they admire, learning attitudes from them that can lead them down an individual path of change (Brown & Trevino, 2014). Research indicates that people follow role models more often than they follow leaders who simply provide instructions (Brown & Trevino, 2014). If you want to influence workplace culture or make change happen, then role modeling is where it should begin!

There are two forms of role modeling: implicit and explicit (Mayer et al., 2012). Implicit role modeling occurs when leaders exhibit desirable qualities without making an issue of them; for example, placing family first sends an unspoken signal about the importance of work–life balance. Explicit role modeling occurs when leaders openly express values such as "I promote diversity because it's important to me." However, both forms can dramatically affect employee attitudes and ethical behavior (Mayer et al., 2012).

Culturally intelligent leaders can be influential in building an environment that celebrates diversity by acting as role models. Showing openness, being curious about various cultures, and adapting behaviors accordingly all help foster intercultural acceptance. Furthermore, research has linked leader curiosity directly to team CQ (Chen et al., 2010): When leaders model cultural learning, their employees become more comfortable taking intercultural risks. Leading by example and openly working on cultural development are keys to collective improvement.

Being a culturally intelligent leader means acting as an example to others while encouraging others to carry out this vital work. Here's the deal, folks: Mentoring emerging marginalized talent, recognizing and appreciating employees' allyship efforts, and admitting when we don't know it all—these things keep the momentum going strong and flowing forward like nobody's business. You don't have to just trust me on this: I've shown you the research!

The CQ Leadership Continuum

Let's talk about the CQ continuum. A detailed visual representation of this continuum and its various stages can be found in the Appendix (see Figure 10). This tool allows leaders like you to reflect on how effectively they lead diverse teams while developing plans to increase their cultural consciousness.

As you embark on your leadership journey, having the appropriate mindset and skill set is vital—however, you will need to adapt them depending on the context. That's where the three main stages of cultural intelligence in leadership come in as benchmarks for evaluation—these apply equally across cultures.

First up is the Red Zone: culturally inflexible leadership. No one wants to find themselves in this zone! Leaders at this stage tend to impose their cultural values onto everything, including communication patterns and decision-making processes. They surround themselves with people who share similar opinions. This tendency could quickly turn into an unethical situation that fosters biases.

Moving on, we enter the Yellow Zone: culturally emerging leadership. These leaders tend to be more accepting of cultural differences but still need to make more effort to understand what drives different communities. They might flex their approach occasionally but often stick with familiar patterns—which doesn't help their team reach its full potential.

Finally, we enter the Green Zone, where magic truly happens: culturally intelligent leadership. Leaders operating in this realm focus on building bridges between cultures and breaking down cultural barriers, searching out hidden voices to ensure authentic inclusion, and co-designing systems that consider everyone's knowledge equitably. These leaders really are rock stars!

Now is the time to assess yourself and your cultural leadership capabilities, set goals to increase CQ, and foster diversity within your team. Please use the color-coded continuum elements provided below to help guide your self-reflection and goal-setting process. Make this journey count by taking advantage of every chance to make a positive difference.

Red Zone: Culturally Inflexible Leadership

Ethnocentric mindset: Believes that one's cultural values/ways are superior and dismisses differences as irrelevant.

Self-awareness deficit: Holds assumptions about others based on unexplored cultural biases.

An uncompromising leadership style: Imposes one's preferences/style and marginalizes diverse needs.

Monocultural decisions: Takes unilateralist approaches without considering the cultural context.

Homogenous teams: Restricts representation; diminishes diversity value and limits its representation.

Yellow Zone: Culturally Emerging Leadership

Tolerance stance: Accepts cultural differences on a surface level but makes little effort to understand deeper meanings or integrate diverse perspectives.

Partial self-insight: Acknowledges the impact of personal culture at an intellectual level but lacks nuance when applied across situations.

Inconsistent flexibility: Sporadically adjusts leadership communication/policies when cultural gaps become apparent, but falls back into familiar/comfortable behavior patterns.

Emerging cultural cues: Takes account of data trends from across cultures when making decisions; however, implements them only if all parties are included.

Shallow integration: Supports diversity numerically on teams without providing psychological safety for nondominant groups to contribute authentically, thereby failing to maximize capabilities.

Green Zone: Culturally Sensitive Leadership

Culture-bridging attitude: Appreciates cultural differences as assets, forms connections across divides, and integrates cultural insights.

Self-awareness around blind spots: Is aware of how one's personal cultural lens impacts what one sees, reflects on identify bias, and works to broaden perspectives.

Situationally-skilled flexibility: Adopts behaviors, language, and policies to foster cross-cultural harmony and belonging.

Decision-making that integrates cultural wisdom: Solicits inputs early and comprehensively from all groups involved and co-creates solutions that reflect community values.

Building psychologically safe and empowering team cultures: Ensures that all talent feels respected and valued and can freely provide skills and ideas through equitable policies that foster a sense of belongingness.

Cultivating CQ and inclusive leadership is a fascinating journey of growth and transformation that never ends. It's becoming clearer and clearer: Investing in personal development is worth *every* penny.

Developmental Milestones

Now let me offer some helpful developmental milestones to consider.

First up is self-awareness. Understanding your biases and perspectives is vital for creating an inclusive environment. Next comes decision-making. For a leader, making fair and informed choices while considering all perspectives can make or break an inclusive workplace environment. And don't underestimate trust building! Building strong bonds within diverse teams is essential—when everyone feels included and valued, positive transformations abound.

Second, don't forget progress assessments. Regularly checking in with yourself helps to create intentionally empowering environments and ensure that every individual has an equal chance to thrive—hence the importance of promoting equity and creating a sense of belonging, much like creating an inviting home where everyone feels at ease.

Case Study: Cultivating CQ at TechVista

Jeremy, the CEO of TechVista, an expanding technology company, recognized the need to build CQ among his leadership team as his workforce became increasingly diverse in culture, generational status, physical and cognitive abilities, and location. The realization came after a series of incidents highlighted the lack of cultural understanding in the organization.

In one instance, a talented Malaysian employee resigned, citing a lack of inclusivity and understanding from her manager, who had repeatedly dismissed her ideas and excluded her from crucial meetings. The employee's manager incorrectly assumed that the employee's quieter demeanor indicated a lack of engagement and initiative and failed to recognize that her culture valued harmony and respect for authority.

In another incident, during a team-building exercise, a Nigerian team member felt uncomfortable with his Western colleagues' direct and aggressive communication style. The team member's reluctance to engage in the debate was perceived as a lack of interest, leading to his ideas being overlooked and his contributions undervalued.

Furthermore, minority employees reported a lack of senior role models who could provide meaningful guidance tailored to their cultural backgrounds. They felt that their unique perspectives and challenges were not fully understood or addressed by the predominantly white male leadership team.

To better understand the organization's cultural dynamics, Jeremy assessed senior executives' cultural perspectives using tools like the Cultural Intelligence Scale (CQS) and the Intercultural Development Inventory (IDI) (see the Appendix for links to these tools). The results revealed significant gaps in empathy, adaptability, and inclusive decision-making among the leadership team.

Some executives held Western-centric views, which valued direct debate as an indicator of engagement. This led them to mistakenly perceive team members from other cultures, particularly those from African backgrounds, as disengaged or inactive when they did not conform to these communication norms.

As tensions mounted and productivity suffered, Jeremy realized that urgent action was needed to bridge TechVista's cultural divides and create a more inclusive and culturally intelligent organization.

Case Study Questions

1. What proactive measures could Jeremy have taken to identify and address cultural issues before they escalated into resignations and unproductive team dynamics?

2. How can Jeremy effectively communicate the findings from the cultural perspectives assessment to his leadership team and gain their buy-in for the proposed CQ development initiatives?

3. What additional components or activities would you recommend to enhance the effectiveness of Jeremy's Culturally Intelligent Leader's Mindset development program in fostering CQ among TechVista's leaders?

4. How can Jeremy ensure that the mentorship program and multi-demographic advisory councils continue to thrive and evolve as the company grows and new employees join the organization?

5. What other metrics or indicators would you suggest Jeremy use to measure the ongoing success and impact of the CQ initiatives on the organization's culture and performance?

Case Study Resolution

Recognizing the critical need to address the cultural divides within TechVista, Jeremy took decisive action to develop the CQ of his leadership team and foster a more inclusive organizational culture.

Jeremy established a comprehensive Culturally Intelligent Leader's Mindset development program aligned with the eight competencies outlined in this chapter. The program included biweekly reflective sessions during work hours, providing a safe space for executives to explore their cultural biases, blind spots, and privileges. Quarterly cultural immersion experiences were organized that exposed leaders to diverse communities and perspectives, and monthly coaching circles facilitated deep discussions and sensemaking around cultural challenges.

To ensure that the development of CQ was not limited to the leadership team, Jeremy instituted a mentorship program that paired emerging minority talents with directors and VPs. The active engagement and success of mentees in the mentorship program was made part of the mentors' performance metrics, which underscored the importance of diversity and inclusion to the organization's success. The mentorship initiative provided minority employees with access to senior role models who could offer culturally relevant guidance and support while fostering greater understanding and empathy among the leadership team.

In addition to introducing the mentorship program, Jeremy piloted a series of measures intended to promote inclusive decision-making and create a culture of openness and collaboration. Ideation sessions using anonymous input-gathering software were implemented, ensuring that all voices were heard and valued, regardless of cultural background or communication style. Participatory budgeting on pilot projects enabled employees at all levels to contribute to the company's direction, which fostered a sense of ownership and engagement.

Jeremy also formed multi-demographic advisory councils composed of employees from various cultural backgrounds, generations, and abilities. These councils collaborated on product development and policy reviews, providing diverse perspectives and insights that enriched the company's offerings and practices. By seeking out and valuing the input of these advisory councils, Jeremy demonstrated his commitment to co-creation and his openness to feedback from all members of the organization.

Just one year these initiatives were implemented, TechVista experienced a significant transformation in its organizational culture. Innovation flourished as diverse ideas and perspectives were freely shared and explored. Retention rates, particularly among minority employees, improved dramatically as individuals felt valued and empowered to express their opinions without fear of judgment or retribution.

The success of Jeremy's efforts to cultivate CQ at TechVista highlights the importance of proactive and committed leadership in creating inclusive and diverse organizations. Jeremy demonstrated that leaders can effectively bridge cultural divides and create environments where all employees can thrive by assessing cultural perspectives, providing targeted development opportunities, and fostering inclusive decision-making.

Through his culturally intelligent leadership, Jeremy not only transformed the mindsets of those in leadership positions but also implemented systemic changes that embedded cultural intelligence into the organization's fabric. Jeremy positioned TechVista for continued success in an increasingly diverse and interconnected world by ensuring that these changes were sustainable.

Advancing Your Leadership Journey

Reflection Questions

1. Which of the eight components of the Culturally Intelligent Leader's Mindset framework do you consider to be your strongest, and which do you believe is most in need of improvement in your leadership approach?

2. Reflecting on your past experiences, can you identify instances where a lack of CQ may have hindered your ability to lead effectively? What did you learn from those experiences?

3. How can you leverage the Cultural Intelligence Leadership Continuum to assess your current CQ level and set specific growth and development goals?

4. What steps can you take to create a psychologically safe environment for your team or organization that encourages open dialogue, diverse perspectives, and inclusive decision-making?

5. How can you role-model CQ and inspire others in your organization to embrace the Culturally Intelligent Leader's Mindset?

Practical Application Activity

Commit to developing a culturally intelligent leader's mindset. Try this:

- The Cultural Perspective-Taking Exercise

Select three cultural groups with which you have little personal experience and do some research on each to broaden your understanding. Look for sources such as academic articles, cultural framework models, or interviews with individuals from those cultures. Explore topics like cultural values, communication norms, workplace motivations, and leadership preferences unique to each cultural group.

Once you've developed an in-depth knowledge of each group, it's time to get creative. Imagine you're managing an employee from each cultural background. Step into their shoes and consider how you would adapt your management style to show that their perspectives were considered. Take some time and jot down 2–3 paragraphs about each situation that reflect how to make connections more effective, culturally attuned, and mutually understanding; sharing them with a peer or mentor may yield further insights.

Now that we have completed this powerful growth planning activity to expand your capabilities, let's step back and examine the key learnings from this chapter.

Key Takeaways

1. The Culturally Intelligent Leader's Mindset comprises eight essential components: self-awareness, cultural empathy, situational attunement, inclusive decision-making, psychological safety, equitable access, reciprocal adaptation, and role modeling. Cultivating these skills allows leaders to effectively navigate diverse contexts and foster innovation and collaboration across cultural differences.

2. Developing CQ is an ongoing journey that requires leaders to confront their biases, challenge assumptions, and seek out diverse perspectives. Tools such as the Cultural Intelligence Scale (CQS) and the Intercultural Development Inventory (IDI) help leaders to assess and expand their intercultural abilities over time.

3. The Cultural Intelligence Leadership Continuum serves as a valuable tool for leaders to assess their current level of cultural and set goals for growth

and development across the three zones: Red (culturally inflexible), Yellow (culturally emerging), and Green (culturally sensitive).

4. Enabling cultural development entails confronting biases and barriers while offering equal access to global experiences, leadership training programs, and advancement opportunities. Leaders can drive improved organizational performance in an increasingly globalized world by creating psychologically safe environments and adapting their approach.

Part 2

Navigating the Dimensions of Cultural Intelligence:
A Deep Dive

Chapter 5

Developing Cognitive CQ Discernment

To truly cultivate cultural intelligence, we must begin by looking within ourselves and engaging in candid self-reflection. Simultaneously, we must maintain a sharp awareness of the context in which we operate and demonstrate a profound respect for the kaleidoscope of perspectives that surround us. As Moua (2010) noted, "Culturally intelligent leaders must create an environment where diversity and culture flourish, and where conflicting values can be safely expressed and explored through dialogue" (p. 14). Unfortunately, we often judge unfamiliar behaviors reflexively, through biased lenses, without considering all possible contexts. As leaders who seek to deepen our cultural understanding, we must first recognize our inherent human limitations when it comes to fully grasping perspectives outside our dominant paradigms.

Structured cultural frameworks come into play here to facilitate successful navigation across diverse regions with varied histories and priorities. For instance, some cultures value harmony more, while others place more importance on communication or scheduling issues. By considering factors like comfort with uncertainty, individualism vs. collectivism, and so forth, we can better accommodate practices that differ from our inherited preferences while adapting them appropriately.

Let's examine this example further. In some cultures, direct critique may be considered simply efficient rather than intentionally aggressive. In other cultures, specifically in symbolic cultural traditions (such as those of Japan or Middle Eastern countries like the United Arab Emirates), elaborate hospitality rituals for welcoming guests may signal respect, but in a way that might seem foreign to other cultures without proper context. Structured cultural frameworks, such as Hofstede's Cultural Dimensions (see Chapter 2 and the Appendix), provide valuable insights into these differences. Although they may not be complete, as generations and cultures shift, they still serve as helpful guides when navigating cross-cultural interactions. As Earley and Mosakowski (2004) noted, frameworks like Hofstede's provide vital starting points for approaching cross-cultural differences gracefully and thoughtfully.

Leaders seeking to deepen their cultural understanding should first acknowledge that we struggle to fully comprehend perspectives outside our dominant paradigms. Sometimes we judge unfamiliar behaviors just because they're different; but by applying frameworks such as Hofstede's Cultural Dimensions, we can navigate and learn more about predictable differences between regional norms.

Culturally intelligent leaders recognize the value of getting input from peers with diverse cultural backgrounds. By listening actively and asking questions instead of making quick judgments, they gain valuable insight into different communication styles, what motivates individuals, and policies that resonate with culturally diverse teams. When conflicts arise, leaders with CQ must analyze root causes carefully before mediating to find common ground between all involved.

Cultural discernment requires leaders to accept that they don't know everything, to have the courage to face challenges, and to remain committed to learning. So let's empower marginalized voices, include them in our strategies, and keep learning from one another as we work to create an inclusive and culturally aware world together.

Structured Cultural Frameworks: Unveiling Predictable Differences

As leaders strive to foster cultural discernment, they may turn to conceptual frameworks that expose differences in norms across diverse regional histories. Such frameworks help us grasp what matters in terms of harmony, acceptance of hierarchy, open and transparent communication, or scheduling paradigms prioritizing universalist efficiency assumptions—to name but a few elements!

Hofstede's Cultural Dimensions (see Chapter 2 and the Appendix) is a prime example of a framework that provides valuable insights into how different cultures operate. This framework examines levels of uncertainty avoidance, individualistic or collectivist orientation, and comfort with power distance among various groups. By exploring these spectrums, leaders can gain a deeper understanding of complex dynamics that might initially seem confusing when viewed through a single cultural lens. Moreover, these frameworks offer context-specific insights into the drivers of behavior across various world paradigms.

Once leaders acquire this knowledge, they can better recognize potential challenges and approach them mindfully. With this understanding, leaders can quickly identify potential issues and employ mindfulness when confronting them. They learn patience because they realize that sometimes cultural differences require situational learning rather than making assumptions based on cultural preferences; different cultural norms exist and may be suitable in other circumstances. It's like knowing when it is best to engage in heated debate versus opting for tactful ambiguity—these leaders have it covered!

And let's keep sight of our ultimate goal here: Adopting these insights can help leaders navigate the complexities of multicultural environments more successfully by cultivating CQ and encouraging inclusive dialogue. In that way, they can create an environment where everyone gets on board, respects each other's backgrounds, and works collaboratively toward success, regardless of the various players' different cultural roots.

Next time someone mentions conceptual frameworks, note that they are about gaining some cultural street smarts—like becoming a global traveler without leaving your desk (although a vacation to a new land wouldn't hurt, either!). Accept their wisdom with open arms and watch as your understanding improves.

Going Beyond Static Frameworks

Although these static frameworks can be fascinating and provide a crucial initial understanding of cultural orientations, they are not enough in today's constantly evolving world.

Think about it: We're all connected and constantly exposed to music, movies, and the internet; therefore, our identities are becoming an amalgamation of different eras and cultures. No longer can people be classified simply according to age or where they're from. It's much more complicated now!

Leaders who truly grasp this issue know that academic knowledge alone won't cut it; instead, they immerse themselves in various environments to stay current and adaptable in their thinking and their openness to various groups and behaviors. Blending traditional practices with modern efficiencies is only part of the picture; balancing the conservation of our heritage with the acceptance of change is also essential.

Static frameworks provide us with a starting point, but adaptive leaders fully understand the complexities of cultural dynamics. They know that things are still emerging and developing, meaning we must continue broadening our knowledge and remaining flexible in our thinking to stay on the cutting edge of today's ever-evolving world.

Leader Blind Spots in Applying Frameworks

Now let's take a look at leader blind spots when it comes to cultural frameworks. After all, these frameworks are meant to aid us in comprehending the complex global environments that are shaped by diverse social and geopolitical journeys (Hofstede, 2003). They offer patterns for preferences, communication conventions, and what not to do so we don't plunge headfirst into cultural confusion. They map key dimensions along spectrums while deciphering generations of observation and then wrap all that into visually pleasing summaries that promise foolproof understanding of cultural differences (Hampden-Turner & Trompenaars, 2006).

But do these frameworks actually live up to their promises? Although they provide simplified decision rules and elegant shortcuts, what these frameworks cannot capture is the ever-evolving nature of cultural contexts across time and place. Nor can they fully explain our hybrid backgrounds that cannot be summarized with formulas; as individuals, we constantly negotiate our way across a spectrum, seeking a balance between various ways of being.

Surface knowledge of cultural frameworks may lead to overconfidence among global leaders who lack cross-cultural humility (Johnson et al., 2006). Unquestioningly adhering to cultural models without acknowledging their limitations is our greatest weakness. We need to remember that intellectual capital alone will not suffice in reaching across infinitely diverse human contexts, and moral courage and self-reflection must also play their parts.

There are three issues, in particular, that have an enormously detrimental impact on historically marginalized individuals and organizations, threatening progress and making life harder for people. Let's look at these three issues here.

Initial confusion arises from **assumptions of similarity**. These involve projecting dominant beliefs onto various groups without asking if they agree.

Before making assumptions or drawing conclusions about anyone, we must seek consent and receive validation about what we're thinking.

Next is **presentism**. This occurs when we judge unfamiliar behaviors based solely on current norms, without considering the historical context. We must remember that differences exist for a reason!

Finally, we must work to free ourselves of **stereotyping**, which is our tendency to group people based on simplified categories. Stereotyping does not lead to anything positive. It's like trying to understand a symphony by listening to only one note—you miss out on the rich complexity and beauty of the whole! So why not embrace diversity and celebrate humanity's fantastic tapestry instead? Not only is it the right thing to do, for all the reasons we have already discussed in this book, but it will also make life more exciting and vibrant.

By acknowledging these gaps in our cultural frameworks, we leaders can take responsibility for our dominant perspectives. We need to create space for others beyond clichéd tropes—this is indeed everyone's duty, and particularly, each global leader's obligation.

Assumptions of Similarity

One of the biggest blunders a leader can make is assuming everyone thinks and acts just like them without checking to confirm it. That kind of assumption amounts to projecting your personal preferences and idiosyncrasies onto the entire team or customer base without even double-checking—talk about a recipe for disaster (Caprar et al., 2015)! Although it might be tempting to think that what works for you should also work for everyone else, researcher Geert Hofstede warns against taking this approach, because leaders who overlook cultural differences set themselves up for failure if this bias goes unchecked; leaving this bias in place severely diminishes cognitive CQ (Caprar et al., 2015).

Even in performance metrics and qualifications, we rely too heavily on narrow ethnocentric benchmarks to assess merit. By doing this, we overlook alternative cultural pathways to excellence, such as community organizing roles that demonstrate capability just as much as Ivy League credentials but often go unnoticed because of rigid hierarchies. If we want genuinely responsive services, we must move beyond homogenous archetypes toward a greater multiplicity of experiences.

So how can we avoid falling into an assumption trap? One approach is to include diverse perspectives when making decisions and engaging in product development. Bring advisory councils that include voices from diverse backgrounds into strategy meetings, get feedback from focus groups with members from various cultural segments, and check the data before making assumptions (Livermore, 2015). Otherwise, you may end up with some ticked-off, resentful people; miss out on incredible innovation opportunities; or even misidentify crucial needs.

Presentism

Presentism may be a fancy term, but it is a real issue that can seriously compromise a leader's cultural discernment. Instead of understanding practices in different cultural environments as intended by their originator, we end up judging them solely by today's standards—talk about missing the mark!

Let's consider our modern workplace: With flexible schedules and video calls that lend themselves to casual attire, informal work styles have often replaced more businesslike attire. Younger workers generally seem comfortable with these new work norms—they like flexible hours and casual attire when video chatting, and they enjoy speaking their minds freely in virtual settings. However, some more experienced leaders from traditional corporate environments might view this change as threatening their established reporting structures (Aldrich, 2014).

We need to stop projecting our present ideas onto the past! Although some old practices may appear outdated, we must understand their context and investigate their origins before we reject or condemn them. Dig deeper instead of making snap judgments! Next time you encounter something unfamiliar, take a step back. Consider its historical context and cultural evolution before jumping to conclusions based solely on the present context. Be open to learning from past events while celebrating cultural intelligence!

Tendency Toward Stereotyping

Cultural models often contribute to inaccurate generalizations about communities that are based on biased observations, leading to stereotyping about individuals and prejudices against them (Kankanhalli et al., 2016). We should take particular care not to reduce diasporic hybrid identities into conventional ethnic categories that only reinforce boundaries rather than breaking them down. For example, a second-generation immigrant may identify with both their ancestral culture and the culture of their birth country, resulting in a unique hybrid identity that cannot be easily categorized.

Keeping things simple by categorizing them can be appealing, but we must avoid arbitrarily assigning people to groups. Critical theorists have voiced concerns over evaluating cultural groups without taking into account the minority perspectives within each larger group; don't forget that though we so often look at the differences between cultures, there are many marginalized cultural groups even within each culture (Jack & Westwood, 2009). We must remember that categorizing differences can create inequitable relationships (Shenkar et al., 2008).

As leaders who employ cultural models, we must first undertake our own solemn self-examination. We should ask ourselves whether our frameworks hide biases that we harbor even though they appear to be scientific. By courageously confronting latent prejudices and welcoming different viewpoints, leaders can move toward responsible leadership that does not perpetuate stereotype threats; by searching out marginalized voices and insights during every phase of applying what might seem to be perfectly solid models, we can move closer to social justice (Jack & Westwood, 2009; Kankanhalli et al., 2019; Shenkar et al., 2008).

Avoiding Interpretation Pitfalls

Conceptual models can help us better understand different cultures in an advanced and responsible manner; however, let us not ignore their power dynamics, even in seemingly convincing scholarly works (Jack & Westwood, 2009). Adhering to any theory without questioning it may prove dangerous, leading to polarization and the oversimplification of thought processes.

Therefore, we must remain open to diverse perspectives and build relationships across power, perspective, and identity boundaries. We need to be mindful of pitfalls that can arise as we shape our theories—for example, being unconscious of our privilege. This way, we create space for diversity while not oversimplifying individual experiences.

Relying too heavily on frameworks and theories can lead to oversimplification and the perpetuation of dominant perspectives. In the next section, we will explore the limitations of cultural frameworks in more detail.

Remember, solidarity comes from our shared commitment to moving beyond our usual ways of thinking and understanding, which lies in the journey that each of us undertakes and that we all undertake together as we celebrate all the beautiful facets of humanity that defy any framework.

Limitations of Frameworks

Conceptual models can be invaluable when navigating unfamiliar cultural environments, providing leaders with a roadmap of do's and don'ts, motivations, and communication norms for leading in unknown waters (Hofstede, 2001). However, we must remember that depending exclusively on these models can lead to false confidence if we fail to account for lived experiences and the real constraints of communities. That is why responsive leadership must supplement these models with insights from people themselves by actively listening for local voices, tracking changes, and prioritizing stories, because stories help ground facts in wisdom (Hofstede, 2001).

One common misstep leaders make is relying too much on broad national frameworks, overlooking the rich tapestry of diversity that lies within. Although such broad frameworks might give a general impression of cultural preferences in any particular country, they fail to capture all its nuances and variations (Leung et al., 2014). Culture is dynamic, shifting and developing among various groups and generations. Therefore, leaders must be attuned to these differences and approach every interaction with an open mind.

Let's not overlook identity, either: As complex, multidimensional beings, we are all balancing multiple aspects of our identities, including ethnicity, religion, profession, education level, age, and more, that shape our experiences and decisions as we go through life (Ganesh & McAllum, 2012). External categorizations cannot fully capture the complexity of identity. Some cultural frameworks oversimplify and generalize, failing to account for individuals' unique experiences and intersectional identities.

Therefore, the responsible application of cultural frameworks requires us to acknowledge their inherent limits. We must integrate contemporary diversity by amplifying local voices and paying attention to changes happening around us. Learning surface-level facts will not suffice; instead, we need to embrace an interdisciplinary developmental perspective that encourages us to explore cultural dynamics with curiosity and vulnerability—a perspective that can shift and adjust, just like the world itself keeps shifting.

Credibility issues arise when we consider the ethics of engaging with communities that have not consented to measurement methodologies and applications (Caprar et al., 2015). Simplifying things mathematically has its own kind of integrity, but it risks repeating the patterns of the dominant power dynamics by silencing marginalized voices, which should, in fact, be the ones to shape such work. To avoid unintended exploitation, we need to refrain from using one-sided research approaches; to achieve justice, we need fair collaborations and early anonymized focus groups (Kankanhalli et al., 2019). In efforts toward justice, it is crucial to empower marginalized communities and allow them to drive change from within. This means giving them a platform to share their experiences, insights, and ideas and ensuring that their voices are heard and valued in the decision-making process.

External frameworks alone cannot create an equitable approach that incorporates inputs from those affected populations. But by acknowledging our ignorance and our knowledge gaps and listening to others' stories and experiences, we can recover hope in meaningful ways and move toward reconciliation by amplifying voices from outside the established paradigms.

Lack of Generational Nuance

Cultural models on a national level may often fall prey to the oversimplification of diversity. When we aggregate data, we risk missing out on individual experiences that shape our understanding (Leung et al., 2014). Cultural shifts do not happen overnight—they emerge slowly over generations.

Policies, infrastructure, and technology changes can have far-reaching ramifications for different age groups. Furthermore, as people grow up in various environments, their values and motivations change accordingly; hence, what is needed is more than just a one-size-fits-all approach to understanding cultural differences.

Cultural evolution also differs across regions, creating additional complexity. Instead of just looking for similarities among them all, we must identify any differences as they emerge and monitor them over time.

To manage these complex challenges responsibly, we should approach cultural frameworks as guides rather than rigid rules. Our insights should constantly adapt to reflect the ever-evolving nature of culture—prompting the question, "Who will recognize, understand, and take responsibility for implementing this enormous diversity?"

Missing Intersectionality

Cultural frameworks may need to catch up with new understandings about the complexity of identity (Atewologun, 2018; Crenshaw, 2017). Relying solely on broad cultural categories is overly simplistic. In truth, we need to go beyond general categorizations and investigate all influences—from ethnicity and occupation through region and family background—that make up our multifaceted communities today.

As Nkomo and Hoobler (2014) noted, when we rely solely on external lenses such as nationality or gender to understand identities, we miss the many layers that intersect and shape them. For instance, first-generation college students of color face unique challenges arising from socioeconomic considerations and campus environments. Unfortunately, these challenges often remain unrecorded in national statistics, which only scratch the surface.

Let us also remember our mobile expatriates, who must navigate a delicate balance of dual national allegiances across multiple spheres. Their experiences are often left out of mainstream expatriate research, which focuses solely on corporate outcomes—which is like looking at just the tip of an iceberg but missing all its depths!

We must take an inclusive approach to more fully recognize and nurture the diversity that exists, including intersectional factors like economic class backgrounds, migration generations, abilities, and sexualities. We must listen, understand, and support individuals on their unique journeys.

Here's the thing: We cannot merely impose assumptions or disconnect ourselves from experiences of systemic inequality. In contrast, cultural humility requires us to ask questions, build relationships, and take risks. Through this process comes true wisdom.

Cultures Continually Evolve

Cultural ossification, or cultural stagnation, is a legitimate risk when it comes to frameworks. The mere existence of frameworks might suggest fixed traits, even though that is not the intent of their creators (Caprar et al., 2015). The architects of these frameworks recognize this potential loss of fluidity, but they hope that novices will use the frameworks as starting points for development instead of as rigid stereotypes. We must stay relevant by keeping pace with the changes around us!

Technology and diasporic influences continuously transform how we negotiate our identities within countries, particularly for the younger generations who are immersed in digital environments from an early age. As a result, cultural goalposts are constantly moving, so we cannot assume that what worked in the past will continue working now; we must listen carefully and adjust as necessary.

We will never be able to fit all individuals into neat little identity boxes. Diasporic diversity challenges traditional majority–minority dynamics, and projections still struggle to capture its essence. Statistical models may also need to be more flexible when used to understand belonging and identity. We must seek out various inputs and adapt our forecasting methods to stay ahead.

The responsible application of any framework recognizes the ever-evolving nature of culture rather than fixating on static states (Leung et al., 2014). Surveys should be conducted regularly to monitor incremental shifts in value adoption. However, numbers alone will not do: We must also collect employee stories and analyze any training differences over time.

Make sure to take account of ongoing changes rather than just past insights. Weighing factual updates alongside contextual interviews to stay current ensures that the way in which we apply the frameworks will remain responsive; statistical models alone cannot offer us the complete picture.

Supplementing Frameworks

Conceptual models serve as a kind of GPS for comprehending culture, but using them responsibly means finding the appropriate balance between quick fixes and actual community experiences. That is where participatory input comes in! When leaders acknowledge the limitations of simplification while including community voices in decision-making processes, simplification becomes less of an issue, and everyone gets their say at the table. Tracking generational shifts and prioritizing narratives helps to ground facts in a way that goes beyond surface-level stereotypes. Hearing the voices of all involved individuals and groups and staying informed as things evolve is of the utmost importance to ensure that we don't miss anything important by oversimplifying things. No one can fully grasp another human being without person-to-person encounters and the forming of relationships, and it is sharing human experiences that makes life worthwhile.

Let's be clear. To make progress, we must all take collective responsibility and accept the diversity that makes our world unique and vibrant. This is not some abstract concept: It involves people with real identities and real stories who need our solidarity when dealing with the complexities of identity.

Leaders who recognize this and stand in solidarity with those affected are taking an essential step toward liberation for all of us.

Seeking Community Input

Conceptual frameworks are created by taking samples of diverse respondents and searching for commonalities. The goal is to form usable models that simplify complex differences into something we can all comprehend. However, we must ask ourselves whether this process, as currently practiced, is even ethical. If minority subcommunities aren't included, their unique perspectives could be lost forever.

Mathematical simplification can be helpful, but it can also contribute to maintaining dominance if it marginalizes nondominant voices. We must resist the one-way flow of knowledge and embrace collaboration. Placing affected populations at the core can prevent intellectual colonization and produce more equitable theories (Caprar et al., 2015). To reach solutions, it is necessary to listen to minority focus groups. They can reveal assumptions that need correcting and highlight details we might otherwise overlook.

As a concrete example, financial literacy programs often struggled to effectively engage South Asian immigrant communities. However, when women-only focus groups were conducted, they revealed specific household money management dynamics unique to these communities. This insight allowed program designers to tailor their approach, resulting in more culturally relevant and successful financial literacy initiatives (Leonardo & Porter, 2010).

At the core of all of this, it is critical to understand that even seemingly homogenous groups contain various intersections that influence our perceptions of them as we try to predict their behavior and preferences (Carter, 2013). Using the techniques of business anthropology, such as ethnographic research, participant observation, and in-depth interviews, will allow us to dig deeper into these intersections. These methods involve immersing oneself in the culture, observing and participating in daily activities, and conducting detailed interviews to understand the culture and its various subgroups better. It's like having cultural insiders who can explain why certain behaviors may align with historical constraints and priorities. This knowledge empowers us to make informed decisions rather than relying solely on external standards (Jordan, 2012).

When we design solutions to bring about lasting change, we must involve the community. Our solutions will be infinitely more effective if we listen to and support community members' goals than if we force our ideas onto them. Voices that have long been silenced must finally be heard—justice cannot be achieved through technical orchestration alone (Johnson & Onwuegbuzie, 2004).

Conceptual models provide excellent starting points, but we need to remember that they cannot fully capture the complexity of real-life dynamics. Therefore, we must work to understand each other better, approaching our work with empathy and curiosity. After all, what awaits discovery through these meaningful connections is nothing less than our shared humanity.

Gathering Qualitative Insights

Collecting qualitative information and stories can add depth and richness to the data. Culturally intelligent leadership requires us to pay close attention during meetings as well as to any assumptions that are being made and any unconscious projections that may surface because of our biases or unconscious projections we may make. Let us ask ourselves: Are we making claims without evidence? And do certain communication styles dominate conversations while others go unnoticed? Transparency is vital when it comes to learning and growth.

It is crucial that we examine our existing policies and practices. We need to evaluate how flexible they are in truly meeting the needs and concerns of different individuals and groups, using tools like psychological safety assessments to spot hidden gaps. Workplace Strategies for Mental Health offers an online psychologically safe team assessment that can help identify areas where our practices may be falling short of creating an inclusive environment (see the Appendix for the link to this assessment).

Disaggregating data by identity variables enables us to better visualize diversity within seemingly homogeneous scores. We must recognize which individuals or groups might still be facing constraints, even if overall trends for a particular group, or for marginalized groups in general, have improved. This recognition enables us to make progress with conscious and incremental goals in mind.

To achieve a deeper understanding, we must seek out different perspectives and narratives—particularly those that are marginalized in the existing systems. Anonymous surveys can offer safe spaces for people to share their experiences and offer crucial data points. By blending quantitative patterns with qualitative nuances, we can empower leaders to navigate complexity more successfully while moving away from binary thinking. Remember, there is no one-size-fits-all approach, and there is no shortcut. It's important to embrace diversity and seek input from multiple sources.

Tracking Changes Over Time

The responsible application of a cultural framework recognizes that things are constantly shifting rather than remaining fixed in one spot (as we noted above, in the section titled "Cultures Continually Evolve"). Technologies and generational shifts continue to influence our mindsets and experiences, so we must remain abreast of this ever-evolving cultural landscape to stay current with what is relevant.

In efforts to keep track of these shifts and changes, it is invaluable to conduct regular organizational culture surveys. Such surveys provide quantitative data by analyzing media consumption trends and employee stories in an attempt to detect shifts in attitudes toward training initiatives. Furthermore, segmenting focus groups according to cohorts and communication channels allows us to detect variations in the momentum of adoption and adjust our strategies accordingly. Forecasting the future requires more than data analysis: It requires listening to emerging voices and perspectives as we consider what lies ahead.

Building Cognitive CQ Skills

CQ involves more than simply knowing about different cultures—it requires the skills to effectively apply that knowledge in different situations (Johnson et al., 2006). Building your CQ muscle is all about flexing those diversity management skills and diving headfirst into complex decision-making (Ang et al., 2007). Think of it as a workout routine for your brain, like bench-pressing weights for professional growth!

To increase cognitive CQ, you must consciously expand your cultural repertoire. That means training your mind to pick up subtle cues, consider different perspectives, and welcome unfamiliar cultural frameworks (Leung & Chiu, 2010). Doing this improves communication, relationships, and collaboration across differences (Leung & Chiu, 2010).

How can one develop cognitive skills for CQ? By strengthening the critical capacities (Bird et al., 2010) that are necessary for cultural discernment. By honing these four key abilities—perspective-taking, systems thinking, balancing of generalizations and specifics, and adaptive forecasting—you can enhance your cultural discernment, enabling you to avoid miscommunications and adapt more quickly in cross-cultural situations. We will now look more closely at these four techniques that can build intercultural awareness, perceptual acuity, and behavioral repertoires.

Perspective-Taking

Perspective-taking is about putting yourself in someone else's shoes and trying to see things from their perspective. It can be like shifting gears in your brain, giving you access to new cultural lenses and ideas (Leung & Chiu, 2010). Leung and Chiu (2010) found that exposing yourself to different systems of cultural meaning changes how your brain operates regarding perspective-taking: Building new pathways makes you more adaptable across cultures.

Tadmor and colleagues (2009) also discovered that multicultural experiences increase our capacity for complex and nuanced thinking—again, giving our brain a workout. And, as they say, a little exercise goes a long way! Imagine the power of stretching your cognitive capacity, exploring various cultural logics, and strengthening your adaptability muscles.

Bird et al. (2010) discovered some encouraging data for global leaders: People who are very good at perspective-taking have an edge in terms of their international management potential. Their flexibility, creativity, and knowledge of the global business landscape make them standout leaders, because perspective-taking is an impressive skill and can lead to a competitive advantage. So take note: Perspective-taking may give you an edge as well.

Immersing yourself in foreign films, literature, art, or travel will broaden your perspective-taking skills. However, as Leung and Chiu (2008) pointed out, if you have a genuine desire to understand other cultures, you will need more than just expose yourself to it. Journaling about your experiences or having conversations with cultural informants can elevate your cultural understanding to new levels. This kind of activity builds adaptability for intercultural success.

Systems Thinking

Systems thinking is another invaluable skill that can strengthen our cognitive abilities and increase our cultural intelligence. It involves considering the larger picture—understanding the cultural contexts, relationships, and root drivers behind cultural dynamics—to better understand cultural ecosystems and why specific patterns emerge the way they do. Hofstede (2003) suggested that cultures function like a collective programming of our minds, passed down through generations and reinforced by reciprocal institutions.

By honing this systems thinking ability, you will gain the ability to anticipate cultural resistance when significant shifts occur, or to identify subtle social cues that otherwise often go undetected. Systems thinkers can make more discerning cultural observations by spotting power structures or picking up norms through gestures. Think of it as having your very own Spidey-Sense!

Ng et al. (2012) conducted research that demonstrated how systems analysis can result in superior cultural judgments and significantly boost cognitive CQ. This means that those with a more robust capacity for and grasp of systems analysis have an enhanced ability to process cultural understanding to make more informed decisions.

Are you trying to improve your systems thinking muscle? Visualization techniques that map out relationships between different factors, such as causal loop diagrams, can be highly effective at building that muscle: Imagine connecting the dots and visualizing how different cultural variables intertwine and influence each other. Also, studying real-world cultural case studies from a systems perspective will significantly expand your sense of contextual clarity and your pattern recognition skills—soon, you will start seeing connections where others might miss them! To push your thinking further, you can study models that account for complex, non-linear changes, which offer another level of advancement: the ability to master an understanding of cultural dynamics regardless of circumstance.

Balancing Generalizations and Specifics

Navigating new cultures requires a delicate balancing act between broad frameworks and specific situations—it's a way of reaching an understanding without falling prey to stereotypes. Navigating foreign cultures can be a formidable mental exercise that tests your capacity to evaluate cultural knowledge based on new evidence.

Generalizations may provide an initial starting point, but don't become attached to them. Skilled cultural navigators act like detectives, identifying affirming and conflicting signals from cultural environments and adjusting their frameworks as necessary. This process is about becoming acutely aware of your cultural surroundings and adapting your understanding accordingly.

Making judgment calls involves weighing current evidence against sociocultural history as a whole. It means keeping yourself informed of specific cultural nuances, behaviors, and events happening now while always keeping the broader historical and cultural context in mind. By continuously comparing and analyzing different cultural contexts, you can increase your cultural intelligence and adapt to new environments faster.

Here's an insider tip: Asking good questions and recognizing patterns against the background of your existing cultural knowledge can help you update your understanding without losing your sense of the big picture. A synthesis of broad perspectives and attention to details is where true cognitive flexibility and cultural intelligence thrive (Ang & Van Dyne, 2008).

Adaptive Forecasting

The advancement of CQ requires adapting your cultural forecasts to the changing cross-cultural situations rather than trying to make exact predictions every time. In other words, adaptive forecasting focuses on updating scenarios based on new cultural evidence, not on trying to get it exactly right.

Klein and Hoffman (1992) conducted fascinating research on cultural judgment. They discovered that adaptable experts who collected sparse cultural cues, generated multiple hypotheses from those cues, and adjusted their strategies based on their observations demonstrated superior sense-making than novices who clung to fixed forecasts while disregarding contradictory signals.

If you want to enhance your cultural predictive abilities, it is important to embrace uncertainty and constantly refine your working theories (Mendenhall et al., 2008). Seek out disconfirming cultural evidence to challenge your existing mindset. By repeatedly testing and adjusting your assumptions based on new information, your mental models will come closer to reflecting the ever-evolving realities, and having an expansive mental library of patterns will help you quickly recognize familiar dynamics even in unfamiliar contexts.

Here is the exciting part: Any changes you make now will only strengthen your future judgments, and conducting debriefs after the event can advance your predictive capacities even further. Review your forecast scenarios and compare them with actual outcomes; keeping track of how effectively your judgments worked will strengthen your adaptability, helping you navigate cultural ambiguity more easily.

Developing Cognitive CQ Through Inclusive and Equitable Decision-Making

One essential step for effective decision-making is carefully evaluating both the process and the outcomes of decision-making— including participation rates, psychological safety assessments, and consensus levels—to see whether the benefits are reaching diverse communities equitably (Mitchell et al., 2014). Tracking the leading indicators of inclusive processes and the lagging indicators of equitable results is crucial in creating equitable solutions.

Collective debriefs can be very valuable! Regular debriefs with your team let you identify cultural assumptions, blind spots, and communication misunderstandings together—it's like revamping your mental models for future decisions (Halverson et al., 2004). Encourage team members to reflect together transparently, as this increases the awareness of subtle dynamics that might otherwise undermine equitable collaboration and helps you to develop cognitive CQ faster.

Inclusive Decision-Making Processes

As leaders, we must seek input from various cultural viewpoints and listen without judgment (Hajro et al., 2017). Although incorporating inclusive practices might initially seem complex, research shows that inclusive processes can increase creativity, accuracy, and collective intelligence (Phillips et al., 2004). So where should we start when it comes to inclusive decision-making? Leaders need to frequently analyze their biases and power dynamics to unearth hidden assumptions (Cook & Glass, 2013). By becoming conscious of our subconscious perspectives, we create space for alternative worldviews to be heard loud and clear.

One helpful framework for discovering blind spots is the Ladder of Inference (Argyris, 1990), which maps reasoning chains from observations to conclusions. A visual representation of this framework can be found in the Appendix (see Figure 11). The Ladder of Inference helps us recognize how our perceptions and assumptions can affect our beliefs and actions. The Ladder of Inference consists of seven steps: observing data, selecting data, adding meaning, making assumptions, drawing conclusions, adopting beliefs, and taking actions. By examining each step of the ladder, we can identify where our subjective filters may influence our interpretations and lead to hasty judgments. This process allows us to challenge our assumptions and objectively consider alternative perspectives.

However, examining our subjective filters is only half the story. If genuinely innovative alternatives are to be successfully discovered and implemented, decision-making bodies must seek input from diverse cultural voices, particularly those of minority groups. Integrating dissent and debate into institutions promotes constructive disagreement; we can incorporate conflicting advice to find complex solutions (Roberto, 2005). To develop innovative alternatives, we must heed wise counsel from across ages, races, genders, and beliefs. And by seeking out diverse perspectives and encouraging constructive debate, we can create a more inclusive decision-making process that leads to better outcomes.

Leaders must also remain abreast of innovative techniques designed to minimize bias and increase equitable participation, such as participatory budgeting, which allows community members to determine directly how part of a public budget should be spent through informed proposals and voting. Giving people power over where their money goes is key to creating transparency and democracy. At the same time, anonymous ideation software acts like a magical tool by collecting suggestions from everyone without regard for demographics—so that fresh and unfiltered ideas flow! Furthermore, design thinking sessions enable decision-makers to immerse themselves in marginalized groups' experiences, which helps them to develop empathy and compassion.

Now, when seeking diverse input, we must listen with empathy. Being patient gives people time to explain their logic without interruptions from outside sources; thoughtful questions may reveal an even more profound understanding and lead to finding common ground among us all.

It is also important to explain how different voices influence our decisions. Acknowledging the contributions of others helps to build trust (Groysberg & Slind, 2012). Inclusive decision-making requires ongoing self-reflection, power analysis, diverse representation, empathetic listening, and transparency. Communicating the decision-making process and how the advice was implemented demonstrates accountability while strengthening relationships and future collaborations.

Cultural Equity Analysis

Regarding inclusive processes, leaders must ensure that the outcomes of the decisions being made benefit various cultural groups fairly and equally. Therefore, leaders should conduct a thorough cultural equity analysis for each major decision (City of Seattle, 2012). Think of this analysis as an assessment that examines how various identity groups will access the resources and opportunities resulting from a given proposal, in an attempt to distribute advantages equitably.

How does this analysis work? Well, first of all, leaders need to establish which cultural subgroups will be affected and collect demographic information on factors like race, ethnicity, gender, age, disability, and residential geography. This data gives leaders an in-depth knowledge of conditions that different groups face, including their advantages and any barriers they encounter. It is important to gather this data because even well-intentioned initiatives intended to benefit everyone may inadvertently favor majorities with greater access or power (City of Seattle, 2012).

Once that step has been taken, leaders can project how each decision is likely to affect each subgroup by asking questions such as whether resources will flow equally across communities or who might face marginalization or harm from the decision. By quantifying the potential consequences of such decisions, leaders can reveal hidden cultural biases within these decisions even before implementation occurs.

Once we know that our projected impacts are unequally distributed, leaders must revise their proposals to ensure fairness among subgroups. For example, a city's plan to improve public transportation by increasing bus routes might benefit more affluent neighborhoods, as they tend to have better infrastructure and more political influence. To reduce this disparity, the city could conduct a cultural equity analysis to identify underserved areas and allocate resources to improve transportation access in those communities. Cultural equity analysis is an effective means of mitigating adverse impacts. Drawing on data analysis, outcome modeling, and solution refinement to ensure fairness for all, this analysis enables leaders to make more informed decisions and build more inclusive organizations. As leaders, let us embrace this approach together, for greater insight.

Mitigating Bias for Cognitive CQ

Effectively navigating cultural complexity requires that we identify and clear any biases that impair our judgment. These could take the form of systemic barriers, everyday microaggressions, or deeply embedded mindsets that perpetuate inequities across different groups (Sue et al., 2007). Having the courage to confront such prejudices head-on through education and empathy can increase our cognitive CQ.

Let me share an experience from my own career that highlighted the significance of leaders' addressing bias and of organizations' adjusting policies to honor employees' cultural preferences and needs. At one point, my schedule needed to be flexible so I could provide care for my elderly mother with disabilities, who required special assistance. At that time, my organization provided generous maternal and paternal leave benefits, because it recognized the importance of supporting employees with young children. However, the organization failed to offer any leave for elder care, even though caring for an aging parent presents challenges and responsibilities similar to those involved in caring for a child. Ironically, the organization acknowledged the value of family care in one context but overlooked it in another, simply because it involved a different kind of family structure.

My manager at the time had the nerve to suggest I place my mother in a nursing home as a solution to my scheduling difficulties! That comment exposed a significant lack of empathy and cultural sensitivity, not to mention the organization's blind spot. Many cultures around the world prioritize taking care of elders at home rather than seeking institutional solutions for care. That comment demonstrated the significance of CQ: understanding diverse viewpoints while creating space for different priorities in a workplace environment.

This experience taught me that implicit biases are rooted in deep-seated assumptions—in this case, about mainstream nuclear family structures. Expecting employees to prioritize the policies of the organization over their own cultural caregiving traditions implies that the Western individualistic paradigms are superior, but family structures and definitions differ greatly across cultural groups; we must recognize their depth of value instead of simply favoring traditional parental roles (Hofstede, 2001). By acknowledging and accommodating employees' diverse family structures and caregiving traditions, organizations can create a more inclusive and supportive work environment that values cultural differences and promotes employee well-being.

Addressing Cognitive Biases and Assumptions

Prejudice can result from systemic factors as well as from individual shortcomings; combating it requires self-introspection at every level, including on an individual basis. Even well-meaning leaders may unwittingly hold biases that influence their interactions. An excellent way to begin the process of self-reflection is to take implicit association tests, which can help raise self-awareness about our reflexive tendencies toward stereotypes (Greenwald et al., 1998). These tests, such as the Implicit Association Test (IAT) developed by researchers at Harvard, the University of Washington, and the University of Virginia, measure the strength of associations between concepts (e.g., race, gender) and evaluations (e.g., good, bad) or stereotypes (e.g., athletic, clumsy). These free tests are available online at https://implicit.harvard.edu/implicit/ and can be taken by anyone. The results help individuals recognize their implicit biases and work toward mitigating them. Recognizing our impulse to stereotype can help build humility about snap judgments that might prejudice us, ultimately helping us to be open to counterevidence from outside sources.

Recognizing privilege is also an integral part of cultivating CQ. If we assume that policies serve only our own cultural needs, we must acknowledge any unearned advantages we enjoy. Critical examination helps reveal deeply embedded cultural barriers that seem normal or fair to most (McIntosh, 1989). As leaders, our role is crucial in driving both institutional and personal change.

Fostering Pluralistic Attitudes

Cognitive CQ can be strengthened when we embrace pluralistic mindsets that prioritize fair coexistence (Bennett, 2004). Instead of expecting minority groups to conform to dominant cultural norms, pluralism encourages adaptability when we are faced with complexity. Supporting religious gatherings, accommodating extended family duties, and alleviating transportation limitations can increase our organization's retention rates, and training about the sociohistorical forces that marginalize specific groups can help us to build better judgment in specific situations. Finally, creating environments that celebrate minority identities spurs growth and fosters innovation.

Inclusive practices are intended to go beyond mere tolerance and achieve true justice. However, implementing these practices requires both organizational and individual development. Leaders play an especially significant role in this respect: They can model humble self-critique, make structural adjustments as needed, and foster intercultural empathy through leadership development initiatives.

Let's continue our fantastic journey of cultivating cognitive CQ and making the world more inclusive and accepting! Not only is this an awesome thing to do, but it's also highly beneficial for everyone involved.

Cognitive CQ Competencies for New Leadership Roles

Navigating our increasingly complex world requires cognitive abilities and keeping up with changes in leadership styles. Technological disruption and social transformation are constants; therefore, you must find that sweet spot where all parties involved come together effectively.

Take, for instance, those remarkable human abilities like cultural translation, community facilitation, and diversity strategizing—people who can do these things bring tremendous value by creating connections across differences (Wilson & Daugherty, 2018). Their cognitive CQ makes a powerful statement about who they are as leaders.

Let's use an example to put this concept into perspective: Imagine a cross-cultural moderator with excellent perspective-taking skills who uses that skill to help build trust among team members from different backgrounds. They do this by finding common ground and ensuring all voices are heard (Clark, 2020). For instance, a moderator might organize a team-building activity that encourages members to share their unique cultural experiences and perspectives, thereby fostering understanding and respect among the group members.

Chief diversity officers play a vital role in organizations. They develop and implement strategic initiatives to foster a more inclusive workplace culture. For example, a chief diversity officer might create a comprehensive DEI training program that goes beyond simply raising awareness about diversity issues. The chief diversity officer also works closely with senior leadership to ensure DEI principles are embedded into the organization's policies, practices, and decision-making processes (Williams & Wade-Golden, 2023). Moreover, chief diversity officers often serve as a bridge between the organization and underrepresented communities. They seek partnerships with diverse organizations, attend community events, and build relationships with involved parties to better understand different groups' unique challenges and perspectives.

Community coordinators should also be recognized for their valuable contributions. They act like cultural detectives by gathering clues from gestures and environments to co-create solutions with people. These specialists remain updated by engaging with people, which leads to targeted policies that break down barriers and have real effects (Wilson & Daugherty, 2018). For instance, a community coordinator might organize town hall meetings to gather input from residents about their needs and concerns and then use that information to develop community-driven solutions.

Cross-boundary leadership roles may still be emerging, but the people who take them on are prepared to meet any challenge that comes their way with adaptability, contextual understanding, and cognitive CQ power. That means they're opening doors to new possibilities (Hajro et al., 2017).

Remember that the practical skills we have discussed can unleash your potential. Maximizing the resources you already possess is what matters most.

Case Study: CQ at GlobalBuild: Building Bridges, Driving Success

Amal, the CEO of GlobalBuild, an international construction company, had a proven track record of successfully managing large urban development projects. However, as her company expanded into new regions, she faced unexpected challenges that threatened the success of the company's projects and the cohesion of her team.

In one instance, a misunderstanding between a senior executive and a local contractor in Mumbai led to significant project delays and cost overruns. The executive, accustomed to direct communication and rigid deadlines, failed to recognize the importance of building personal relationships and allowing for flexibility in the Indian business context. As a result, the contractor felt disrespected and became less cooperative, causing the project to fall behind schedule.

In another case, a team of engineers from GlobalBuild struggled to adapt to the communal decision-making process in a Ghanaian village where they were working on an infrastructure project. The engineers, used to making decisions independently and quickly, became frustrated with the lengthy community consultations and failed to build trust with local leaders. This led to misunderstandings about the project's priorities and ultimately resulted in the village's withdrawing its support.

As these incidents multiplied and tensions rose, Amal recognized the importance of cultural sensitivity, realizing that cultural discernment was imperative for GlobalBuild's continued growth and success. She realized that her senior leadership team lacked the CQ needed to navigate diverse business environments effectively, and she decided to take action to reduce this critical skill gap.

Case Study Questions

1. What steps can Amal take to identify the specific CQ gaps in her senior leadership team, and how can she prioritize the most critical areas for development?

2. How can Amal design a CQ development program that not only teaches individual leadership competencies but also drives organizational change and builds a culture of inclusivity?

3. How can Amal leverage cultural mentors and a multiregional advisory council to help GlobalBuild's leaders navigate cultural differences more effectively and build stronger relationships with local communities and partners?

4. How can Amal measure the success and impact of GlobalBuild's CQ initiatives, in terms of both project outcomes and employee engagement and satisfaction?

5. How can Amal ensure that the CQ development program leads to genuine behavioral change and long-term commitment to cultural competence among GlobalBuild's leaders, and what role can accountability measures play in this process?

Case Study Resolution

Recognizing the need to address the CQ gaps in her senior leadership team, Amal took decisive action to develop their cultural competence and foster a more inclusive organizational culture.

Amal began by having her executives complete assessments to gauge their current CQ levels. The results revealed significant disparities between their cognitive and their emotional CQ scores, with many leaders still assuming that Western communication styles and individualistic incentives were universally effective across all cultures.

Drawing on this data, Amal designed an intensive 10-month cultural intelligence development program. The program began with a two-day workshop that introduced key cultural frameworks, debunked common stereotypes, and included implicit association tests to uncover unconscious biases. This immersive experience served as a powerful wake-up call for GlobalBuild's leaders, challenging them to confront their assumptions and expand their cultural perspectives.

Amal paired each executive with a cultural mentor from one of the company's target markets to reinforce the workshop learnings and provide ongoing support. Through regular video calls and in-person project site visits, these mentors now offer invaluable guidance and insights into local business practices, communication styles, and cultural nuances.

Amal also established a multiregional advisory council comprising architects, engineers, and community leaders from GlobalBuild's key markets. This council provides critical input on local needs, preferences, and expectations, helping project teams to avoid costly misunderstandings and tailor their approach to the specific cultural context.

To ensure that CQ remains a top priority, Amal tied a portion of executive bonuses to the advisory council's cultural resonance ratings. This bold move sent a clear message: that cultural competence is not just a nice-to-have but a core leadership expectation that directly increases the bottom line.

Within a year of implementing these initiatives, GlobalBuild saw a dramatic turnaround in its global performance. By submitting culturally attuned proposals and fostering strong local partnerships, the firm won a series of high-profile contracts in new markets. Internally, team members from diverse backgrounds reported feeling more valued, respected, and empowered to share their unique perspectives and ideas.

Amal transformed GlobalBuild's approach to global business and unleashed the potential of her diverse workforce through her commitment to CQ development. Her story is an inspiring example for other leaders seeking to build bridges across cultures and drive success in an increasingly interconnected world.

Advancing Your Leadership Journey

Reflection Questions

1. How can you, as a leader, seek out diverse perspectives and narratives within your organization to gain a more comprehensive understanding of cultural dynamics?

2. How might your own cultural background and experiences influence your perception of cultural frameworks, and how can you maintain an open and adaptable mindset?

3. What strategies can you employ to balance the use of generalizations and specific cultural knowledge when navigating new cultural contexts?

4. How can you foster a culture of inclusive decision-making for your team, and what steps can you take to ensure that diverse voices are heard and valued?

5. What personal biases or assumptions might be hindering you in developing cognitive CQ, and how can you work to overcome these barriers?

Practical Application Activity

- This activity gives participants hands-on experience in breaking down decisions using quantitative data and projecting outcomes regarding ethical considerations, building up critical cognitive CQ capacity along the way.

Conduct a cultural equity analysis on any current or upcoming decision by using the following steps.

1. Define all cultural subgroups that could be affected.

2. Accumulate demographic information that highlights group advantages/barriers.

3. Model predicted outcomes—Will impacts be equitable?

4. Revamp proposal elements until fairness is attained.

5. Adapt decisions while monitoring metrics by subgroup.

Let's summarize our discussion's main points and takeaways to solidify our understanding of cognitive CQ discernment.

Key Takeaways

1. Developing CQ requires leaders to seek out diverse perspectives, challenge assumptions, and maintain an open and adaptable mindset when navigating cultural complexities.

2. Structured cultural frameworks, such as Hofstede's Cultural Dimensions, can provide valuable insights into cultural differences. However, they should be used as starting points for deeper understanding rather than as rigid stereotypes.

3. When applying cultural frameworks, leaders must be aware of potential blind spots, such as assumptions of similarity, presentism, and the tendency toward stereotyping; and they must work to mitigate these biases through self-reflection and inclusive practices.

4. Fostering inclusive decision-making processes, conducting cultural equity analyses, and recognizing and reducing cognitive biases are essential steps for developing cognitive CQ and creating equitable solutions that benefit diverse cultural groups.

Chapter 6

Cultivating Emotional CQ Across Cultures

One essential ingredient for leadership excellence is emotional CQ. Emotional CQ is all about understanding people from diverse cultural backgrounds on an emotional level while responding to them in ways that demonstrate your true comprehension of their unique background and experience—almost like having superpowers!

Imagine entering a room full of people from various cultures: With emotional CQ, you don't just see a crowd; instead, you witness an intricate tapestry of expressions and behaviors within that crowd. Because you can detect subtle cues, you recognize their emotional states expressed through smiles, body language, and tones of voice.

Emotional CQ goes far beyond simply recognizing subtle nuances; it's about using that knowledge to bridge cultural divides and foster an inclusive environment where everyone feels seen, heard, and truly understood. Furthermore, adapting your behaviors based on cultural awareness ensures smooth cross-cultural interactions. To embark on the path of cultural intelligence, we must first humble ourselves in the mirror, then open our eyes to the world around us, and finally, open our hearts to the beauty of different perspectives.

But let's be honest for a second: Developing emotional CQ can sometimes be unnerving. Yes, it means leaving behind familiarity for unfamiliarity. But that's okay, because you're not on this journey alone; you're part of an expansive global community that is as dedicated as you are to encouraging positive cross-cultural interactions.

At its core, unpacking unfamiliar behaviors involves digging deeper into their emotional undertones. Instead of immediately jumping to conclusions, pause, truly listen, and try to understand what others mean by their behaviors. Consider different cultural contexts and step outside your own worldview when opening yourself up to different perspectives—you might begin appreciating life-stage transitions, oral traditions, and community gatherings more fully than before, and you might grow in the understanding that individual ambition is not always at the forefront. Motivations may also come from the collective wisdom of groups rather than from personal ambition alone.

As leaders, how can we foster openness among our teams? One effective strategy is to explicitly share our own particular cultural values, styles, and needs with them. This sharing creates a safe space where team members feel empowered to express themselves freely while also offering their unique perspectives. It sends the message that all are learning together, and that mistakes are allowed along the way!

Emotional CQ plays a huge role in effective leadership. Visionary leaders go beyond mere transactional efficiency to inspire entire communities. Their contagious hope spreads throughout organizations long after they've moved on—helping to ensure their organization flourishes for years after they leave the scene.

As leaders, we mustn't shy away from discussing complex subjects such as discrimination, systemic inequities, and barriers to advancement. Instead, let's be bold and approach these conversations with patience and compassion. The goal should always be understanding and growth rather than defensiveness or avoidance.

Mentorship can help us develop connections by acknowledging cultural norms regarding hierarchy. We show empathy and support when we check in regularly with individuals as they juggle professional, family, and spiritual identities.

Rejoice in the beautiful accomplishment of enhancing CQ and fostering a culture of inclusion where every individual feels valued and heard. By celebrating teachable cross-cultural moments, we help model reconciliation behaviors while building organizations that prioritize diversity and representation at all levels. Isn't that something worth celebrating?

Remember that leadership potential lies within everyone, not just authority figures. Let's empower all to lead and create an environment where everyone can flourish—when all our unique experiences combine, something magical happens!

Emotional Intelligence vs. Emotional Cultural Intelligence

Emotional Intelligence (EI) and emotional cultural intelligence (emotional CQ) share many similarities, and both highlight our ability to understand and manage emotions effectively. But whereas EI focuses primarily on our emotions and social interactions, emotional CQ takes it one step further by examining how emotions are managed across cultural contexts.

In 1990, psychologists Peter Salovey and John Mayer introduced the concept of emotional intelligence and defined it as "the ability to monitor one's own and others' feelings and emotions, to discriminate among them, and to use this information to guide one's thinking and actions" (p. 189). EI is about understanding our emotions and how they manifest themselves in interactions. EI provides superpowers that enable us to regulate emotions, motivate ourselves, show empathy, and navigate social situations successfully. But EI may not suffice when working across cultures—that's where emotional CQ comes into play.

Emotional CQ refers to our ability to identify emotional cues when engaging with people from diverse cultural backgrounds. Emotional CQ acts as an interpreter that decodes how emotions are expressed and what motivates people from different parts of the globe. With emotional CQ, leaders can tailor their behavior based on cultural nuances such as power distance or uncertainty avoidance and transform the multicultural leadership landscape.

Here is another intriguing point. Whereas EI is primarily concerned with individual emotions and interpersonal interactions, emotional CQ expands that perspective by considering group-level emotions and their effects on communities. Leaders who have emotional CQ can identify the unique emotional realities of subgroups while avoiding broad generalizations. In other words, they intuitively understand the emotional dynamics that influence policies and identities.

But here's the catch: Emotional CQ isn't one-size-fits-all; it requires adaptability and an awareness of cultural conditions to be applied effectively. EI provides the foundation, and emotional CQ builds upon it by giving knowledge of dynamic landscapes across diverse dialects.

Why does emotional CQ matter so much? Emotional CQ helps leaders successfully manage cultural differences, foster unity, and embrace diversity—essential traits in this ever more interdependent society. Emotional CQ allows organizations to retain talented employees, foster inclusivity, and avoid cringeworthy cultural faux pas. Emotional CQ isn't just some abstract concept—it can be an invaluable asset to leaders who want to make a potent contribution to our multicultural society.

Ahmad and Azad (2019) and Keung and Rockinson-Szapkiw (2013) conducted intriguing research that conclusively demonstrated that leaders with strong emotional and cultural discernment abilities tend to lead global teams effectively. Furthermore, these leaders facilitate innovative outcomes and boost organizational performance. There is an apparent correlation between having high emotional CQ and adopting transformational and empowering leadership styles that foster organizational resilience. High emotional CQ could be just what your organization needs to take its performance to new heights. So embrace your emotions, celebrate different cultures, and use emotional CQ to lead you toward success!

Emotional CQ's Organizational Impacts

Workplace emotional CQ can be a game-changer! Though often underestimated as a "soft skill" that supplements technical expertise, emotional CQ has proven its worth in managing talent diversity, building trusted partnerships across differences, and cultivating cultures where everyone can maximize their strengths.

Studies conducted by Rockstuhl et al. (2011) and Groves and Feyerherm (2011) demonstrate that leaders with high emotional CQ have an incredible effect on critical executive performance behaviors such as collaborating cross-culturally, retaining minority talent by creating a sense of belonging, increasing productivity by embracing psychological safety measures, and driving diversity-fueled innovation.

As it stands now, empathetic leaders become beacons for those who have historically endured burdens by showing empathy toward experiences of discrimination, openly discussing system blindness regarding unseen barriers, and listening with an open heart (rather than a hardened mindset). This kind of treatment makes people choose to remain and contribute instead of feeling punished or sidelined.

Organizational leaders must recognize that talent follows talent. Therefore, when organizations prioritize equity efforts to reduce turnover, absenteeism, and reluctance to fully engage as part of their sustainability interests (rather than just trying to mitigate harm indirectly), they align better with contemporary social justice expectations. That leads them, in turn, toward reduced harm while simultaneously meeting sustainability requirements. What you have then is a win-win outcome.

As global society becomes ever-more complicated because of changes in demographics, technology, and the environment, effective leadership becomes more challenging. To productively address all the uncertainty, we must go beyond simply balancing sheets. We need cultural capacities that span far and wide. This is why developing emotional CQ skills is absolutely critical: They allow for the transformation of the workplace and the revitalization of the community. Emotionally intelligent leadership ensures that staff remain inspired while meeting diverse customer demands and giving voice to historically marginalized community priorities. In other words, emotional CQ skills provide a foundation for organizational resilience.

Leveraging Emotional Discernment for Inclusive Decisions

Organizational leaders, you already know this: You're trying to navigate a difficult landscape of policies and strategies while trying to satisfy everyone. That isn't easy; with demographics and perspectives fluctuating all around, making decisions can feel like treading on minefields!

But there are solutions. Identify representatives from various cultural backgrounds early on. Just having different viewpoints is not enough; you need to explore their motivations, assumptions, and reluctances, so that the dominant paradigms won't override the voices of those facing structural barriers.

Let's consider meetings. Simply having ethnic diversity doesn't guarantee psychological safety; we need leaders with emotional CQ who understand the power dynamics at play. Sometimes subordinates feel intimidated about raising their concerns with executives directly. Therefore, try embedding anonymous input channels, conducting cultural impact assessments, or having focus group discussions. These are all ways to foster an environment where everyone feels free to speak their truth.

Cultural differences can lead to communication gaps. For example, passionate dissent may be seen as engaging in debate in some Asian contexts but perceived differently in Europe. Good leaders understand how to adapt their messaging styles to each situation to ensure that ideas are heard despite possible cultural discomfort.

And don't overlook the importance of listening. Some individuals might be more reserved in sharing their opinions, and you have an obligation to draw out these individuals, with patience and compassionate listening. You'll learn a lot by taking the time to truly comprehend another individual.

Another thing you can do is take an introspective approach to discern the hopes and fears that are associated with the policy initiatives intended to benefit historically disenfranchised groups. If we are to effectively explore the relevant issues, it is necessary to create safe discussion spaces where all perspectives can come together without judgment and build a richer context. Think of these places as sacred ground where different opinions and insights can come together and inform each other before any final decisions are made.

Effective leadership involves more than simply representing diversity (although that is important). It is dependent on taking the time to understand the emotional realities of those in your team or community—including looking beyond your own experiences and privilege. You must also explore the hopes and disappointments that minority communities have felt as a result of limited opportunities or broken promises from leaders who lack this understanding.

Here's the thing: As leaders, we cannot remain stuck in our comfortable echo chambers. Instead, we need to embrace discomfort and vulnerability when engaging with different cultures. Doing this requires that we anchor ourselves in values like dignity, compassion, belonging, and accountability. Emotional CQ enables us to observe, listen to, and seek common ground among colleagues while taking in their pain points and aspirations and building solid relational foundations. Even conflict can have creative potential when handled carefully, and the groundbreaking policies that serve human well-being also offer real economic returns.

The Role of Empathy and Perspective-Taking in Leadership

Leadership has changed drastically in recent years. Gone is the "do as I say" era, when bosses dictated everything to their subordinates and used power and authority as weapons against them. Today, we need new leaders who focus more on serving others and inspiring people's best qualities to come out.

So, what does this new leadership entail? It involves humility, compassion, and flexibility for adapting to different situations, all of which are hallmarks of effective leadership. This new culture requires that we recognize different perspectives, behaviors, needs, and styles—that we put ourselves in other people's shoes and try to understand their points of view. And it requires the skill and patience to not brush differences under the carpet but instead make every effort to understand why people see things differently.

Leaders who genuinely try to understand what motivates others can build trust even when everyone does not always agree. In contrast, empty gestures won't cut it: We must address issues like representation, psychological safety, and equal opportunities to bridge gaps and foster an equitable workplace for all. Be wary of any efforts to force everyone into one mold. Instead, we need to redefine hiring, communication, development, and overall operations so that everyone feels included and celebrated for their differences—this ends up making us stronger.

But here's the catch: When it comes to measuring impact, we need to keep in mind more than just privacy protocols, work styles, and motivational preferences. Keeping things real means taking a holistic approach. Forget quantitative productivity measures alone! Embrace qualitative indicators such as community health, generativity, and ecological sustainability—doing so will result in a series of "aha" moments that will have a pronounced effect!

Embracing diversity and inclusion opens up a world of possibilities for organizations. By adapting our language and decision-making processes to resonate with diverse audiences, we enable excellence without forcing individuals to choose between their professional fulfillment and personal identity. Greater discernment allows us to convert universal assumptions into inclusive engagement mechanisms, honoring different heritages while celebrating the richness of subjective experiences. Let's break down the barriers that limit diversity's potential and unleash its fullest power!

As leaders, regularly exercising our emotional CQ will enable us to navigate the complexities of our diverse world with grace and authenticity. Although the term "code-switching" may carry negative connotations for some, it's important to recognize that adapting our communication style to different contexts is a natural and necessary part of effective leadership. (See also chapter 7, "Physical CQ.") Just as you wouldn't use the same "colorful" language in a professional setting as you might at home, successful leaders understand the importance of tailoring their approach to resonate with diverse audiences. By developing this skill, you can effectively communicate ideas across generations, demographics, and global contexts while remaining true to yourself.

Remember that intercultural ambidexterity plays a critical role in our rapidly morphing communities. As people embrace multidimensional diasporic identities—those characterized by mobility, digital fluency, and blended histories—it becomes essential to develop the abilities of empathetic discernment and agile perspective-shifting. Leaders with these traits remain relevant during constant change while remaining sensitive to the dynamic interweaving of fluid forces that ultimately channel collective potential.

Emotional cultural intelligence is pivotal in helping us navigate today's competitive environment. By allowing us to understand that our abilities aren't finite resources but are instead extraordinary assets to be shared with others, emotional CQ helps foster an environment in which each individual's talents can flourish fully and are used efficiently.

Now let's open up dialogue and collaborate to discover the power of intercultural adaptability. Through diverse perspectives combined with innovative thinking, we can create transformative effects unlike those we've seen before!

Developing Digital Empathy in Remote Teams

With video conferences replacing water cooler chats and messaging taking the place of hallway gossip sessions, remote staff may feel alienated in their workplaces. As leaders, we need to foster an atmosphere of belonging, but traditional team-building methods that focus on in-person bond-forming activities won't work virtually; therefore, we need to get creative!

Consider this: Camera angles and lighting options can drastically change online appearances. Deciphering authentic emotions when everyone simply appears as a face is challenging enough, but cultural norms surrounding emoting also vary greatly across regions. Given all of this, leaders risk misreading contexts when they cannot fully see the environment or share the communal rituals that naturally foster intimacy.

But fear not! We can still make a powerful difference. Emotional awareness and regulation are key, as is showing up authentically when engaging in virtual interactions by turning our cameras on and signaling psychological availability. Furthermore, we can practice situational discernment to interpret expressions, even with annoying video delays!

Now comes the exciting part. We can use innovative tools and techniques to bring our team closer. Imagine collaborating on whiteboards while chatting, brainstorming collectively, and engaging in discussions on equal terms—regardless of everyone's physical location. In addition, visual notetaking keeps things coherent across time zones.

Add some life and energy to your virtual meetings by incorporating fun activities. From show-and-tell sessions to virtual laughter to yoga across those little video windows, new ways of connecting will make these two-dimensional confines feel alive and exciting. Thanks to innovative apps, leaders can stay connected outside of formal strategy meetings. Co-development can continue uninterrupted, like the Energizer Bunny! Don't worry about running out of ideas or losing momentum; technology makes brainstorming sessions accessible 24/7. You can use its power for continuous collaboration to propel your strategies further. It's crucial, however, to remember that although technology enables round-the-clock connectivity, it's important to respect personal boundaries and work-life balance. Avoid putting expectations of 24/7 availability on your colleagues or yourself. Instead, use these tools to facilitate flexible collaboration that accommodates diverse schedules and work styles, ensuring a healthy and sustainable approach to virtual teamwork.

Let's also pay attention to the importance of celebrating our peers! With public sharing channels for shout-outs, milestone celebrations, and acknowledgment of team achievements, this positive energy keeps morale high and uplifted. Plus, we can switch up locations for stand-up or all-hands meetings, giving all staff a taste of different cultures and contexts.

To ensure that everyone feels included, we can provide translations for public artifacts like company mission statements or core values to ensure that everyone can understand the references in these public artifacts. And here's another fun idea: Let's create team swag kits featuring our logo and hand them out—this is a great way to reinforce team identity! But let's retain the personal element. Making space and making time for personalized communication is still vital in building strong bonds that ensure everyone feels heard and valued.

Digital empathy is a cornerstone of leadership in distributed working environments today. Empathetic leaders truly understand the unique challenges and opportunities in each region, considering factors like cultural perspectives, situational constraints, and technical barriers. By breaking down the assumptions and biases that presume every remote working condition is the same, these leaders can bridge accessibility gaps and maximize the potential of all locations.

Sometimes written messages cannot adequately express emotions and intentions, so humility and positive intent should always be assumed when writing and reading them. We have all experienced how easily messages can be miscommunicated in the absence of face-to-face interactions, but digital empathy brings minds from various parts of the globe together, creating solid bonds while encouraging collaboration.

Technology can be an effective tool in unifying teams globally, but true success depends on leaders' having the technical knowledge and emotional CQ to unite their teams on an intimate level. Communication with team members should involve listening, understanding, and showing genuine interest, even when geographical distance separates you. Who says traditional practices cannot be modified for remote cultures? Empathy goes a long way toward breaking down geographic barriers. Here's the deal: purpose-driven teams equipped with cutting-edge technologies and led by compassionate remote leaders can thrive across distances. The key to their success lies in creating shared experiences, orchestrating collaboration, and enhancing the effectiveness of leadership in remote settings.

Navigating Crisis and Care Across Cultures With Emotional Discernment

Though our world is more interdependent, showing care and concern for staff while being culturally sensitive can be challenging. This doesn't mean making assumptions or treating everyone equally; good intentions can go astray if we don't fully comprehend cultural nuances.

Consider the different family systems, bereavement protocols, and work-life balance expectations across cultures. Direct touch may be appropriate in some Latin countries, while in more reserved contexts, such as some Asian countries, the same touch might be an unacceptable crossing of boundaries. It all boils down to understanding what's right in each culture.

Establishing what I refer to as *compassion literacy* begins with increasing cultural self-awareness. To avoid projecting our biases onto others, we must examine how our cultural background shapes our assumptions about caregiving. Understanding workplace motivation, mental health perceptions, and communication styles across cultural teams is essential for prioritizing staff well-being without passing judgment on different ways of doing things.

Flexibility is also essential when developing inclusive policies. Instead of adhering to the dominant cultural norms, policies should be tailored to accommodate diverse family care models and holidays. Communication should also be developed with cultural differences in mind—adding cultural guides, avoiding confusing idioms, and offering feedback that aligns with cultural norms can go a long way toward showing empathy and understanding.

The first challenge in leading across cultures is to understand all the perspectives involved. This step is vital, but tricky. Creating an accurate assessment requires gathering inputs from different regions while listening empathetically and paying particular attention to those experiencing more anxiety than usual.

Vulnerability can work wonders. Leaders who show openness and rally their teams around an inspiring purpose rather than focusing solely on market performance can alleviate unrest and build collective trust amid uncertainty. In a crisis, it might be appropriate to temporarily change policies to address the hardships and provide updates regarding steps the organization is taking to regain organizational trust.

For instance, during the COVID-19 pandemic, Ravi, the CEO of a mid-sized tech company, boldly decided to temporarily suspend performance reviews and instead implemented a "check-in and support" system. This shift allowed managers to focus on their team members' well-being and adapt to the challenges of remote work. The result was a notable increase in employee engagement and a stronger sense of community, even as everyone navigated unprecedented challenges. Furthermore, tailoring communication styles to the different processing styles of team members shows genuine care for each person who faces unique struggles, forming the basis of solidarity among the team.

When times become tough, caring leadership and community partnerships will help you through them. Pay attention to marginalized voices, too, as their input is essential in rebuilding better. Boldly uphold minority capabilities instead of sitting back and waiting. Cross-cultural compassion and emotional CQ will guide your journey to resilience.

Remember, empathy is power!

Fostering Resilience Across Differences

Change is inevitable. And although it may be difficult at first, it offers invaluable opportunities for growth and discovery. Organizations must remain flexible and resilient if they are to survive in today's uncertain climate.

Today's successful companies don't rely on old-school strategies that play it safe. Instead, they invest in building resilience. Successful businesses today understand that success lies not in rigidity but in being flexible enough to face any challenge that comes their way.

Leaders, take note: You are the key to cultivating emotional and cultural intelligence in your teams. Emotional intelligence means being aware of, managing, and controlling our emotions when uncertain situations arise. Instead of becoming anxious when things go sideways, cultivate courageous optimism instead. Resilient organizations recognize diversity as an asset and create inclusive environments where different cultures can unite to unleash their creative powers and innovation. However, this process takes patience. Forcing conformity, on the other hand, may only exacerbate and compound any challenges caused by diversity.

Culturally intelligent leaders strike a balance between short-term goals and long-term vision. In a problematic financial situation, it can be tempting to slash costs indiscriminately for an instant fix to the budget. The problem is, that kind of procedure often leads to the alienation of top talent in the long run. We need safe spaces where teams can process their thoughts and address challenges with realistic attitudes. Leaders can help their teams recognize fears, navigate challenging situations, and collaborate to generate groundbreaking solutions for everyone involved. So let's embrace uncertainty and turn turmoil into transformation; together, we've got this. We've got this even in a cross-cultural context!

Remember that building interpersonal resilience also depends upon leaders' commitment to nurturing bonds and welcoming diversity despite the occasional conflicts that may arise. Leaders who can foster good faith and show grace when cultural misunderstandings arise help their teams to address growing pains together while creating agreements and restoring mutual value. It is not about winning arguments but about creating a sense of unity. So, take that leap onto the rollercoaster of change and watch yourself thrive!

Resilient leadership fosters creativity by exploring partnerships outside of established networks. That approach means leaders can add diversity into the mix, spark breakthrough innovations, and avoid the stagnation caused by overspecialization. Instead of reacting reflexively, fearing ideas that come from outsiders, or delaying the reception of new ideas with excessive caution, resilient leaders judge the ideas themselves and evaluate their potential, regardless of who or where the ideas come from—resilient leaders recognize that substance lies beneath the surface.

To foster a resilient organizational culture, it is crucial to create an atmosphere that welcomes unfiltered dissent. This can be accomplished by, among other approaches, accepting small-scale failures as learning experiences and pivoting quickly based on staff sentiment, grassroots council feedback, and predictive analytics data. These small-scale failures, sometimes referred to as "micro failures," are not intentionally planned by leadership to undermine their teams. Rather, they are inevitable missteps that occur naturally during any project or initiative.

For example, imagine a cereal company that decides to launch a new flavor without conducting sufficient market research. The new cereal hits the shelves, but sales are disappointing, and customer feedback reveals that the flavor profile misses the mark. Instead of viewing this as a devastating failure, a resilient leader would see it as a valuable learning opportunity. They might encourage the product development team to analyze customer feedback, identify areas for improvement, and use these insights to inform future product launches. By embracing these micro failures as opportunities for growth and learning rather than as events to be avoided at all costs, leaders can cultivate a culture of experimentation, innovation, and continual improvement.

Leaders who actively listen and pay attention to signals from both mainstream and periphery spaces can adjust their direction seamlessly. Organizations in which leadership is shared, such as student organizations where students outnumber authorities, do well to embrace the discomfort associated with relinquishing preeminence in order to discover the untapped talent that lies in marginalized voices—the voices that contribute to diversity's authentic life force and foster an inclusive and resilient culture.

One essential characteristic of resilient leadership is using contextually informed decisions to navigate uncertainty. As we have seen, no one-size-fits-all approach will work. Resilient leaders understand the necessity of tailoring engagement strategies and measurements of success to align with cultural values in their community.

Resilient leaders use a deliberate decision-making process to mitigate risks and anticipate potential shocks. They carefully evaluate the risks and gaps that have been identified, run prototype-constrained experiments with diverse inputs, and plan iterative contingency options so that they're prepared for unexpected disruptions or surprises in the future.

Resilient leadership goes beyond strict adherence to traditional approaches. Given today's accelerating economic, political, and technological rate of change, such methods often must change in the face of ever-evolving challenges. Thus, leaders who want to make their decision-making process resilient embrace adaptive capacities over short-term efficiency, keeping themselves ahead of the game.

An adaptive mindset means thinking beyond rigid forecasts and investing in real options—real choices with actual returns. Finding a balance that allows them to remain nimble while still maintaining their core capabilities requires leaders to use emotional and cultural intelligence. Instead of relying on fear-based reactions, they lift their teams up with growth mindsets to foster seamless collaboration.

But resilience goes beyond simply weathering storms. True resilience turns crises into opportunities, just as we saw with turning mistakes into chances for learning. Where some might become immobilized at roadblocks, resilient leaders view these obstacles as opportunities to grow and innovate. Over time, they form deep partnerships, which provide invaluable insights that inform their decision-making process. Resilient leadership involves employing multiple approaches: informed decision-making, adaptive skills, emotional intelligence, collaboration, and numerous collaboration platforms. Leaders who use such strategies can not only navigate uncertainty but also open up countless paths of growth and success.

Resiliency and adaptation don't just mean surviving. They mean thriving! Finding joy in each step along your journey means maximizing every opportunity and every twist and turn. Stay flexible and curious, and keep pushing forward to capture the many possibilities available to you!

Managing Responses With Cross-Cultural Agility

Resilience is the cornerstone of successful leadership. It means managing roller-coaster emotions, adapting like a chameleon, and creating solid connections—connections even Cupid would be jealous of! When life throws curveballs their way, resilient leaders don't simply dodge them, but catch these unexpected pitches and turn them into opportunities for growth and innovation. They understand that setbacks don't lead to dead ends but rather are detours along the road ahead that will ultimately lead them to their goal of success.

Imagine an inclusive workplace in which resilient leaders foster an atmosphere of acceptance. Like DJs mixing different perspectives, these leaders use tools such as the Kübler-Ross Change Transition Model (Kübler-Ross, 1969) to guide their people through the emotional rollercoaster of change with ease and grace. The Kübler-Ross Change Transition Model, originally developed to describe the stages dying and later applied to working through grief, has been adapted to understand how individuals react to significant organizational changes. This model describes five stages (denial, anger, bargaining, depression, and acceptance) that individuals often experience when faced with significant change or loss. These stages provide a framework for understanding the emotional journey people undergo during major transitions, whether personal or professional. Visual representations of the model can be found in the Appendix (see Figure 12).

Resilient leaders encourage small failures, knowing that each stumble is another step closer to greatness. When it's time for team debriefs, resilient leaders gather around a metaphorical campfire where everyone shares the lessons they have learned, allowing all to discuss their struggles openly and then leave with the renewed confidence to face uncertainty head-on.

And resilient leaders go even further! When conflicts arise, resilient leaders become adept at restoring harmony by channeling their inner diplomat to reconcile differing viewpoints and bring about a resolution. Restoring mutual value through finding common ground may involve winning arguments less often; resilient leaders simply realize the value of diversity by seeking partnerships beyond the usual suspects. They inspire creativity while keeping things fresh!

Resilient leaders are true masters of long-term growth. They're the ultimate daredevils of change, always looking forward to new horizons. Their organizations constantly evolve under their guidance, so there are no siloed divisions or rigid plans holding back progress. Instead, these leaders assemble dream teams of talented individuals with a range of expertise and skills who can easily tackle new priorities and adapt to changing circumstances. These dream teams help an organization avoid the stagnation and outdated metrics that lead to frustration and dissatisfaction among employees. Resilient leaders understand that every challenge requires an original response, and they have the skill sets to juggle resources and prevent burnout. Resilient leaders show us that success means accepting change gracefully while adapting and flourishing, regardless of circumstance.

Sustaining Positivity With Emotional CQ

Companies often feel inclined to play it safe during uncertain times and wait until things settle down, hoping that things will improve on their own. However, doing the opposite may reveal unexpected opportunities that might even seem contradictory. But here's the deal: Emotional CQ can provide incredible advantages that other options don't.

Think of it this way. Unlike their peers, who might panic under troubled circumstances, successful leaders with experience navigating adversity approach setbacks from a different angle, seeing them as opportunities to pivot and innovate—almost as if they have this secret sauce that drives success! Visionary leaders tend to cultivate a mindset of optimistic realism, staying grounded while simultaneously thinking big—they learn to balance pragmatism and ambition. Their team members are encouraged to find solutions to adversity instead of becoming too discouraged by it all.

And when chaos strikes, these leaders don't waste time playing the blame game. Instead, they highlight all their victories, including the losses they have avoided by taking proactive measures, giving their team the message: "Hey everyone, look what we've achieved! Look how well we handled unpredictable situations!"

Here's the secret sauce: Shifting the focus from problems to solutions. Resilient leaders take a proactive approach by employing design thinking—that creative process that inspires out-of-the-box thinking. They encourage their teams to develop innovative solutions to their current challenges. Their message is: "All right, we may have this issue, but I know we can find an awesome solution!"

Of course, these leaders also don't just plunge headlong into an investment without checking it out first. They strike a balance between cautious skepticism and calculated risk analysis, neither overly careful nor reckless, like walking a tightrope. But they understand that waiting for perfect information is unrealistic, so instead, they celebrate small wins as milestones toward bigger goals, with an attitude that says "Hey, progress is progress, no matter how small."

Flexible game plans are essential for leaders. Emotionally intelligent leaders adapt and adjust without overcommitting resources; they sprint and take short breaks in between heats. Town hall meetings don't just serve as regular updates—they become parties where everyone gets inspired and aligned, giving team members the feeling of "Let's all band together to conquer this chaotic market!" This is opportunistic realism, my friend. It doesn't involve ignoring challenges or living in an idealistic bubble. Instead, it requires acknowledging and confronting the challenges head-on while believing that positive change is always possible. This mindset allows leaders to unlock new opportunities and drive momentum forward even during turbulent times.

Psychological safety is necessary for resilience and cooperation when things become unpredictable. Culturally intelligent leaders understand this concept well, creating environments where team members feel safe to express ideas, take calculated risks, and learn from mistakes without fear of negative consequences. They see setbacks as growth opportunities and support pilot projects that allow for experimentation. By fostering this sense of safety, leaders encourage innovation and adaptability, which are crucial for navigating uncertain times. It all boils down to creating a culture of trust, open communication, and continuous learning—something that every forward-thinking leader knows is essential for success.

Culturally intelligent leaders don't just sit back and wait—no! Instead, they get involved and make things happen. From adjustments and accountability measures to team involvement and engaging everyone on their journey—all this matters in the process of finding the most efficient path ahead. But these remarkable leaders don't stop there. They are unstoppable forces of positivity who model optimism and communicate clearly, and their behaviors, language, and symbols support this magical phenomenon that spreads throughout their organizations.

Resilient leaders know how to remain calm under temporary turmoil; they're like Zen masters in business. Not afraid to admit they don't know all the answers, these resilient leaders remain confident in their teams' abilities while investing in training, wellness, and celebration rituals; encouraging a collaborative environment; and accomplishing incredible feats together. When you create an environment where conversations flow easily, personal connections flourish, and information is freely exchanged, success will follow accordingly. Not only will your organization benefit, but so will its wider community as resilience is created with every positive action.

Resilient leaders excel when times get rough. Their optimism helps their teams easily overcome uncertainty while paving new paths for success. Amid all the chaos, they bring agility and the ability to bounce back. When these conditions exist, there is no limit to what can be accomplished—it becomes an endless growth journey!

Cultivating Collective Care Practices

We can certainly all vouch for how critical personal resilience is over time. Maintaining it is essential for our long-term survival, and our incredible leaders play a significant role in ensuring this happens.

Let's delve a bit deeper. Think about this: When our emotional reserves become depleted, pushed to their limits without any respite or restoration, everything is at risk—all at once! That is why resilient cultures emphasize the significance of breaks for recharging, psychological wellness practices, and open discussions, all of which normalize vulnerability while encouraging everyone to have balanced workloads that don't result in a collision course toward meltdown.

However, in the long run, this approach will also require a robust and holistic support system for our outstanding leaders themselves to protect their own well-being in the grand scheme of things. Once they reach their limits and become emotionally depleted, like anyone else, they may experience severe issues of empathetic fatigue and depletion—not something anyone wants!

So how can we face down this beast? By practicing mindful self-care. Leaders must step up and prioritize their own well-being within the organization, showing discipline, willpower, and enthusiasm when times get uncertain or when their energy reserves get depleted by burnout. We need them strong when the going gets rough!

Self-care isn't simply about managing crises; it goes much deeper. Self-care involves developing sustainable routines that prioritize wellness. No more sacrificing ourselves on the altar of selflessness—this mindset shift is about creating a healthier engagement with work environments that inspires us all to jump out of bed each morning (well, maybe not quite literally, but you get my point).

Get ready, because I'm about to reveal helpful insights into how organizations can ace self-care. One approach we employ is encouraging our teams to take contemplative breaks as often as possible. And remember our psychological wellness rituals! Yes, we need them—let's set some boundaries, folks! No more inbox overload and burnout—let's have honest conversations that make vulnerability an everyday part of life. Let's also prioritize sustainable workloads, because working like an incessant machine is no badge of honor! Let me share this insight: When we take genuine care in treating ourselves well, this creates an inevitable chain reaction that increases our functioning capacity and our collective performance.

Resilient leaders understand the significance of creating an encouraging culture and hosting regular team reflection sessions. Doing these things helps everyone navigate fluid challenges more easily, as they can process emotional states before diving deeper into specific scenarios. It's like taking a breather before running that marathon.

Resilient leaders don't take things so seriously! Creative and resourceful leaders find innovative ways to encourage fresh ideas and out-of-the-box thinking. For instance, literally leaving behind the conference room walls and scheduling walking meetings instead not only stimulates creativity but also helps team members break free from some of the groupthink syndromes that can arise from sit-down meetings, whether virtual or in the flesh—plus, a little fresh air never hurts anyone!

Resilient leaders are adept at optimizing productivity through work rhythms. Recognizing that our energy and mental focus, as well as the physical demands of our tasks, fluctuate throughout the day, these leaders match their teams' schedules with these biological flow states to maximize productivity—ultimately reaching that sweet spot where everyone's firing on all cylinders.

Resilient leaders also employ another strategy for success: investing in professional coaches who provide valuable assistance by encouraging healthy venting, helping broaden perspectives, and creating resilience plans. These coaches can provide invaluable support during times of uncertainty for individuals and groups alike—they create safe spaces for discussions to open up dialogue about problems beyond our immediate concerns. It's like having your cheerleader, confidante, and strategist all rolled into one!

And resilient leaders understand the power of social connectivity to foster strong team bonds. To this end, they encourage community-building activities like sharing meals, participating in wellness group exercises, engaging in collective training fundraisers, or volunteering for worthy causes—nothing brings people closer than having something in common and filling up on tasty food! Seriously, though, camaraderie and purpose provide an atmosphere that uplifts us beyond pursuits that are about superficial status.

Did I mention vulnerability? Resilient leaders demonstrate their resilience by openly sharing their difficulties. Resilient leaders foster trust and camaraderie between all members by being vulnerable and showing that they're human, just like everyone else on the team. Think of it like having your superhero support group: Everyone can openly discuss victories and challenges without judgment being applied against anyone.

Resilient leaders serve as invaluable guides in an uncertain world, providing us with safe spaces to reflect, foster creativity, and stay on the path toward success. They create strong bonds among their followers while instilling laughter, camaraderie, and an awareness of what it takes to thrive in today's challenging environments.

Last but not least, resilient leaders create structural support systems to bolster the resilience of their workforce. They go above and beyond by offering generous caregiving leave, sponsoring family activities, providing lifetime mentorships, organizing mental wellness programs or retreats, or simply recognizing biological proclivities and nurturing them during distress—leaders enable their workforce to flourish despite challenges.

So you see, resilient leaders understand that resilience is a shared responsibility and requires collective effort. Relying solely on heroic leadership can fracture teams; true strength lies in sharing responsibilities. By prioritizing self-care and coordinated care in their leadership practices, leaders help organizations and communities flourish. Resilient leadership doesn't just focus on hitting bottom lines but is about fulfilling collective goals while meeting individual human needs.

Addressing Privilege Gaps Through Emotional CQ

It is fascinating how leaders from dominant ethnic groups sometimes overlook specific issues, like the risks of exclusion and the emotional effects of their policies on minority groups. I guess maybe they haven't experienced marginalization themselves; nonetheless, this lack of experience perpetuates imbalances and cultural dissonance, leading to blind spots.

But there is hope! Through humility and by seeking empathetic input, leaders can expand their awareness beyond the dominant paradigms and work toward justice. Although it will take work and effort, it will pay dividends.

At first, dominant group leaders must engage in some serious self-reflection. Instead of pretending they are colorblind or progressive just for show, they will have to acknowledge any gaps in their understanding and look within, truly making themselves aware of all their own hidden advantages, such as the social access, career mobility, and freedom from racial anxiety they might possess. Once they are aware of these advantages, they can begin leveling the playing field and having honest discussions about power and equity issues.

Securing empathetic input is of the utmost importance for leaders. They need to make time to engage with marginalized communities as actual humans instead of as researchers trying to gain insights. It's about building trust and understanding the struggles these communities are going through. Having local mentors can make all the difference—they can provide leaders with insight into cultural pain points and the challenges faced by minorities. In addition, it is vital to create safe spaces where people can express themselves. These safe spaces can be physical, such as designated rooms or areas in the workplace, or else metaphorical, such as systems that allow for anonymous questions or feedback where individuals feel comfortable sharing their experiences and concerns without fear of judgment or retribution. These spaces should be designed with input from marginalized communities to ensure they meet their needs and foster a sense of belonging and trust.

And now let's also talk about discomfort. It is often uncomfortable to hear feedback that challenges your belief as a leader that your organization is a true meritocracy, where success is based solely on individual merit and not influenced by systemic barriers or biases. However, leaders who embrace humility are willing to apologize for organizational failings and acknowledge the systemic barriers that contribute to representation gaps. Rather than blaming individuals, they accept responsibility and strive to make things right.

But change can only occur through genuine co-creation with marginalized voices and projects designed to benefit them. When all affected parties have equal representation at the planning table, true transformation happens.

The steps outlined here provide leaders with a framework for overcoming blind spots and achieving meaningful inclusion. Although this process takes time and requires self-reflection and responsibility on everyone's part, amazing things can happen when decision-makers lead by example and champion efforts for justice—it all starts by looking inward and being open to learning and growing!

Sparking Innovation Through Emotional Attunement

In today's diverse society, organizations cannot expect groundbreaking ideas to flow effortlessly if they just stick with traditional brainstorming methods. But here's the thing: When you create an environment where employees feel free to express their creativity and share unique viewpoints, magic happens!

Leaders with emotional CQ understand that innovation cannot be forced upon groups who do not share similar viewpoints; instead, they create environments where everyone feels safe taking risks, reflecting on ideas, and finding game-changing solutions.

Moreover, having a diverse team or just including marginalized individuals is not enough. Leaders must devote time and resources to building partnerships, credibility, and trust among team members, setting up anonymous channels so people can voice their thoughts and concerns, and ensuring that ideation processes are equitable by giving equal consideration to every contribution, from initial sparks of creativity to fully developed concepts.

But it isn't all just brainstorming, either. Everyone's input and perspectives are invaluable throughout the process, from stress-testing ideas and challenging assumptions to ensuring they serve a relevant community. That is why diverse user panels, customer advisory boards, and grassroots groups are essential—they help keep things honest and accurate!

Now it gets interesting: When disagreements arise (and they will), leaders with emotional CQ know precisely how to address them. By digging deep and discovering common ground instead of forcing people into conformity, savvy leaders find a path forward that honors all parties involved, especially bicultural or multicultural employees who can seamlessly switch codes—they bring so much value!

At their core, intercultural innovation playbooks focus on creating sustainable partnerships. Their purpose is to elevate marginalized creators while celebrating diversity—because no single culture holds all the answers to great ideas or to identifying future opportunities.

By fostering an environment where diverse perspectives and emotional experiences are valued, leaders can tap into their teams' full potential and drive innovation that resonates with a wide range of audiences. This approach leads to more creative solutions and reinforces the importance of inclusivity and cultural understanding in the workplace.

Case Study: Embracing Inclusivity at AdventurePro

Alex, the CEO of AdventurePro, an outdoor gear and apparel brand, has built a successful company driven by a passion for connecting people with nature. During a recent company retreat, Alex and his team discussed the lack of diversity in the outdoor industry. The conversation turned to the challenges faced by differently abled individuals who often feel excluded from outdoor activities because of a lack of suitable gear and support.

This discussion struck a chord with Alex, who realized that AdventurePro had been unintentionally contributing to this exclusion by focusing solely on the needs of its current customer base. He recognized that the company's product designs and marketing strategies had not considered the unique requirements and perspectives of differently abled individuals.

In a company-wide meeting after the retreat, Alex shared his newfound perspective and vision for expanding AdventurePro's reach to become more inclusive. "Everyone deserves the opportunity to experience the joy and freedom of the great outdoors," he said, his voice filled with conviction. "It's our responsibility to make that possible, but it will require each of us to step up and develop our emotional CQ."

Alex knows that to achieve this goal, his entire organization will have to significantly improve its emotional CQ—through research and product development, testing, marketing, and sales. He realizes that the company needed to find innovative ways to create gear that are both functional and accessible, ensuring that differently abled individuals can fully enjoy their outdoor experiences.

Case Study Questions

1. How can Alex assess the current level of emotional CQ within his organization and identify areas for improvement to support the company's inclusivity goals?

2. What strategies can Alex employ to foster a culture of empathy and understanding among his employees, particularly in departments that have limited direct interaction with differently abled customers?

3. How can AdventurePro's research and product development teams apply emotional CQ to create innovative and inclusive gear and apparel that meets the unique needs of differently abled individuals without compromising functionality?

4. What role can emotional CQ play in AdventurePro's marketing and sales strategies to authentically connect with and serve the differently abled community while avoiding tokenism or exploitation?

5. How can Alex ensure that AdventurePro's commitment to emotional CQ and inclusivity remains a long-term priority, even as the company continues to grow and face new challenges?

Case Study Resolution

Recognizing the importance of emotional CQ in achieving AdventurePro's inclusivity goals, Alex took a multifaceted approach to embedding this competency throughout the organization.

First, Alex partnered with a diversity and inclusion consultant to conduct an emotional CQ assessment across all departments. The results revealed that although employees generally had positive intentions, many needed more knowledge and skills to understand and meet the needs of differently abled customers.

To fill this gap, Alex launched a company-wide training program to build empathy, active listening, and perspective-taking skills. The program included workshops, role-playing exercises, and guest speakers from the differently abled community who shared their experiences and challenges with outdoor gear and apparel.

During one particularly potent session, a guest speaker named Maria, who used a wheelchair, shared her story of wanting to join her family on outdoor adventures but feeling unable to do so because of the lack of appropriate gear. "I've always dreamed of exploring the trails with my loved ones," she said, her eyes glistening with emotion. "But I've never been able to find gear that accommodates my needs while still being functional and reliable. It's heartbreaking to feel so left out."

This story hit home for many AdventurePro employees, who pledged to do better in designing and marketing truly inclusive products. Alex also established an inclusive design task force, bringing together employees from research and product development, marketing, and sales to collaborate with differently abled advisors. This task force worked to identify unmet needs, gather feedback on product ideas, and work with a diverse range of users to thoroughly test all new offerings to ensure they were functional and accessible.

To further embed emotional CQ into AdventurePro's culture, Alex introduced the "Different Yet Able" program and campaign. This program recognized employees who consistently demonstrated exceptional understanding and inclusivity toward differently abled individuals in their work. These champions served as role models and mentors, helping to foster a culture of empathy and respect throughout the organization.

As a result of these initiatives, AdventurePro successfully launched a new line of adaptive outdoor gear and apparel that received widespread praise from the differently abled community. The products were celebrated for their innovative designs that seamlessly combined functionality and accessibility, enabling differently abled individuals to enjoy their outdoor experiences fully. The company also saw increased employee engagement and retention, with many citing the inclusive and emotionally intelligent culture as a key factor in their job satisfaction.

By prioritizing emotional CQ and inclusivity, Alex not only expanded AdventurePro's market reach but also positioned the company as a leader in accessible outdoor gear and apparel. The "Different Yet Able" campaign resonated with customers and employees alike, showcasing AdventurePro's commitment to creating an inclusive community where everyone can enjoy the great outdoors. Alex's dedication to building a culture of empathy and understanding is an inspiring example for other business leaders seeking to create more inclusive and successful organizations.

Advancing Your Leadership Journey

Reflection Questions

1. How can you, as a leader, cultivate a deeper understanding of the emotional nuances and expressions present in different cultural contexts to build stronger connections with your team members?

2. How can you adapt your communication style and approach to foster a sense of psychological safety and belonging for individuals from diverse cultural backgrounds?

3. How might your own cultural background and emotional experiences shape your perception of others' emotions, and how can you develop a more empathetic and inclusive mindset?

4. What strategies can you employ to navigate emotionally charged situations or conflicts that arise from cultural misunderstandings, and how can you foster a culture of open dialogue and mutual respect?

5. How can you leverage emotional CQ to create a more inclusive and equitable workplace culture that values and celebrates the unique emotional experiences and expressions of all individuals?

Practical Application Activity

Commit to developing and implementing an emotional CQ growth plan.

- Take an emotional CQ assessment, such as the Cultural Intelligence Scale (CQS) or the Intercultural Effectiveness Scale (IES) (see Appendix), to identify areas for improvement in your emotional CQ across cultural contexts.

Set one or two specific, measurable goals, such as reading cross-cultural literature, watching films that showcase diverse emotional experiences, or engaging in cultural immersion activities, to illuminate your empathy blind spots.

- Identify a mentor who has demonstrated expertise in cross-cultural conflict resolution and schedule regular discussions to learn about their mediation principles and strategies for navigating emotionally charged situations in diverse cultural settings.

Initiate a grassroots conversation within your organization about implicit biases and exclusion, focusing on creating a safe space for open dialogue and gathering input from diverse perspectives to inform inclusive policies and practices that consider individuals' emotional needs and experiences from different cultural backgrounds.

As we conclude our exploration of ways to cultivate emotional CQ, let's reflect on the most critical insights and lessons learned.

Key Takeaways

1. Emotional CQ builds upon the foundation of emotional intelligence by emphasizing the importance of understanding and managing emotions when engaging with individuals from diverse cultural backgrounds. This approach

enables leaders to foster stronger connections and adapt their behaviors accordingly.

2. Cultivating emotional CQ allows leaders to create a culture of trust, navigate conflicts arising from cultural differences, demonstrate resilience during crises, and harness the power of diverse perspectives to drive innovation and inclusivity in their organizations.

3. Addressing privilege gaps requires leaders to self-reflect, seek empathetic input from marginalized communities, and collaborate with diverse participants to create equitable policies and practices that promote social justice and inclusion.

4. By embracing vulnerability, maintaining a positive outlook, and prioritizing collective care, emotionally intelligent leaders can guide their teams through uncertain times, foster a sense of belonging, and build the resilience necessary to thrive in an ever-changing world.

Chapter 7

Physical CQ: Developing Behavioral Agility Across Cultures

Leaders today have unprecedented diversity within their teams, comprised of people from many cultural backgrounds coming together for global projects. It is no longer enough to simply have technical expertise—organizations now require cross-cultural discernment skills to maximize team potential in an increasingly globalized world.

In practice, leaders need to adapt their communication styles to connect with people from diverse cultures. This includes not only spoken words but also nonverbal communication, such as body language, gestures, and facial expressions, which all have distinct meanings across cultures.

For example, take eye contact: As we mentioned earlier, it can be perceived differently depending on the context in which it is taking place. In Western cultures, direct eye contact can often be taken as a sign of credibility, whereas some Asian and Indigenous cultures may perceive direct eye contact as being too aggressive. Other components of nonverbal communication that come into play and affect how others see you can include the firmness of a handshake, the proximity of the participants in a conversation, and the fluctuation of voices.

As a leader, you must recognize cultural differences and adjust your nonverbal behavior accordingly. Otherwise, you could unwittingly offend or alienate your team members. Imagine, for instance, pointing to someone with your index finger, thinking it was friendly, only to discover that this gesture may be considered rude in certain parts of Asia or Africa.

Another mistake you will want to avoid involves interrupting others while they speak; this is a sign of disrespect almost everywhere, but particularly so in Arab and Asian cultures. Allowing the soles of your feet or of your shoes to show can also be a sign of great disrespect, and you should take care never to let it happen—it could have severe repercussions for the influence of your leadership and the cohesion of your team.

Cultural conditioning also plays a large part in our interpretation of the nonverbal cues we receive from others, leading us to make assumptions without even realizing it. For instance, people in certain cultures often display a more stoic demeanor than we Westerners might be used to. This may indicate not lack of interest, but rather politeness. Similarly, failing to laugh at an attempt at humor can often be misconstrued as rejection when, in reality, the context is not considered an appropriate one for laughter.

Observing the subtle variations between cultures regarding silence during conversations is fascinating. People from some cultures experience discomfort during moments of silence, while others consider that very same thing as a sign of deep thoughtfulness. These nuances in verbal tone and body language can create challenges in cross-cultural communication.

Yet these seemingly complex challenges can be surmounted relatively easily. By honing our emotional reading skills and becoming more aware of nonverbal cues, we can avoid inadvertently insulting others. Additionally, leaders with this nonverbal versatility tend to create stronger connections among diverse backgrounds, thereby increasing harmony and understanding among their team members.

Adapting Communication Styles

So how can leaders increase their physical CQ? I'll describe some key strategies.

Immersion experiences provide invaluable opportunities for personal development. Taking on expat assignments, volunteering abroad, or exploring cultural hubs in your own region offer excellent chances to experience unfamiliar social norms. Engaging in greetings with people from other cultures, observing conversational postures that catch your eye, and even learning about dining table customs can be eye-opening. These immersive experiences will leave a lasting impact and increase behavioral adaptability.

As you learn how to behave in other cultures, you will become adept at code-switching— consciously or unconsciously adapting your expressions, gestures, and proximity comfort to fit local norms. Code-switching might seem inauthentic to some, but it's a crucial skill for leaders navigating diverse cultural contexts. Code-switching helps people blend seamlessly into different environments while avoiding awkward public miscues. Though it can initially feel uncomfortable, practice in it will make you more proficient.

Mirroring is another powerful strategy. This involves mirroring your dialogue partner's posture, hand motions, and eye contact rhythms. By adopting matching energy levels, seating orientations, or gesticulation tempos, you can build deeper connections while creating psychological safety for both parties. Mirroring sends signals of solidarity that bridge cultural differences.

The next strategy is favoring curiosity over certainty. Instead of making assumptions or feeling embarrassed over not nailing a traditional handshake perfectly (for example), adopt a learner's mindset. Embrace what's unfamiliar and be curious about its underlying logic; ask questions, show interest, and let your humble curiosity drive the dialogue. Not only will you gain respect, but you might turn awkward interactions into opportunities for mutual growth and learning.

At this stage, leaders also need to create feedback channels. We all have blind spots regarding our behaviors, mainly unconscious social habits, so leaders should provide open and honest feedback opportunities. Take time for self-reflection on multicultural interactions and nonverbal disconnects that might have gone undetected. Review recorded speeches, as they could reveal body language red flags that need to be altered. Collect anonymous input to evaluate your leadership communication style. This way, you can continually improve.

Let's dive deeper into the journey of improving your physical CQ. It's not solely about avoiding cultural gaffes (although that is undoubtedly key); it's also about expanding your behavioral repertoire and unlocking leadership influence. Being able to read nonverbal cues allows people to form trusting relationships. Creating an atmosphere in which everyone feels respected and valued brings truly remarkable results.

Moving at the Right Pace

Leading diverse teams in an ever-evolving environment is like navigating through a shifting landscape: You must know when to stroll, jog moderately, or sprint, based on changing conditions and your team members. Change must be orchestrated in such a way that it works effectively. Start off slowly, by setting down inclusive policies and creating psychological safety for open conversations, and then, once this foundation has been set, moderate changes won't provoke as much pushback from your employees.

Do not underestimate the need for bold moves, such as during conflict flare-ups or problematic patterns that lead to marginalization. Quick action may be vital for saving relationships and keeping talent from leaving; sometimes, that will require breaking the rules slightly to get things back on track—it's all about finding that balance!

Communication is of the utmost importance. To avoid accidentally insulting team members of different generations or ideologies, we need to be sensitive when choosing our words, making sure not to offend those of different ages or perspectives. It's best to find common ground gradually before adapting our approach as necessary—it's like dancing together, mirroring each other's styles and cues without becoming polarized or heated.

But occasionally, emotionally charged exchanges will arise, and they must be addressed directly in ways that range from challenging assumptions to facilitating complex discussions. Finding the balance between conviction and respect is the key here. You will need to create space for cathartic release, and reconciliation should always be your goal.

Cross-cultural leadership requires special skills. You must read the room and respond accordingly, from adapting and transitioning frameworks to building foundations or sparking breakthroughs. Think of yourself as being like an experienced diplomat, drawing out the best in everyone while managing all the complexity associated with diversity.

So, it all boils down to finding that balance: Being bold when necessary and approaching communication with care and respect are crucial steps in leading your team toward sustainable unity while appreciating individual differences.

Adaptability in Nonverbal Communication

Adapting our nonverbal communication across different cultural contexts is a crucial skill. This adaptability involves being aware of and modifying our body language, gestures, facial expressions, and spatial preferences to align with diverse cultural norms. It requires a keen sense of observation, empathy, and flexibility. By adjusting our nonverbal cues appropriately, we can build rapport, show respect, and, ideally, avoid unintentional offense. This adaptability extends beyond mere mimicry; it's about developing a genuine understanding and appreciation for the subtle nuances of nonverbal communication in various cultures.

Physical Greetings

Our body language and actions say so much when we meet someone new. From that slight nod or awkward high-five to an accidental fist bump mishap, each aspect of human interaction speaks volumes about who we are as individuals. And it's not all about dodging handshakes in today's era of social distancing. Instead, it should be about appreciating the art of understanding and respecting diverse cultural norms—because something as small as bowing gracefully can set the tone for future relationships to bloom or fail altogether. Don't underestimate the power of physical greetings.

Calibrating Expressiveness

To truly express ourselves emotively, we must be conscious of cultural comfort levels when communicating emotionally. Finding that sweet spot between overdramatizing ourselves and being too composed requires a delicate balance. What might resonate with Latin or African audiences may not connect as strongly with Asian Pacific audiences. Adapting accordingly and knowing norms helps build meaningful connections while preventing unintended misunderstandings. Although many people desire to "keep it real," it's important to recognize that what's considered "real" or authentic varies across cultures. Being culturally aware means understanding and respecting these differences in emotional expression.

Nonverbal Encouragement

When you're engaging in collaborative conversations, nonverbal signals are crucial for maintaining smooth interactions and creating an environment where all members can contribute freely without regard for status differences.

Imagine that you're sitting in a meeting, listening to someone passionately discuss an idea they believe in, but nobody seems engaged with what is being shared. There is no need to panic, though; nonverbal cues can save the day.

You will send a clear signal of interest by mastering open gestures and friendly eye contact. But that isn't all! While discussing an idea, someone makes a hilarious joke, filling the room with laughter and positive vibes. That laughter is nonverbal communication in action—like adding some zesty flavorings to a bland meal to turn it into an explosion of taste.

Being conscious of our nonverbal signals allows us to create an environment where all ideas can flourish, not just our own. We need to be intentional with nonverbal communication if we want innovation to grow and bring out the best in everyone involved. Please don't underestimate the power of nonverbal cues, as they connect us all and unleash collective brilliance.

Nonverbal Cues for Conflict Mediation

Let's discuss how nonverbal signals can make an enormous impact when leaders face cross-cultural situations that become heated or divisive. Reading body language and adapting yours can be crucial for finding peaceful resolutions to heated disagreements.

Skilled mediators excel at demonstrating situational awareness through facial expressions. Their concerned looks mirror others' distress, creating an atmosphere of mutuality and connection. And let's not forget body posture; open stances without crossed arms indicate we're available to hear all perspectives.

Here's a quick tip: Use measured proximity to find that balance between giving people space and showing them you're fully engaged. *Measured proximity* involves being conscious of the physical distance between you and others and adjusting it based on cultural norms and the level of rapport. At the same time, provide intentional cues that show you are truly listening instead of passing judgment on the speaker's thoughts or ideas.

Once we've established psychological safety using nonverbal methods, we can begin bridging disparate perspectives through strategies like subtle head nods or matching speech pace and pausing patterns to create an atmosphere of resonance—it's like everyone is speaking the same language, only with their bodies.

Hand motions can also provide great nonverbal support. By including these nonverbal cues in our conversations, we can transform emotions into reasoned discourse—which should always be our aim.

Let me describe a time when I successfully mediated an extremely heated situation between two department heads. Nonverbal signals played an incredible role in turning around this wild encounter. Initially, angry gestures were flying around. To replace them, I used open palms as an effective yet subtle signal that I wasn't taking sides. Instead, I stood right in the middle, sending a clear message of finding common ground.

As I began our discussion, I focused on their mutual interests to change the tone and set a framework for finding compromises. I maintained steady eye contact to demonstrate my entire presence—that I was there listening and understanding their perspectives—and used periodic affirmative nods and smiles to create a safe space wherein honesty could flourish.

It might seem surprising, but defensive body language can quickly soften when we reengage and start working on innovative solutions. Our purposeful nonverbal cues can pave the way for the breakthroughs we seek.

So, when it comes to high-stakes interactions, remember that successful communication hinges on aligning our signals and creating a sense of resonance. As circumstances evolve, remember to adjust nonverbal messaging accordingly. Keeping yourself attuned while avoiding unchecked reactions can be critical for creating lasting harmony and results.

Cultivating Cross-Cultural Communication Dexterity

As we've noted, leaders can foster responsive influence by cultivating emotional and social discernment and by adapting their behaviors to cultural norms. And the good news is that nonverbal adaptability is a skill that can be developed through practice alone.

Let's delve deeper into some practical methods that can expand our unconscious nonverbal repertoires. There is no need for pantomimes and mimicry—what we need here is genuine rapport built through simple calibration and commitment.

Mastering nonverbal versatility is paramount for leaders who want to guide their global teams with emotional and social intelligence. Leaders who intentionally cultivate this skill set can expect significant improvement in their leadership abilities. With geographic barriers crumbling away in our interconnected world, being able to exert resonant influence quickly overshadows formal authority alone, so developing nonverbal adaptability is well worth your consideration.

Let's examine some practical strategies for developing this essential competency. First up is immersive nonverbal skill building. One way to hone adaptability could be through sustained international volunteering. Immersing yourself in various cultures allows you to practice greeting rituals, vocal alignment, and listening gestures that vary by culture. Doing this will develop your adaptive muscle memory as you gain familiarity with your host culture's nonverbal cues, such as senior colleagues' matching the depth of their greeting bows or handshake firmness being calibrated according to norms of intimacy. These subtle adjustments signal situational credibility and establish rapport quickly and effortlessly.

Practice and exposure will enable you to experience how understanding nonverbal cues in different cultures can simplify tense situations. Instead of unwittingly causing distrust through your micro-expressions, you'll develop an intuitive sense of body language that enhances communication. Over time, these adaptable behaviors become second nature, making navigating various cultural settings effortless.

You will develop habits that naturally signal cross-cultural welcome with time and practice. Your conscious efforts will become unconscious competence over time. As part of this reflective practice, it can be beneficial to review past exchanges by noting successful moments for reinforcement, as well as areas requiring improvement. Keeping a learning journal may be helpful for capturing insights and monitoring your progress over time—this practice goes a long way toward strengthening conversational skills and developing meaningful cross-cultural connections.

One practical approach for building rapport is to seek external feedback. Bicultural coaches can offer invaluable insights by reviewing video debriefs of your speeches, discussions, and conflict mediation sessions. Their insight includes giving guidance on subtle language cues that you might miss because you are not a native of that culture. Expert eyes can help highlight areas where further rapport-building opportunities lie.

Leaders can tune into their unconscious tension indicators to detect inconsistencies between words, body signals, and any other mismatches. These unconscious tension indicators could be subtle changes in your own facial expressions, body language, or vocal tone that develop when you feel discomfort or unease in a cross-cultural interaction. For example, you might notice yourself furrowing your brow, tensing your shoulders, or speaking more rapidly when faced with an unfamiliar cultural situation. By paying attention to these physiological responses, you can identify areas where you need to adapt your nonverbal communication.

It's like reading a hidden language that shows where leaders may be over- or under-demonstrating in a given situation—they might even discover themselves unwittingly draining their audience's energy by maintaining an uneven pace. Reflecting upon these cues provides valuable insights into blind spots and helps to hone situational skills.

Coaching conversations open up a whole new world of developmental planning for leaders. Through such discussions, leaders can discover nonverbal listening cues, proactive gestures of invitation, and the significance of culturally appropriate spaces and vocal tonalities. It's like building your toolbox of superpowers. Through instruction, guidance, and practice, leaders become experts at easily adapting to diverse environments while effortlessly reading the room, making an impression that amazes everyone.

On top of all this, implicit biases cannot be overlooked. Leaders can watch for subtle physiological tension and anxiety during intercultural encounters that might indicate unconscious projections of cultural bias that need to be explored. A leader actively works on dismantling biased mental reflexes by paying attention to facial expressions, vocal cues, and personal space interactions. Expanding our comfort zones by becoming inclusive individuals instead of running from growth opportunities can be immensely empowering. Who knew that growth could be so life-changing?

Building adaptive versatility takes more than awareness; it also requires courage and vulnerability. Acknowledging our initial discomfort when faced with differences, and then holding ourselves accountable to learn about other cultures and become more tolerant—it's like searching for hidden layers of prejudice. We can make real strides as inclusive leaders by approaching these challenges with empathy rather than shame. Society may stymie our ideals of equity, but with some humor and determined effort, we can pave a pathway toward more extraordinary capability building.

Decoding Digital Body Language

Navigating age-diverse teams can be an immense challenge for leaders. Recognizing generational gaps when conveying and decoding nonverbal signals can be especially important in today's digital era, when remote work has become more prevalent. Older demographics tend to rely more on in-person interactions, whereas young generations born into tech culture instinctively use virtual body language through chat apps, emojis, and video platforms.

Failing to bridge this nonverbal divide can alienate talented individuals or cause them to miss out on the subtle cues provided by nonverbal messaging—this can be a particular problem, for instance, for seasoned professionals unfamiliar with virtual communication channels. They may feel overwhelmed by the rapid-fire multimodal communication used by their Millennial or Gen Z colleagues, such as chat messages speeding back and forth with multiple chat windows open at once (the speed at which these messages are sent is itself a nonverbal cue); immediate responses using emojis or emoticons; and comments, memes, and laugh-inducing pictograms flooding their Slack or WhatsApp team channel. Veteran team members accustomed to slower deliberation may perceive this fast-paced dialogue as chaotic and distracting noise. At the same time, younger digital natives view this rapid back-and-forth as part of a nonstop practical brainstorming session.

Text-based messages offer some engaging lessons. Have you noticed how often people use emojis or character stylizations such as ALL CAPS to emphasize tone or urgency when communicating online? Additionally, without vocal inflection or facial tension, periods at the end of simple words like "Sure" and "Fine" can serve as passive-aggressive punctuation. GIFs and memes provide emotional context to written statements that might otherwise be overlooked. Unfortunately, leaders from older cohorts may miss these nonverbal digital cues altogether, leading to misinterpretations of the intended sentiment.

And video calls. Oh, the joys of video conferencing! An interesting observation has emerged from this form of communication: Younger employees tend to feel comfortable showing off their intimate living spaces, complete with adorable pets and kids who wander into view from time to time. But this informality may give an unprofessional vibe to more traditional staff who prefer formal office backdrops that clearly distinguish work from home personas. Conversely, younger colleagues may perceive Boomer managers' lack of background material as robotic or as their having something to hide.

So what can be done about all this? Here are a few potential solutions:

First, onboarding training focusing on common kinds of digital nonverbal messaging among Generations Y and Z can go a long way toward solving this issue. By raising awareness of leader biases, such as assuming that all generations communicate in the same way or that certain digital expressions are universally understood, leaders can develop a more nuanced understanding of generational differences in communication styles. This increased understanding can foster empathy and help leaders adapt their own communication to better connect with team members from different generations.

Using mirrors before live-streaming video calls helps you become aware of unintended background distractions that might appear during calls. Position a mirror behind your camera to see what others see, and adjust as needed.

Emoji guides, such as Emojipedia (), are handy references that explain the meanings and appropriate usage of various emojis and digital expressions. These resources can assist with communication issues and reduce confusion and miscommunication, especially for those less familiar with digital lingo.

Gathering insights through separate generational focus groups, especially when using tools like Slack, can be extremely helpful in identifying and addressing gaps. Encourage open discussions about preferred communication styles and any challenges in interpreting digital body language.

Finally, a generous dose of nonjudgmental patience goes far toward helping leaders appreciate and comprehend these rapid virtual mannerisms. Approach generational differences in digital communication with an open and curious mindset.

As is true of other aspects of communication, nonverbal signals carry generational differences that necessitate code-switching when working remotely in digitally driven work environments. Taking the time to acquire decoding skills and establishing a decoding infrastructure can help to preclude having younger and older talent alienated from each other because of unfamiliar technology-enabled teaming styles involving emojis, GIFs, rapid chat volleys, or context collapse across life domains. Intentional bridge-building today ensures equity tomorrow.

Case Study: Bridging the Generational Gap at StyleHaven

Fabian, a seasoned executive at StyleHaven Apparel, had built a successful career by leveraging his charisma, expertise, and traditional leadership tactics. However, as the company expanded and brought in a wave of Generation Z employees, Fabian struggled to connect with and motivate this new cohort.

Fabian's traditional approach to communication, which relied heavily on in-person meetings, formal presentations, and hierarchical decision-making processes, failed to resonate with the younger employees. They preferred more flexible, collaborative, and tech-driven ways of working. Fabian's attempts at humor and casual conversation often fell flat as he struggled to understand the cultural references and digital terminology used by his Gen Z colleagues.

Moreover, Fabian's leadership style, which emphasized individual achievement and long work hours, clashed with Gen Z's values of work–life balance, social responsibility, and team-oriented goals. He found it challenging to adapt his motivational strategies and feedback methods to align with their preferences for frequent, informal check-ins and a strong emphasis on personal growth and development.

As a result, Fabian noticed a growing disconnect between himself and the younger team members. Collaboration and productivity began to suffer, with Gen Z employees feeling misunderstood and disengaged. Fabian recognized that his traditional tactics needed to be changed to align with Generation Z's values, priorities, preferred channels, and cultural trends.

Case Study Questions

1. What aspects of Fabian's communication style might be contributing to the disconnect with Gen Z employees?

2. How can Fabian adapt his leadership approach to better motivate and engage Gen Z team members?

3. What steps can Fabian take to bridge the generational gap and foster a more collaborative, inclusive work environment?

4. How might Fabian leverage technology and digital platforms to enhance communication and connection with Gen Z colleagues?

5. What role can reverse mentoring play in helping Fabian better understand Gen Z's values, preferences, and cultural trends?

Case Study Resolution

Recognizing the importance of physical CQ in bridging the generational gap at StyleHaven Apparel, Fabian took a multifaceted approach to developing this competency and fostering a more inclusive work environment.

First, Fabian partnered with a generational diversity expert to conduct a physical CQ assessment across all departments. The results revealed that although Fabian and other seasoned executives had strong technical skills and industry knowledge, they needed help to adapt their communication and leadership styles to connect with Gen Z employees.

To diminish this gap, Fabian launched a company-wide initiative to build nonverbal communication skills and generational awareness. The initiative included workshops, role-playing exercises, and reverse mentoring programs that paired seasoned executives with Gen Z employees. These sessions focused on understanding and adapting to different communication preferences, cultural references, and digital platforms.

During one particularly powerful reverse mentoring session, a Gen Z employee named Liam shared his perspective on the importance of work–life balance and social responsibility. "For my generation, it's not just about climbing the corporate ladder," he explained. "We want to work for companies that value our well-being and positively impact society. We feel more engaged and motivated when leaders understand and support these priorities."

This information struck a chord with Fabian, who realized he needed to adjust his leadership style to align better with Gen Z's values. He began incorporating more flexibility into work arrangements, offering opportunities for community involvement, and emphasizing the company's commitment to sustainability and social responsibility.

Fabian also consciously tried to adapt his communication style, turning to digital platforms like instant messaging and video conferencing to facilitate more frequent and informal interactions with his team. He participated in social media challenges and learned to use emojis and digital vocabulary to connect with younger colleagues.

To further embed physical CQ into StyleHaven Apparel's culture, Fabian introduced the Bridging Generations program. This program celebrated employees who demonstrated exceptional skill in fostering cross-generational collaboration and understanding. These champions served as role models and mentors, helping to create a more inclusive and adaptive work environment.

As a result of these initiatives, StyleHaven Apparel saw a significant improvement in employee engagement, productivity, and retention across all generations. The company was recognized as a generational diversity and inclusion leader, and it attracted top talent from seasoned professionals and Gen Z graduates.

By prioritizing physical CQ and generational inclusivity, Fabian boosted StyleHaven Apparel's performance and positioned the company as an employer of choice in the fashion industry. The Bridging Generations program made sense to employees and job seekers alike, and it showcased StyleHaven Apparel's commitment to creating a workplace where all generations can thrive. Fabian's journey in developing his physical CQ is an inspiring example for other business leaders seeking to navigate the challenges and opportunities of a multigenerational workforce.

Advancing Your Leadership Journey

Reflection Questions

1. How can you enhance your awareness of nonverbal cues and their cultural variations to improve cross-cultural communication in your team?

2. In what ways might your own nonverbal communication style be interpreted differently by people from other cultures, and how can you adapt to provide clarity and respect?

3. What steps can you take to create a psychologically safe environment that encourages open dialogue about cultural differences in nonverbal communication?

4. How can you use the power of nonverbal communication to build trust and rapport with team members from diverse cultural backgrounds?

5. What personal biases or assumptions might influence your interpretation of nonverbal cues, and how can you overcome these barriers to develop your physical CQ?

Practical Application Activity

Commit to developing and implementing a physical CQ growth plan.

- Identify three specific nonverbal communication patterns common in your own culture, and research how these patterns might differ among cultures. Using role-playing exercises with a trusted colleague or friend, and practice adapting your nonverbal communication to align with these cultural norms.

- Over the next month, pay close attention to how your greetings, posture, and gestures change depending on the cultural context of your interactions. Keep a journal to record your observations and reflect on any insights gained.

- Seek feedback from at least three colleagues or community members from different cultural backgrounds regarding your nonverbal communication style. Ask them to provide specific examples of when your nonverbal cues were culturally appropriate and when they might have been misinterpreted. Use this feedback to inform your ongoing physical CQ development.

As we wrap up our discussion of Physical CQ and developing behavioral agility across cultures, let's reinforce our understanding by reviewing the key takeaways from this chapter.

Key Takeaways

1. Nonverbal communication—including gestures, proximity, and eye contact—plays a crucial role in cross-cultural interactions. Leaders must be aware of cultural variations in nonverbal cues to build connections and avoid misinterpretations.

2. Developing physical CQ involves expanding the unconscious nonverbal repertoire of the person who engages in immersive cultural experiences, practices code-switching techniques, and seeks external feedback from intercultural coaches.

3. When working with diverse teams, leaders must be intentional about change management and communication. Although it's important to consider team readiness, there are times when leaders need to take decisive action to drive needed changes, even if the team is not entirely prepared. Leaders must find the right balance between modulating change and taking bold measures to resolve conflicts, reduce marginalization, and create a more inclusive work environment. This may involve challenging the team members to step out of their comfort zone and adapt to new ways of working and communicating.

4. Bridging generational divides in digital communication is crucial for remote leaders. Ensuring that all team members understand and feel included in the use of emojis, GIFs, and rapid-fire chat styles can contribute to a more inclusive work environment.

Part 3

Harnessing Cultural Intelligence:
Strategies for Inclusive Leadership and Sustainable Success

Chapter 8

The Growth Journey: Strategies for Developing CQ Leadership

Effective leadership today involves managing diversity, cultivating trust-based relationships, and leading teams across cultural differences. However, successfully developing these intercultural leadership skills requires humility, courage, and an open mindset (Van Dyne et al., 2012). But don't worry; this chapter offers practical strategies and important milestones to unlock inclusive excellence and unleash collective potential through CQ.

First, it's crucial that we both acknowledge our limitations and recognize our growth potential. Gudykunst and Kim (1984) noted that to minimize our ethnocentric tendencies, we must first identify any biases that skew our perception and judgment of unfamiliar cultural practices. This self-awareness is the foundation upon which we can build our CQ.

Dweck's groundbreaking 2008 research on growth mindsets and neuroscientist Marian Cleeves Diamond's 1988 work on neuroplasticity provide compelling evidence that our abilities, including CQ, can be developed and enhanced through effort and experience. Dweck demonstrated that leaders who embrace a growth mindset are more likely to welcome challenges and learn from failures, enabling them to expand their capabilities over time. Similarly, Diamond's research on Einstein's brain revealed that the human brain can change and improve with enriching experiences, which highlights the importance of exposing ourselves to diverse cultural contexts and perspectives.

By combining the insights from the work of Dweck and Diamond, we can approach CQ development with a powerful combination of self-awareness, a growth mindset, and a commitment to seeking out enriching cross-cultural experiences. This approach enables us to challenge our biases, learn from our mistakes, and continuously expand our cultural understanding and adaptability.

In Chapter 4, I introduced the Culturally Intelligent Leader's Mindset framework as the cornerstone of becoming an incredible leader. However, we know that it is not enough to talk the talk. To effectively align our values and behaviors, we require structured development plans that track how we are moving closer to our personal goals (MacNab & Worthley, 2012). This is where the Intercultural Readiness Check comes into play, which we will introduce in this chapter. Cultural risk-taking, dealing with ambiguity, and adapting to change are critical aspects of experiential growth opportunities (Paige, 1993). Let's gear up and prepare to start learning immersively now.

Immersive learning experiences can be transformative. Directly confronting new cultural dynamics can provide moments of epiphany, new insights, and fresh perspectives (Johnson et al., 2006). However, once we return home, we might lose momentum; therefore, periodic reinforcement through coaching or communities of practice is crucial to sustaining our growth (Eisenberg, 2013).

Inclusion efforts will hit an impasse unless we address the systemic barriers that limit access for marginalized groups (Castilla, 2008). Unfortunately, cultural training and similar initiatives do not always lead to equal opportunities across diverse identities (Hajro et al., 2017). For lasting change to occur, we need individual and structural interventions that encourage adaptation from all corners (Mavletova, 2013), with leadership playing an essential role in orchestrating all this change.

Progress along the Cultural Intelligence Leadership Continuum is like an eternal journey toward cultural consciousness—there is no endpoint! But do not despair: Milestones help keep us on the right path and maintain momentum over time. Regularly reviewing our blind spots, seeking feedback, and aligning our behaviors with our intentions is how we can build momentum and keep it going.

Assessment: Mapping Out the CQ Journey

Expanding your CQ involves embarking on an adventure of self-discovery—uncovering biases and blind spots that might prevent you from reaching your fullest potential. By employing various assessment methods, you can measure your awareness of cultural differences and track your progress and critical lessons learned along your journey.

Diagnostic evaluations should not be seen as definitive assessments of your capabilities; given the cultural context, relying too heavily on standardized scores may reinforce biases and stereotypes about marginalized groups (Hajro et al., 2017). Instead of accepting them without scrutiny, let us critically assess the limitations of these diagnostic tools to achieve more ethical evaluation practices.

Various tools can be used to assess your intercultural readiness and identify areas for improvement objectively. Let's look at a couple of common ones here. The descriptions below include links to the assessments, which can also be found in the Appendix. (These tools are described in greater detail in the earlier chapters of this book.)

The Cultural Intelligence Scale (CQS): Developed by Van Dyne, Ang, and Koh (2008), this tool measures abilities across several dimensions, including metacognition, cognition, motivation, and behavior. While readers can refer to Van Dyne et al.'s original CQS for a comprehensive academic assessment, Harden Consulting Group has developed a free quiz based on this foundational research to help you explore your cultural intelligence strengths and growth areas. Your results might reveal various patterns - for example, you may find that while you have a strong knowledge of cultural differences, you might benefit from developing more adaptability in cross-cultural situations. Or you might discover that while you're highly motivated to engage with people from different cultures, you could enhance your understanding of specific cultural norms and values. You can access Harden Consulting Group's free CQ quiz here: https://hardenconsulting-group.com/cq-quiz

The Intercultural Development Inventory (IDI): Unlike the CQS, the IDI offers a more qualitative insight into your approach to cultural differences. It places you on a continuum from denial to adaptation, providing greater self-awareness of your own ethnocentrism or behavioral inconsistencies while motivating you to bridge intentions with behaviors—in other words, acting like a guide through different stages of understanding and growth. The IDI is accessible for evaluation at .

The Intercultural Readiness Check (IRC): This assessment integrates elements from the previous models while adding dimensions such as cultural risk-taking, coping with ambiguity, flexibility, and interest in different cultures. The IRC can help assess capability "gaps" that require you to undergo particular experiences to expand your comfort zones. It guides you in targeting growth edges and shows your progress along these experiential markers. Explore your intercultural competencies with the IRC here:

The Cultural Orientations Indicator (COI): This tool offers insight into your preferences, tendencies, and cultural values, compared them with national or workplace norms. By understanding your score patterns on scales that measure things like universalism vs. particularism and neutral vs. emotional orientation, you can adapt your style to improve your relationship-building and communication. However, it should be noted that COI tends to focus more on enhancing existing capabilities than on advancing new ones. To measure your cultural orientations using the COI, refer to the assessment link in the Appendix.

These assessments provide an initial awareness, but it is always crucial not to fall into the trap of reinforcing stereotypes. This is why further exploration involving contextual interpretation, group narratives, and open dialogue is essential for creating a more nuanced understanding of cultural truths. With all of these tools and approaches at your disposal, enhancing your intercultural readiness should come naturally.

Development Planning: Charting the Course

CQ development can be an exhilarating journey. However, moving forward on this path requires deliberate personal planning that helps set and motivate us in the right direction. With clear goals and an understanding of why these cross-cultural capabilities matter to us as we progress, we can avoid becoming bogged down in the overwhelming complexity of the project. Together, let's go deeper to explore how to chart an inspiring yet grounded developmental course.

To begin with, we must narrow our focus to identify the key competencies we need to develop. Assessment tools help us measure our intercultural flexibility, empathy, and decision-making patterns, and any gaps between our values and behaviors (Van Dyne et al., 2012). Once we have set our growth goals and our timelines for reaching them, we will develop and adjust them according to the results of each assessment tool as we use it—assessment thus becomes our secret weapon!

For example, someone with a high cognitive CQ score but a low emotional CQ would benefit from developing their ability to regulate emotions and show empathy in cross-cultural situations. On the other hand, leaders who struggle to adapt their verbal and nonverbal communication in culturally diverse settings should focus on improving their physical CQ, as this is crucial for fostering effective intercultural interactions and inclusive environments.

Setting ambitious targets is excellent, but we should not leave them just hanging there once we have set them. Instead, we must work backward from our desired capabilities and establish milestones to help us make better decisions, foster inclusive processes, and ensure cultural representation (MacNab & Worthley, 2012). Reaching our goals will have far-reaching effects, and to get there, we need to employ mechanisms that will reinforce our development. Have you considered rotating programs, community exchanges, or mentorships as tools for embedding newfound capabilities (Blake-Beard et al., 2011) and building cultural muscle memory? Such ongoing encounters offer us a way to solidify our accomplishments.

Keeping tabs on our progress is crucial; we must gather data on our performance against equity and inclusion metrics. Then we want to see evidence of how we have applied our newly acquired skills. Both qualitative indicators and equitable access outcomes tell us much about our capability journey (Kankanhalli et al., 2019). As soon as we combine all these pieces, we create a cycle of discovery, planning, application, and reflection that helps us tap into our infinite potential to contribute to society.

Creating Growth Goals

Here's the deal: To step up your game and expand your capabilities, you've got to set specific CQ goals. After assessing the areas where you need improvement, create measurable objectives to motivate your growth (MacNab & Worthley, 2012). Push yourself out of your comfort zone regarding thinking and behaving differently. Then, once you have identified areas for improvement, it is time to set your specific goals. Make them SMART goals: specific, measurable, attainable, relevant, and time-bound. For instance: "Over the next quarter, I plan on joining two intercultural book club conversations to better my understanding of systemic inequality issues." See what I did there?

However, this is about more than checking boxes and fulfilling tasks; we want to see real growth and integration here, including making inclusive decisions, increasing belonging for marginalized groups, and creating a diverse team that can handle anything that comes their way. Once your goals are accomplished, you will watch their impact ripple throughout your crew.

Now, I'm not suggesting waiting a year before looking for progress; instead, set out smaller quarterly milestones that lead toward your annual objectives and build on one another to give you a sense of progress (Bandura, 1977). Do not overlook small victories—they count.

Here's another great tip: Consider linking your goal tracking with some coaching or community forums so that someone is holding you accountable and helping to keep the motivation flowing strong.

Structuring Development Initiatives

Formal learning initiatives provide concrete evidence of development by creating opportunities for you to elevate marginalized voices into everyday work environments. Without structures supporting capability advancement across an entire organization, the pressures to assimilate into the dominant culture fall unevenly on minority groups as they seek to integrate their identity between their personal and professional selves (Mavletova, 2013). Let's investigate mechanisms that enable sustainable adoption.

Rotational programs that temporarily place leaders in unfamiliar cultural contexts get them out of their inherent tendency to see things from their own context by immersing them in foreign team dynamics and community needs (Silzer & Dowell, 2009). Navigating Indian caste systems or African American opportunity barriers fosters humility while uncovering shared hopes.

Skill-based volunteering with historically excluded communities fosters reciprocal relationships that lead to unexpected discoveries about the human condition. Deep connections teach leaders to use privileges responsibly. Mentorships that connect emerging talent with seasoned professionals from similar cultural backgrounds provide supportive sounding boards that promote resilience on leadership journeys (Blake-Beard et al., 2011). Together, we can reframe challenges as growth opportunities.

Regular intercultural exchanges through work assignments, community collaborations, and guidance frameworks foster the acquisition of lasting capabilities in an inclusive atmosphere. Structured programming equitably distributes developmental responsibilities so that marginalized team members can contribute authentically without fragmenting their identities between the personal and professional realms: Inclusive climates that last are formed from the bottom up, not from the top down.

Learning Approaches to Develop CQ

Maintaining momentum on your CQ journey requires tailored learning approaches that match your goals and help you adapt to the ever-evolving challenges you encounter. Let's discuss some focused mechanisms designed to foster transformed mindsets, push boundaries, and reinforce new behaviors through shared discovery. Here is the crux: If you are to maximize learning efficacy, your development activities must align with the insights gleaned from your assessment results. Otherwise, your capability-building efforts could end up as scattered attempts that do not address your core limitations—something we certainly want to avoid! For lasting progress and development, implement a personalized intervention aimed at your own personal emotional, cognitive, and behavioral competencies. Doing this will allow you to advance and expand in a way that works for you.

Now let's talk about structured initiatives, such as rotational programs, mentorships, and simulations. They provide opportunities to fully immerse yourself in lessons and directly apply them to your daily life. Real-world skills development becomes easy when you are supported by peers who share your vulnerabilities—a dynamic best fostered by rotational programs, mentorships, and simulations. Peer communities offer invaluable support when you are navigating this tightrope of growth!

Advice from an expert (yes, me!): Short-term interventions do not work; they quickly evaporate into thin air. If changes are to last, institutional ecosystems must provide an environment that protects the cultural ideals we hold dear.

Changing Our Perspective Through Immersive Learning

Transformative learning involves challenging assumptions and adopting fresh perspectives, like entering an emotional and cognitive rabbit warren to explore different cultures (Illeris, 2014). Imagine what it would be like to participate in an intensive cultural immersion experience that includes group dialogues in an effort to seek and find collective meaning. Having experienced such immersive learning programs myself, I can tell you that they are amazing! Immersion puts you right into the thick of cultural dynamics, causing powerful perspective shifts. A great example is the National Outdoor Leadership School's adaptable leadership curriculum that uses wilderness expeditions. These programs truly take learning to the next level by fostering cultural agility among participants who must simultaneously navigate uncertainty (Aldrich, 2014).

Diversity is also key: Deliberately gathering a range of demographics and cultures in the immersion experience can amplify the breadth of each person's outlook through peer exchanges. Such meetings reveal the privileges and the barriers that shape each of our paths, helping us to develop cultural intelligence while emphasizing our intersectional identities (Mendenhall et al., 2008).

But let's also think about post-immersion reinforcement. Since we want our new perspectives to stay with us, coaching conversations can provide invaluable support in making sense of our intense emotional awakenings; they can help us to channel our inner justice warrior (Mendenhall et al., 2008) and distill the complex dilemmas we face through dialogue.

Pushing Our Comfort Zones

Something remarkable occurs when we explore other worldviews outside our comfort zones. Our awareness expands, and we understand the different cultural realities viscerally. Although it might feel awkward or even uncomfortable at first, once we push through, something beautiful emerges: shared hopes and humanity.

Cultural mentorships offer invaluable opportunities to understand the challenges that others are facing by pairing program participants from disparate backgrounds in an interactive learning experience. Over months of engagement, in safe spaces, mentors and mentees share their trials, successes, and lessons learned (Blake-Beard et al., 2011). Moreover, both parties gain wisdom by providing insight to one another.

Reciprocal perspective-taking is another effective strategy for building empathy. By volunteering in historically marginalized communities and engaging in role reversal simulations, we gain glimpses into existing structural inequities; similarly, role reversal simulations help us open our eyes to minority experiences while becoming aware of our own privileges—but all of this must start with deep listening and a genuine willingness to connect.

Becoming a true ally, however, involves going beyond our comfort zones and actively advocating for voices that may otherwise go unheard. By co-creating solutions that are explicitly tailored to the needs of marginalized communities, we can help break through the mainstream policies and cultural norms that otherwise limit those communities from flourishing fully.

As we embark on these journeys of understanding, we may also uncover uncomfortable truths about ourselves (Hajro et al., 2017)—it can be an eye-opening experience, and not always in a happy way. Yet it is necessary if we are to create a more compassionate world.

Coaching, Sponsorship, and Role Modeling

One key to help you and your team grow as culturally intelligent leaders is continuous one-on-one guidance. This personalized approach allows for tailored feedback, goal setting, and progress tracking. In these individual sessions, you can set personalized goals based on assessment results and hold yourself accountable for adopting situationally adaptive behaviors. You can discuss feedback and environmental changes that impact your CQ development. Similarly, you can encourage your staff and colleagues to set their own CQ development goals and provide them with the support and resources they need to succeed. This individualized guidance ensures that each team member receives the specific attention and support they need to grow their cultural intelligence.

As a leader, you must model the behavior you wish to see in your team. By actively working on your CQ development and sharing your journey with your staff and colleagues, you can create a continuous learning and growth culture. Encourage open discussions about cultural differences, share relevant resources and training opportunities, and celebrate the progress and achievements of your team members in their CQ development.

Have you ever found yourself wondering how some aspiring leaders manage to advance their careers while also promoting CQ within their organizations? The secret lies with sponsorship. Having a sponsor helps you navigate your organization and connect with senior decision-makers more quickly than simply having a mentor (who typically focuses just on providing psychosocial support). Powerful sponsors can directly influence discussions about promotion and help to clear obstacles through tacit coordination efforts (Hewlett et al., 2010), which means that your sponsor or advocate can open doors for you that might otherwise remain closed. Additionally, sponsors can help you champion CQ initiatives and gain the support and resources needed to implement them effectively.

Communities of practice also play a pivotal role in fostering culturally intelligent leadership. These groups enable leaders who are navigating similar challenges to gather in an exclusive environment to offer support by sharing their collective insights—that way, they can develop solutions to issues related to cultural diversity and inclusion. By participating in these communities, you can learn from the experiences of others, share your own successes and challenges, and collaborate on strategies for promoting CQ in your respective organizations.

Together, with dialogue as our ally, we can break free of isolation and overcome challenges head-on. Drawing on sponsorship, communities of practice, and other proven developmental formats, you can advance your career and create a ripple effect of positive change throughout your organization. Remember, building a culturally intelligent organization starts with your own commitment to growth and your ability to inspire and support others in their development journey. As you grow and develop as a culturally intelligent leader, you'll inspire others to do the same, ultimately building a more inclusive and effective workforce.

Shared Learning

Individualized learning can help to advance capability development, but collaboratively engaging in dialogue as part of a team brings exciting potential! Here is where cultural truths emerge and multiple perspectives open up—an experience unlike any other. As the starting point, assess your organization's CQ levels. Examine how well its leadership style adapts, how language barriers are overcome, and how trust-based partnerships are formed (Ang et al., 2007). A collective diagnosis can help pinpoint gaps and maintain an organization's humility. Then, consider these incredibly potent options.

Engaging in inclusive leadership simulation modules will enable your team to experience complex intercultural negotiation scenarios that mimic real-life project environments. Furthermore, conducting debriefing sessions aimed at finding superior solutions provides invaluable peer insights that support the team's experiential learning while swiftly expanding the participants' behavioral repertoires.

What's more, consider book and film clubs. These groups provide regular opportunities to increase cultural consciousness by allowing members to discuss often marginalized narratives. Trust me—the eye-opening guided dialogues that result will reveal blind spots you never knew existed. Additionally, by conducting regular check-ins with team members, you can ensure that dominant culture interpretations are challenged and that everyone works together toward a more inclusive understanding. These check-ins involve asking team members to share their thoughts, feelings, and experiences related to the books or films discussed, ensuring that diverse perspectives are heard and valued.

Here's the deal: Group-based activities create supportive spaces for you to practice, test assumptions, and gain confidence in demonstrating the high-level CQ capabilities expected of leaders like you. These activities form part of your collective developmental journey and will lead to system-wide transformation.

Supplemental Methods of Motivational Reinforcement

Maintaining high motivation between formal learning sessions is paramount in developing our CQ. One way of doing this is by using supplemental techniques that reinforce our goals and learning, hold us accountable, and celebrate our progress.

Gamification—the practice of injecting game-like elements into non-game situations (Armstrong & Landers, 2018)—offers a practical and an engaging solution. Gamification rewards your CQ gains with badges for mastering new skills, or leaderboards to track CQ gains, turning the journey to build CQ into an exciting adventure. Additionally, immersive simulation training platforms allow learners to practice skills in realistic virtual environments modeled on intercultural workplace settings, meaning they receive personalized feedback and analytics about their decision-making (Hurn, 2011). The combination of gamification techniques and simulations provides tangible mechanisms for both motivation and experiential development as we seek to continuously build our cultural discernment capabilities.

Digital credentials can also help strengthen your CQ (Oliver, 2019). These dynamic skills passports help track your development across different learning formats—from formal training courses to volunteer experiences abroad. Digital credentials give an impressive visual representation of your CQ expertise, enabling you to see how much your expertise has grown over time and in different environments. They also boost your confidence while keeping your engagement alive for the long run.

Never underestimate the power of enterprise social networks, either: These platforms create spaces for peer learning and knowledge sharing and remind us to stay on track with our cultural goals (Aoun, 2022). Here, you'll find allies who model inclusive mindsets while seeking assistance in applying new perspectives. Besides, who doesn't appreciate an unexpected notification that gives a well-deserved pat on the back?

By adopting these advanced practices, we can foster cultures where all voices—particularly marginalized ones—are recognized and valued. Cultural impact transcends formal interventions. It's about acknowledging progress made, staying connected to cultural insights gained throughout life, and making this all part of daily living. So, let's stay motivated, have some fun, and incorporate CQ into our lives both in and outside of the learning environment!

Tracking Progress

"You manage what you measure" rings true when tracking progress in capability timelines. However, we should take care when using numbers alone, as metrics by themselves will not adequately capture CQ advancement. If this kind of measurement is to be effective, we must also account for subtle social dynamics and long-term community effects (Kankanhalli et al., 2019).

Let's discuss how we can measure our CQ growth appropriately. The first step is to identify significant markers at both the individual and organizational levels; for instance, CQ leadership can be demonstrated by equitable retention and promotion rates, increasing the numbers or proportion of minority vendors/partners, or fulfilling accommodation requests. We must track relevant metrics so that progress is visible over time.

And remember, no one said culture change would be easy! We need to find an appropriate time and frequency for evaluating cultural initiatives—every two to three years seems like a reasonable balance, as this allows enough time for those changes to take hold while keeping things moving along smoothly. Let's also connect these progress reviews to strategy planning meetings to increase accountability.

As we measure all this, we must ensure we are not simply ticking off boxes—or, worse, commodifying marginalized communities without their input (Johnson & Onwuegbuzie, 2004). Conducting regular reviews led by community representatives is imperative if we want a proper assessment that truly measures the impact of our efforts to grow CQ—including indicators like reduced identity threats or safer speaking climates—to make sure we genuinely grasp its worth, measure our impacts responsibly, and empower groups themselves with tools for self-measurement. As we mentioned, strategic tracking should go beyond simply gathering numbers and data; it should focus on understanding context, finding an acceptable pace, and engaging the community to effectively demonstrate the capabilities of our investments and move collectively toward a brighter future.

Let's delve deeper into some essential metrics. Many measurement tools and milestone listings are readily available online and through academic resources, professional development organizations, and specialized consultancy firms. The Appendix of this book provides a list of reliable resources for these tools, including links to reputable online platforms. As you explore these metrics, consider the categories that follow.

Intrapersonal Factors: These measurements emphasize self-awareness, emotional regulation, and motivation in daily life—they show that your capabilities have expanded! For instance, as you reduce implicit association test (IAT) biases (Greenwald et al. 1998), experience shifts in your cultural perspectives brought about through the use of disorienting dilemmas combined with journaling sessions (hello journaling!), and increase your resilience scores (Connor & Davidson, 2003), changes in your measurements will show how your skills are growing over time.

Interpersonal Engagement: Intercultural engagement involves forging relationships across various cultures. Leaders must engage with marginalized communities, speak up against biases with empathy, and coach those in power on the barriers that others face. Remember these milestones to build your confidence!

Group Climate Factors: This is about working toward creating an inclusive team environment. Take the lead as an inclusive role model, facilitate challenging conversations, and ensure that everyone feels psychologically safe to amplify marginalized voices (Wasserman et al., 2008). Anonymous climate surveys can also provide helpful feedback about belonging, trust, and engagement within an organization. Regular pulse checks help keep everyone on the right path and avoid regression.

Organizational Metrics: Organizational metrics measure how effectively CQ is implemented throughout an enterprise. Note any improved innovation rates that result from the implementation of more inclusive decision frameworks; track minority retention and advancement percentages relative to industry norms; and measure the utilization rates of new accommodation policies that show your organization's commitment to equality (Roberson, 2006). Scorecards can help an organization track progress.

As you continue to expand your emotional, cognitive, and behavioral competencies, make sure to set milestone assessments. Take quantitative and qualitative measurements that are relevant, both personally and organizationally (MacNab & Worthley, 2012). If you integrate these measurement systems into the fabric of your organization, CQ will become part of your performance framework. We want meaningful outcomes, not simply going through the motions (Hajro et al., 2017).

Seeking Feedback

Leadership requires understanding that even our best intentions can lead to isolating echo chambers of progress if we fail to seek external input (Hirak et al., 2012). We require feedback to open our eyes to the realities our colleagues face daily and to guide us toward inclusive excellence.

Leaders who embrace vulnerability and encourage input from others build loyalty through transparency (Brown, 2018). We all make mistakes and admitting them helps others see our shared humanity. Building our capacities together is how we progress!

But herein lies the challenge: Without reliable structures for continuous feedback, we risk overlooking our own blind spots, misjudging our community's needs, or missing signals of exclusion that threaten the resilience of our workforce (Wasserman et al., 2008). Therefore, it is vital to create transparent channels of input, such as independent advisory councils, listening circles with minority groups, or equitable participation audits, as such channels allow us to address any shortcomings while maintaining continuity.

Not to be forgotten: We require formalized processes for constructive feedback to demonstrate our willingness to hear truthful arguments, even when they threaten the status quo. Marginalized groups have been silenced for too long—now is the time to end that, and trusted intermediaries can document and help remedy any damage before public confrontation becomes necessary (Kulik, 2014).

Overcoming Blind Spots

Overcoming blind spots is an integral component of successful feedback and inclusion programs. Leaders may fall into certain traps without even realizing it. One common pitfall of assumptions of similarity is projecting our own cultural values onto others instead of seeking their input. To combat this problem, drawing on advisory groups from diverse backgrounds can be helpful (Caprar et al., 2015).

Another danger is our unconscious biases—those unconscious associations that lead to quick judgments of certain groups (Devine et al., 2012). Bias tests can increase our self-awareness so that we can correct these mistakes. As leaders, we must remain mindful of our unintended in-group favoritism (Balliet et al., 2014). Therefore, we must hold regular reviews to ensure equitable access and mobility across the board.

And let's not forget confirmation bias—our tendency to recognize or remember only information that confirms our existing views (Nickerson, 1998). We should actively question our assumptions and seek different viewpoints to address this bias.

By understanding these tendencies, leaders can implement controls such as seeking contrary viewpoints, checking interpretations with minorities, and using metrics to track equitable advancement. This process of uncovering our blind spots continues indefinitely.

Now let's talk about effective feedback channels for making real progress. Communication does not stop at top-down communication; we need input from our frontline teams to assess the effectiveness of our communication, the productivity of our teams, the level of fulfillment that our team members are experiencing, and the support that is being offered to our team members for their career growth (Burke & Dillon, 2016). That is where employee listening circles, inclusion councils, and minority advisory panels come into play—these ongoing forums promote continuous conversation and collaboration while keeping us on our toes and preventing us from becoming too comfortable or complacent!

At every turn, it is imperative that all parties involved in an issue, especially those who have experienced exclusion or bias, share their insights to uncover the kinds of outdated norms, microinequities, and unconscious biases that impede individual advancement (Roberson et al., 2017). By keeping the dialogue alive and fostering an environment in which feedback is valued, we can chip away at blind spots and promote a more inclusive future together. Over time, these practices of openly sharing insights and valuing every voice become deeply embedded in the culture, creating lasting change and a more equitable workplace for all.

Case Study: Transforming Legal Services Through CQ

Kara, a seasoned attorney at Community Legal Advocates, a nonprofit law firm dedicated to serving low-income clients, had built a successful career by leveraging her legal expertise and strong work ethic. However, as the firm expanded and took on more clients from diverse backgrounds, Kara struggled to connect with and effectively serve this new client base.

Kara's traditional approach to client communication, which relied heavily on formal legal terminology and a one-size-fits-all approach, failed to make sense to clients from different cultural backgrounds. Kara's attempts to build rapport often fell flat as she struggled to understand the cultural nuances and unique challenges faced by her diverse clientele.

Moreover, Kara's leadership approach, which focused on hierarchical decision-making and formal business relationships, conflicted with the expectations of many clients and staff members who valued transparent communication and more personalized interactions. Kara struggled to adjust her communication style and business practices to accommodate the diverse cultural norms and preferences of her multinational clientele and multicultural team.

Consequently, Kara observed a widening gap between her management style and the needs of her clients and staff. Client retention rates began to decline, with some clients feeling their unique cultural perspectives were overlooked. Within her team, cross-cultural misunderstandings became more frequent, resulting in decreasing morale and productivity. Kara realized she needed to develop a more culturally intelligent approach to bridge these divides and create a more inclusive and globally minded business environment.

Case Study Questions

1. What aspects of Kara's communication style might contribute to the disconnect with clients from diverse backgrounds?

2. How can Kara adapt her leadership approach to better motivate and engage staff members with different cultural values?

3. How can Kara bridge the cultural gap and foster a more inclusive and understanding environment at Community Legal Advocates?

4. How might Kara leverage CQ to enhance her ability to serve and connect with diverse clients?

5. What role can self-reflection and personal development play in helping Kara improve her CQ and leadership skills?

Case Study Resolution

Recognizing the importance of cultural intelligence in bridging the cultural gap at Community Legal Advocates, Kara took a multifaceted approach to developing this competency and fostering a more inclusive work environment.

First, Kara completed an Intercultural Development Inventory (IDI) assessment (see Appendix), which revealed that she was at an early Minimization stage, focusing too heavily on similarities while overlooking differences. Determined to develop herself further, Kara set a goal of reaching the Acceptance stage within one year.

To achieve this goal, Kara joined a book club that explored systemic inequality, which opened her eyes to the struggles faced by her diverse clientele. She also sought guidance from a mentor, an experienced attorney with a track record of applying cultural knowledge to legal cases. The two met regularly over coffee to discuss culturally appropriate solutions and strategies for connecting with clients from different backgrounds.

Kara also created listening circles where staff from marginalized communities could share their perspectives on firm culture and inclusion. Initially, Kara found these conversations uncomfortable, but by pushing herself outside her comfort zone, she gained invaluable insights that helped her better serve her diverse clientele and create a more inclusive workplace.

To further embed CQ into the culture of Community Legal Advocates, Kara introduced a Cultural Champion program. This initiative recognized employees who demonstrated exceptional skill in fostering cross-cultural understanding and collaboration. These champions served as role models and mentors, helping to create a more inclusive and adaptive work environment.

A year later, Kara retook the IDI assessment, and it revealed significant progress. She had reached the Acceptance stage, demonstrating an ability to recognize and appreciate cultural differences without resorting to stereotyping. Kara continued to strengthen her CQ through ongoing reinforcement programs at Community Legal Advocates.

As a result of these initiatives, Community Legal Advocates saw a significant improvement in client satisfaction, employee engagement, and overall organizational performance. The firm was recognized as a leader in cultural competence within the legal industry, and it attracted a diverse range of clients and top talent.

By prioritizing cultural intelligence and inclusivity, Kara improved her leadership skills and positioned Community Legal Advocates as a beacon of social justice in the legal community. Her journey in developing CQ serves as an inspiring example for other professionals seeking to navigate the challenges and opportunities of an increasingly diverse world.

Advancing Your Leadership Journey

Reflection Questions

1. How can you leverage assessment tools to identify your strengths and areas for cultural intelligence improvement, and what steps can you take to address any gaps?

2. In what ways might your own cultural background and experiences influence your leadership style, and how can you adapt to better serve and connect with people from diverse backgrounds?

3. What role can mentorship, sponsorship, and communities of practice play in your CQ development journey, and how can you seek out these opportunities?

4. How can you create a psychologically safe environment that encourages open dialogue, feedback, and continuous learning about cultural differences within your team or organization?

5. What metrics can you use to track your progress in developing CQ, and how can you ensure that these metrics align with your goals and values as an inclusive leader?

Practical Application Activity

Commit to developing your personal CQ leadership growth plan.

- Create two to three specific development goals that target discernment, empathy, or adaptability gaps through immersive learning encounters.

- Plan to work toward achieving these goals over the upcoming weeks, using timeline milestones along the way.

- Form an accountability partnership to maintain your momentum and discuss the insights gained and lessons learned from your experiences during this journey.

- Reflect on your progress, challenges, and "aha" moments in a journal or through regular check-ins with your accountability partner.

- Review and make any necessary modifications to your next steps based on the progress you have made.

By engaging in this practical application activity and reflecting on your experiences, you'll be well on your way to becoming a more culturally intelligent leader. Let's recap the key takeaways from this chapter.

Key Takeaways

1. Assessment tools, such as the Cultural Intelligence Scale (CQS) and the Intercultural Development Inventory (IDI), can provide valuable insights into your CQ strengths and areas for improvement.

2. Immersive learning experiences, mentorship, and communities of practice are powerful tools for pushing yourself out of your comfort zone and gaining new perspectives on cultural differences.

3. Creating a psychologically safe environment that encourages open dialogue, feedback, and continuous learning is essential for fostering CQ in your team or organization.

4. Tracking your progress using relevant metrics and regularly seeking feedback from diverse constituents can help you stay accountable and ensure that your CQ development aligns with your goals as an inclusive leader.

Chapter 9

The Power of CQ in the Workplace

The world is more connected now than ever, which means there are countless opportunities for collaboration across cultures. This is stimulating and delightful—and it brings challenges. Effective leadership requires us to navigate this complex landscape as our organizations expand beyond geographical and cultural boundaries. That's where CQ—the ability to adapt and thrive in different cultural contexts—comes into play (Earley & Ang, 2003). Think of it as a superpower that equips our teams and organizations to amplify the advantages of diversity.

Culturally intelligent leaders create inclusive environments where employees feel safe, valued, and heard. Their language, their background, where they are from—none of those should diminish their sense of belonging.

Studies have found a positive link between inclusive diversity practices and key performance indicators across organizations. Research by the consulting firm EY shows that, on average, more culturally diverse executive teams have 3% higher profit margins than their peers in the industry (Hunt et al., 2018). Furthermore, Forbes analyses reveal that organizations with the highest rankings in diversity and inclusion enjoy innovation revenues that are 19% higher (Lorenzo et al., 2018). Amazing, right?

Furthermore, McKinsey & Company (2020) discovered that in culturally inclusive companies, engagement levels are 56% higher and workforce retention is 53% greater. It's clear that building a culture of trust and belonging—one that values diverse perspectives and identities—leads to measurable improvements in financial, operational, and human capital outcomes. Conversely, exclusionary or nonadaptive environments seriously undermine effectiveness in these crucial areas.

Our ability to drive innovation depends on our tapping into the full spectrum of the diverse thoughts and experiences of our team members and partners. Remember that generational changes also increase expectations for working environments where everyone's voice matters. Let's dive in and discuss the motivational sources that fuel our engagement on this developmental journey.

Sparking Motivation for the CQ Journey

We've established that CQ is crucial for organizations. Still, to truly create lasting change, we must acknowledge what motivates teams when we are trying to teach them to develop this skill (Earley & Peterson, 2004). Otherwise, we run the risk of failing. Think about it: Giving individuals the power to develop their contextual attunement skills can really excite them! Instead of forcing generic training programs on them, we can offer them customized options tailored to their individual interests and values in such a way as to spark their curiosity, which is vital to the mastery of new abilities and knowledge (Gagné & Deci, 2005). Wise leaders know that forcing rules down from above usually results in either resentment or simply going through the motions; so instead of doing that, let's foster the inner motivation of our teams by encouraging the kind of self-directed development that aligns with their passions and talents. That way, we can help them to unleash their untapped potential and achieve excellence.

Progress is made much faster when we actively pursue activities that align with our growth goals rather than passively consuming information. And here's the key ingredient: We overcome obstacles more effectively when we have internalized our purpose. Connecting our personal development to shared goals and values gives it meaning. Additionally, understanding cultural dexterity in terms of visions of an ethical workplace helps to keep us going strong even when we are outside our comfort zones; tracking progress toward creating inclusive cultures gives our journeys meaning.

When our organization's goals create inequalities or exclusionary practices, morale suffers significantly—so tolerating such practices is an absolute no-no. Instead, we must use CQ to fill any gaps between our purpose and the reality of our workplaces, with leaders like you playing an instrumental role in rectifying those disconnects by continuously aligning the organization's systems with ever-more equitable foundations. Celebrating those small wins reaffirms our progress toward justice, equality, and psychologically safe environments and can boost commitment like nothing else.

Linking CQ and DEI

Inclusive cultures are at the core of everything we've been talking about. But where does cultural dexterity fit into DEI? Great question!

Here's the deal: CQ gives leaders invaluable tools for bridging divides. Culturally adept leaders recognize diversity as a source of innovation rather than something to overcome (Lindsey et al., 2017). Instead of just talking about CQ as something academic or theoretical, they intentionally identify the historical and systemic barriers that have excluded talented individuals because of their race, gender, orientation, or disability status. Then, the leaders take steps to break down those barriers through interventions that aim at equity: This is precisely what CQ stands for.

Psychological safety is the key here. Something magical happens when people feel their uniqueness is valued and their need for belonging is met. Making policies that lack substance is an absolute waste of time. Meaningful participation creates sustainable progress. Equitably redistributing decision-making power is integral to CQ's operating system (Noon, 2018).

However, we cannot stop there. Inclusive organizations are all about empowerment, and leaders who understand that are attuned to the subtleties of inclusion that empower traditionally marginalized groups to participate and make fundamental changes in priorities. Effective communication involves tailoring messages to resonate with people from diverse backgrounds, which requires active listening, empathy, and adaptability. Nurturing allies involves demonstrating humility and finding common ground as we process disagreements amicably, seeking shared goals without dismissing anyone's concerns.

And please don't overlook sensitivity training. It is our tool for developing empathy and emotional intelligence, for helping us recognize how our words or actions might unintentionally diminish or invalidate the experience of oppressed individuals. Celebrating collective successes keeps everyone engaged, motivated, and moving forward together.

Access to resources, development, and advancement opportunities is crucial for unlocking the full potential of all employees. Although recruitment initiatives often focus on diversity, it is equally important to prioritize retention planning and to conduct regular career trajectory audits. By doing so, organizations can ensure that team members from different backgrounds are not marginalized and have equal access to leadership opportunities. By investing in the long-term growth and development of a diverse workforce, companies can foster a culture of belonging, drive innovation, and achieve sustainable success.

Sponsorship programs can be one incredibly effective means of combating the problem that certain groups of employees have not historically been given the chance to advance. These programs pair emerging leaders with executive advocates who provide visibility, networking opportunities, and coaching for career growth. Furthermore, to be truly equitable, growth planning must ensure that minority employees receive meaningful assignments that advance their careers. And finally, we need transparent complaint systems that allow individuals to report microaggressions without fear of retaliation. Regular audits will further ensure fairness across demographic groups.

Efforts to promote CQ and DEI are essential steps toward creating an environment where everyone can contribute meaningfully. So, what is the first step a leader can take?

Listen First

Building strong relationships across differences requires leaders who exhibit patience, compassion, and humility. Taking the time to listen before you react demonstrates a genuine interest in understanding others' lived experiences; otherwise, without the proper context, your well-intended responses may cause unintentional harm (Bruneau & Saxe, 2012). Leaders demonstrate care by creating safe spaces for marginalized voices to express themselves freely, without interruption from leadership figures or other team members (Bruneau & Saxe, 2012), while building the necessary trust to ensure collective healing and progress.

But listening is more than simply remaining quiet and waiting to speak. Someone who is listening actively engages and focuses on the speaker, seeking to understand their experiences without judgment. We call this attitude "cultural humility." It is all about making those vital connections that build trust and foster meaningful relationships. Culturally intelligent leaders notice nuances like tone, body language, and the subtle cues embedded in stories. They practice empathy by placing themselves in others' shoes and then asking open-ended questions instead of making assumptions; these micro-skills help to form the bonds that foster authentic and open sharing of thoughts and experiences.

Identify Needs

The successful management of culturally diverse teams demands an in-depth knowledge of what motivates individuals, regardless of their differences. Various groups often become frustrated because they feel like they are walking on eggshells, not receiving due respect, or both (Jaiswal & Dyaram, 2020; Rosenberg, 2015). Our task as influential leaders should be to tap into the fundamental human needs that lead to these emotional responses—it's like playing detective and uncovering their core motivations! Mastering this skill will enable your team to ease tensions and make significant progress together.

Let's be honest for a second. Underneath our heated policy discussions are universal needs we all share: security, belonging, autonomy, and fulfillment. Isn't it incredible how our experiences shape how we prioritize these elements? As leaders, our job is to foster dialogue in which frustrations can be openly expressed but respect is still always given and maintained. In the workplace, we often encounter "difficult conversations" or "courageous conversations." However, I advocate for a different approach: "change conversations." When guided by the right mindset and tools, change conversations can be powerful catalysts for positive transformation and more benefits than their counterparts. They encourage us to approach discussions with curiosity, compassion, and a genuine willingness to listen and learn, thereby creating a safe space for both parties to express their thoughts, feelings, and concerns openly. By fostering an environment of trust and respect, participants can explore different perspectives, identify common ground, and collaboratively develop solutions that benefit everyone involved. In that way, they strengthen relationships and build a foundation for future collaboration.

Polarization occurs when groups feel threatened, ignored, or disrespected. But if we probe deeper, we will discover the same common human needs underlying all those heated debates (Rosenberg, 2015). Anxiety increases during times of social change because times like these cause power dynamics to shift. By identifying the core unmet needs behind such reactions, using psychological tools like Maslow's 1943 hierarchy of needs, we can more effectively de-escalate situations to discern where the problems lie. Maslow's hierarchy is a motivational theory that suggests that individuals are motivated to fulfill their basic needs before moving on to more advanced needs. The five levels of Maslow's hierarchy, from most basic to most advanced, are physiological needs, safety, love and belonging, esteem, and self-actualization.

It's important to remember that historical challenges and inequalities can sometimes lead to a lack of trust among individuals from different backgrounds. When this happens, some folks may cling to their policies or ideologies even more tightly because they are frustrated about not having their basic needs met. So rather than being open to compromise, they will remain steadfast in their position until their needs are met. That's where leaders come in! These leaders need to understand people's needs and their top priorities. By truly understanding what motivates people, we can navigate the stormy waters ahead and work collectively to make progress.

Reframe Conflict

Leading diverse teams can be challenging, particularly when disagreements arise. But don't panic: Culturally intelligent leaders have quite the toolkit. Have you ever heard of reframing arguments? It's like wearing glasses to see things in a new light. Leaders can turn bitter conflicts into friendly discussions by digging deeper and uncovering the shared cultural experiences that influence our preferences (LeBaron, 2003). Talk about turning enemies into pals! It's all about finding that sweet spot of mutual understanding.

Experienced mediators have some pretty slick techniques up their sleeves for resolving conflicts. One of their key moves is to reframe arguments by finding those shared values and concerns that can bridge even the most significant gaps. And get this—they also consider the cultural influences that shape each side's approach to reaching a resolution. Smart move, right? Not only does this prevent any group from being demonized, but it also upholds the dignity of everyone involved. And you know what? It often leads to finding some common ground between parties that seemed worlds apart.

Culturally intelligent leaders know how to ease tensions by focusing on our universal needs: security, belonging, purpose, and autonomy. And let me tell you, those needs are the secret sauce for finding unity even when it seems impossible. But here's the kicker—even with leaders focused on people's needs, historical inequalities can make things trickier than they would otherwise be, breeding distrust. That's why compassionate leaders look closely at the systems that unknowingly contribute to polarization and compromise human dignity. By understanding these systems and their potentially adverse effects, leaders can bridge differences and transform those false dichotomies into inclusive visions.

Consider a scenario involving a dispute over organizational change. When changes are introduced, tensions can escalate quickly, as individuals concerned about losing their status become defensive when those experiencing inequities call for immediate action. However, by reframing the situation as a collaborative effort toward growth and evolution and an attempt to meet the needs of all parties involved, we can create an environment where both historically privileged and disadvantaged groups feel heard and valued. This approach enables everyone to envision a path forward that honors the dignity of each person and fosters a sense of shared purpose in achieving progress. By shifting our perspective and focusing on mutual understanding and cooperation, we can transform potentially contentious situations into opportunities for growth.

Culturally intelligent leaders know how to defuse conflict like nobody's business. They welcome marginalized perspectives, find common goals and hopes that bring people together, and dig deep to analyze the root causes of conflicts. This approach allows them to ignite innovation, prevent any knee-jerk demonization of one group or another, and treat everyone with dignity and care.

When we base our arguments on misjudgment alone, we're limiting the possibilities. But what if we try to reframe conflicts as misunderstandings? You know, a result of different perspectives? This shift in mindset opens up room for empathy instead of blame. It's all about appreciating the diverse ways we express our shared ethics. And guess what? When we do that, we create this beautiful thing called creative synergy.

Transformative leaders aren't fans of those easy-peasy solutions that pretend to fix complex systemic issues quickly. No, no! They understand that progress comes from embracing diversity with nuance, creating a space where different ideas can come together. This approach fosters an environment conducive to the emergence of wisdom, as multiple perspectives are thoughtfully considered and integrated. By cultivating this inclusive and collaborative atmosphere, transformative leaders lay the foundation for sustainable innovation, ensuring the organization's growth and development are built upon a solid bedrock of diverse insights and experiences.

Call In or Out with Compassion

Culturally intelligent leaders understand that compassionate leadership is crucial when leading diverse teams. Research shows that shaming people makes them defensive rather than inspiring positive change (Sue et al., 2019). The much more effective route is to have respectful conversations in which you seek to understand the source of issues. When responding to sensitive language or behaviors, leaders with CQ recognize the significance of calling in privately and only calling out publicly if needed.

Calling in means showing care and helping others develop. Culturally intelligent leaders understand their team members' different developmental stages and meet them where they are rather than create resentment; they foster transformation by developing relationships and challenging assumptions. Indeed, this is the only sustainable path toward lasting change.

However, when private coaching fails, firmer public boundaries may be necessary. But remember, compassion rather than contempt must be used when calling out individuals or groups. Skilled leaders ensure that their policies prioritize inclusivity and dignity; they rely on community expectations and accountability structures to manage problematic behaviors, while still holding out hope for those willing to learn and grow.

Leaders with CQ recognize that many biases arise from limited knowledge or experiences rather than from malice. While being careful to protect marginalized groups, transformative leaders also create room for growth and learning among those who are causing harm but are willing to change. Sustainable progress relies on calling harmful actions in or out, always with compassion and wisdom, so that accountability and forgiveness can coexist (Sue et al., 2019). What does that mean? Calling *in* involves privately addressing issues with compassion and understanding, while calling *out* involves publicly addressing issues when necessary, but still with compassion and a focus on growth and learning.

Provide Resources to Support Change

Culturally intelligent leaders understand that good intentions alone won't create sustainable change. You need the appropriate resources and interventions (Dobbin & Kalev, 2016). Think about this: Well-meaning efforts falter when they require more resources, such as budgets, staff, and infrastructure. Organizations must go beyond simply recruiting diverse talent; they must also prioritize the equitable retention and advancement of current employees. Leaders who consciously sponsor high-potential professionals from underrepresented backgrounds provide crucial visibility, networking opportunities, and coaching for career growth for those professionals. Additionally, regular inclusion audits can help to sustain accountability by measuring the demographic flows through career milestones within an organization, preventing its leadership from growing complacent.

Transformative leaders don't just sit around daydreaming—they put their words into action. They allocate sufficient funds for diversity initiatives (and even create separate budget lines!), invest in Employee Resource Groups (ERGs), analyze HR data and metrics, and conduct surveys to gauge employee engagement. They even dig into exit interviews to spot cultural gaps in their organizations. This is how you turn priorities into realities!

Structural inclusion requires continuity. One-off initiatives won't cut it. To bring your vision to fruition, you must ensure that resources keep flowing so that cultural consciousness is embedded into every facet of an organization; that is how sustainable transformation occurs.

Leaders with CQ recognize that mere good intentions aren't enough: You must invest strategically to effect lasting cultural shifts. Leaders with CQ understand this reality, so they provide the means for marginalized voices to be heard and confront systemic obstacles head-on with solutions—and yes, this requires an all-out effort from the leaders themselves.

Adaptive Flexibility

If diverse teams are to be led well, we must have leaders who are adept at adapting their support to the various needs of their teams and encouraging excellence from their team members across various cultural styles without expecting everyone to conform to one set of ideals or norms. This kind of leadership means embracing value spectrums ranging from individualistic to collectivistic norms and considering recognition preferences that differ from one person to the next. Some prefer being outspoken and receiving personal recognition, whereas others wish to remain anonymous while contributing to the team's success.

Communication is crucial. Individuals have different communication preferences: Some prefer direct and logical discourse, whereas others use contextual hints and inferences to interpret the overall picture. Remember motivation, too—various things drive people. Some prioritize reaching specific goals, and others see cultivating meaningful relationships as their primary motivator.

Transformational, culturally intelligent leaders recognize that their team members have diverse strengths and preferences. Instead of expecting everyone to conform to a single mold, they craft policies that maximize each person's potential. For instance, when it comes to meetings, finding the right balance between fostering a sense of belonging for all and maintaining team productivity can significantly affect employee morale and performance.

Recognition is also vital. Transformative leaders recognize outstanding performers while celebrating team achievements, acknowledging that some individuals prefer not to be in the spotlight, as noted above. They know how to adapt their recognition strategies to meet their team members' needs and preferences.

Now let's discuss incentives: In all their endeavors, leaders must recognize the importance of balancing the need to complete projects with the need to ensure the continued well-being of their team members. In other words, they must work to sustain project excellence while preventing burnout. When asked "What can leaders do today to potentially save the world?" Jon Clifton, the CEO of Gallup, replied, "Change the way your people are managed" (Gallup, 2023, p. 1). Furthermore, he noted, "Addressing [these] wellbeing concerns and improving engagement should be top priorities among political and business leaders worldwide" (p. 2).

Diversity does not simply refer to cultural differences; it can also be about generational differences. Many Gen Zs and Millennials choose career paths based on their personal values, because they want to make a meaningful contribution and be empowered to effect positive organizational changes (Deloitte, 2023). And beyond that, we also need to take diverse abilities into account. Leadership has to be flexible and adaptive—welcoming and celebrating the diversity of cultural, generational, and ability styles. Leaders should work to engage their teams in ways that meet their employees' differing needs and that foster an atmosphere of trust among employees. This kind of approach is integral for everyone's success; just like when you nurture plants, providing supportive environments will enable growth. Similarly, people thrive when they feel supported and empowered, and resilient organizations thrive when they respect and develop individual capacities.

Addressing Obstacles to Unlock Workplace CQ

Implementing CQ involves candidly assessing and ameliorating the hidden, pervasive barriers that inhibit inclusion. Well-intended leaders often initiate generic diversity programs with the expectation that everyone will buy in, but, unfortunately, we all carry the kind of implicit dominant group norms and unchecked biases that inhibit inclusion. At the same time, organizations continue to unthinkingly use talent tracks and noninclusive communications that exclude some team members from ever being part of the conversation. Now is the time for intentional unlearning: Updated policies and "change conversations" are needed to provide marginalized groups with a safe space where they can bring their whole selves to work (Mor Barak, 2017).

Now let's talk about roadblocks. Have you noticed that newcomers are often expected to fit immediately into the existing culture instead of the organization's accepting them on their terms, with their own authentic expressions of identity? And don't even get me started on how we second-guess someone's competencies simply because their background appears unfamiliar; these unchecked assumptions and unexamined prejudicial assumptions only stunt leadership diversity (Janssens & Zanoni, 2014). We must update our policies and foster compassionate dialogue to create a welcoming work environment.

Power differentials that concentrate authority within majority demographics require immediate rebalancing. We need to increase psychological safety for respectful dissent, and here's the good news: It can be done! With strategic support provided by the communities most affected by inequalities, organizations can create inclusive policies that enrich the entire organization through full-spectrum participation. The barriers that must be overcome take all different shapes and forms. Still, they all stem from the historical experiences and unchecked biases of the dominant group in a given culture or system.

Overcoming Hurdles to Integration

Integrating historically underrepresented groups into talent development may initially seem like an uphill struggle. Still, any obstacles can be surmounted with strategic adjustments to our capability infrastructure and by providing access for all. Studies by Janssens and Zanoni (2014) and by Ardichvili et al. (2014) have proven that although the transitions involved in systematic reforms may cause temporary dips in outputs, their eventual results can pave the way to brighter and more inclusive futures for everyone involved.

Turbulence indicates growth. Pushing boundaries and accepting diversity can build resilience and open new frontiers, as Hewlett et al. (2013) noted. If leaders want to maximize innovation and creativity, we need to be patient during the onboarding process. But when we optimize workflows with the inclusion of diverse perspectives, innovation will surely flourish, and creativity will soar!

Focusing solely on productivity may not effectively capture inclusiveness; to grasp it fully, we need to measure community health, generativity, and ecological sustainability. Leaders who embrace compassion without becoming complacent can lead systems toward equilibrium by giving voice to marginalized groups and providing space for alternative viewpoints, thereby creating environments where all feel welcomed and safe to express themselves openly without fear of their professional advancement sapping their personal identity (Shore et al., 2018).

Diverse perspectives bring abundant energy, creativity, and passion to any workplace environment. Modern mental models acknowledge this fact and use it as leverage for organizational success (Janssens & Zanoni, 2014). It's important that we focus only on productivity metrics, but also think about holistic health and community sustainability when we make our decisions. Culturally intelligent leaders know the value of creating psychologically safe environments where marginalized voices can be heard while unlocking synergies from all those diverse inputs. Remember, this isn't about conformity. We want individuals to contribute authentically without forcing themselves into any mold.

Redirecting the Inevitable Backlash

Workplace changes designed to foster diversity and inclusion can sometimes generate diverse reactions in employees, so as leaders, we must first ensure that we have provided an environment in which everyone feels psychologically safe to express not only their support for the changes but also any skepticism or traditional perspectives (Hewlett et al., 2013). Our ultimate aim should be an open exchange of ideas that challenges the assumptions preventing our organization from reaching its full potential. However, perfection shouldn't be expected; inclusion is an ongoing journey of personal and institutional growth that involves welcoming diversity without restrictions (Shore et al., 2018). One of the ways we can make sure we do that is to prioritize historically marginalized groups in all decision-making processes and to dismantle the barriers that create exclusion (Janssens & Zanoni, 2014).

It's natural to feel anxious when challenging the status quo. But as transformative and culturally intelligent leaders, we must keep an open mind, show empathy, and avoid being judgmental. Moving forward without getting overwhelmed means we must constructively engage with all perspectives. We must educate ourselves, respond to doubts, and consider diverse viewpoints. Inclusivity is about exploring challenges from as many angles as possible and ensuring that marginalized voices are included in our decision-making. In this way, we can discover fresh and innovative solutions that benefit our entire community.

Here's a tip: Embrace discomfort! Yep, you heard me. Embrace discomfort, because that's where growth happens and new possibilities open up. (See the next section for more details on this.) To keep productivity up and improve our bottom lines, we must build accountable structures and form partnerships beyond surface-level interactions (Ardichvili et al., 2014). Leadership is critical, but teamwork, cooperation, and good old courage will help us overcome the fear-based divisions that keep us apart (Hewlett et al., 2013). Oh, and let's remember that celebrating diversity creates a collaboration that benefits each of us (Ferdman, 2017).

There may be temporary instability as we push past previous limits and experience rapid expansion. But that's okay—that's when innovation happens! To ensure that our disruptive ideas lead to meaningful progress, we need to establish clear goals, monitor our efforts closely, adapt our strategies, and create accountability processes based on the insights we gain along the way. Of course, strong leadership sets a direction, but progress requires cooperation and collaboration among different groups within the organization.

Discomfort as a Growth Opportunity

Becoming more adventurous, questioning traditional paradigms, and welcoming diversity are all behaviors that strengthen our capabilities and give us new perspectives. Leaders should avoid attempts at coercion or intimidation and instead empower their staff through inclusion, approaching problems with an open mindset and without presumptions or assumptions. It's about the slow and steady progress achieved through team effort and care. So rather than expecting instant change, let's invest in long-term development and prioritize relationships and people over personal agendas on our journey toward transformation (Hewlett et al., 2013). Let us celebrate how leadership and teams can unite with shared values to pursue justice and reconciliation, giving equal respect to everyone while healing old wounds (Ardichvili et al., 2014).

Growth and personal development depend upon our courage to venture into unfamiliar territories that challenge how we do things. Leaders should aim to infuse enthusiasm into their teams rather than allowing team members to be intimidated—with this approach, we give value to inputs from unexpected sources while challenging preconceptions. When we collaborate as a community, progress happens faster. Together, we can form cultural alliances that withstand setbacks while simultaneously upholding ethical development. By taking steps to uplift marginalized voices and repair historical wounds, we can unleash excellence that was once unthinkable!

We can unlock the untapped potential that unjust systems have long restricted by pushing beyond our current perceptions of inclusion and justice. By acting ethically and with care during this process—something that may initially seem idealistic—we can make the new standards set by reliable accountability systems a reality. Therefore, let's set new benchmarks by elevating those previously excluded from the decision-making tables and establishing new and reliable accountability systems.

Conducting Cultural Audits: Current State vs. Desired State

As organizations strive to harness diversity and inclusion to promote innovation and growth, CQ has become a strategic priority (Hofhuis et al., 2020). Unfortunately, leaders often initiate culture shifts before ensuring they have acquired an accurate sense of their workplace, resulting in disjointed initiatives without buy-in that fail to produce tangible change (Sabharwal, 2014). For this reason, experts stress the value of cultural audits. These evaluations compare the current diversity climate with an ideal vision to provide baseline awareness and a measurement of the constructive progress made over time.

Cultural audits offer a comprehensive approach to gathering data on employee experiences through surveys, interviews, and focus groups. Quantitative participation rates provide insights into engagement levels across various demographic groups, and qualitative feedback offers a more nuanced understanding of an organization's values regarding diversity. This feedback covers many elements, including policies, leadership, advancement opportunities, and interpersonal interactions at both the organizational and the individual levels (Ely & Thomas, 2020). To further refine the analysis, some experts suggest categorizing cultural surveys into organizational, managerial, and interpersonal levels (Sabharwal, 2014). This granular approach allows for a more targeted examination of the factors in the organization that are influencing diversity and inclusion, enabling leaders to identify specific areas for improvement and develop tailored strategies to address any identified gaps or challenges.

Benchmarking your inclusion efforts against your desired objectives allows you to identify the gaps that require extra focus and action (Boekhorst, 2015). Additional initiatives and accountability mechanisms come into play here—they help bridge the space between the current reality and the ideal (Boekhorst, 2015). Generic diversity training strategies often fail to make any fundamental differences, but when your initiatives match the specific challenges in your organization that have been uncovered through cultural audits, magic happens! You'll begin building stronger communities while giving historically marginalized voices greater representation in all decision-making processes.

Here is the key to long-term success: ongoing cultural assessments. That's right: Regular check-ins, conducted perhaps once or twice annually, can track progress on key benchmarks. Conducting assessments allows you to identify emerging needs that may appear over time (Gelfand et al., 2004). When conducting surveys, give equal weight across all hierarchical levels and to all demographic voices. Doing this will enable everyone to participate and elevate marginalized narratives, which will end up supporting the growth of your workers (Hofhuis et al., 2020). With pinpointed data on the barriers that exclude specific subgroups from opportunities, leaders can champion policy reforms that tackle these barriers directly. Cultural audits are your key to moving forward. They allow you to better understand where you stand, identify areas for improvement, and create change that sticks.

Adapting Policies to Promote Workplace CQ

Implementing CQ as a strategic priority involves adapting organizational policies to overcome the obstacles to inclusion that are often overlooked in an organization's standardized paths. Those obstacles to inclusion are what lead to sustained marginalization. Unfortunately, even well-intentioned generic strategies may run into their own problems because of their inclusion of performance benchmarks and talent development criteria that implicitly focus on dominant group norms rather than breaking down stubborn barriers (Shore et al., 2011).

Let's use individual achievements in isolated roles to illustrate this point: When we emphasize personal success in solo roles, we tend to favor majority members who have established networks and cultural capital over those from minority groups, who may, however, possess the kind of excellent interdependence skills that allow them to navigate hostile environments (Janssens & Zanoni, 2014).

Here is something else to remember: Organizations that prioritize diversity without matching that with inclusive practices and decision-making power can risk exploiting their marginalized talent by using the mere presence of diverse team members as evidence of "fairness" without actually valuing their contributions (Mor Barak, 2017).

Let me tell you about an exciting program called Opportunities for New Professionals, implemented by PATH, a nonprofit organization. Organizational leaders aimed to foster CQ among emerging professionals by pairing junior-level staff with senior directors and program officers as mentors who shared similar passions and interests. The program took participants on exciting international trips for cultural exposure and experience, providing an accelerated course in global awareness.

This program had more than just personal development benefits for the participants—it also made a lasting impression and a powerful statement about their organization. Surveys revealed that over 80% of the participants had gained increased cultural perspectives that advanced their priorities and communication approaches with international partners. Focus group discussions highlighted excellent outcomes; participants became more empathetic, patient, and flexible, while learning to accept the uncertainty that occurs globally. They were also able to identify unconscious Western assumptions that had been inhibiting them from creating innovative, inclusive solutions.

The best part? These participants returned with new perspectives and an increased commitment to navigating complexity with humility. They understood and celebrated diversity while working toward a common purpose. By pairing the chance to cultivate individual passions with a program for leadership development, PATH unlocked innovation while strengthening the kinds of inclusive mindsets that foster connections across differences.

Equitable Pathways to Talent Development

Audits have exposed a persistent equity issue, showing how standardized talent tracks can unfairly disadvantage those who don't fit into dominant group norms. Boekhorst (2015) noted that linear timelines for career advancement, idealized work styles, and limited access to sponsorship all negatively affect diverse individuals—but don't worry: I have solutions! We can address these issues by adapting our policies to include equitable criteria, providing tailored coaching sessions, and sponsoring high-performing individuals from minority groups as role models who exemplify success.

Intercultural fluency is also vital to our enterprise. We can achieve it by encouraging cross-departmental rotations, which provide employees with valuable insights that can transfer between business areas. Retention policies also play a crucial role in maintaining our diversity benefits when we structurally incorporate the guidance supplied by marginalized advisors into our decision-making processes. This approach ensures that our diversity benefits continue to be realized, providing continual support for the issues raised by the insights from marginalized communities that mainstream leaders may have missed out on.

And although equitable policies are essential, we must also establish accountability mechanisms to monitor their impact beyond mere intentions. Metrics relating to applications, acceptances, and advances for members of marginalized groups before and after reforms are implemented can help measure the efficacy of the reforms. Simultaneously, conducting pulse surveys—brief, frequent questionnaires designed to quickly gauge employee sentiment and engagement—to gather feedback from subgroups can help identify areas that require further refinement. These short, targeted surveys allow for real-time insights into the experiences of different groups within the organization. This ongoing process, guided by the insights of those we serve, is crucial in reducing barriers to progress and preventing complacency.

Psychological Safety Protocols

Cultural audits have also helped to uncover the risks inherent in the pressures toward conformity that restrict members of marginalized groups from freely sharing their authentic experiences (Gelfand et al., 2004). When those pressures become apparent, swift action must be taken—for example, by creating psychological safety policies with secure reporting procedures that ensure no retaliatory measures. In this way, people can report incidents anonymously without fear of reprisals. We should also provide safe spaces for reporting incidents of minority stress that may otherwise be suppressed because of implicit biases and implicit stereotypes. By doing so, we can collectively address these team members' obstacles through compassionate dialogue and restorative justice. Leadership plays a central role here; Leaders should uphold the unconditional dignity of members of marginalized groups while building the necessary trust to create policies that meet community needs.

Psychological safety is also dependent on regularly engaging mid-level leaders in resolving reported incidents. This tactic helps to model reconciliation practices and strengthen our understanding of each other; rather than simply offering surface-level training without addressing conflicts head-on, we must build the capability to overcome obstacles together.

Last but not least: conflict resolution! Effective conflict resolution strategies are essential for preventing minor issues from snowballing into major problems—let's keep that in mind as we strive to create an improved, inclusive environment. This can involve various approaches, including in-house mediation by trained HR professionals or team leaders, peer mediation programs where colleagues are trained to help resolve conflicts, or bringing in external professional mediators for more complex or sensitive issues. Establishing clear conflict resolution protocols and communication channels is also crucial. By implementing these strategies, organizations can address conflicts early and constructively, fostering a more harmonious and inclusive workplace.

Community Advisory Boards

Vision statements may sound lofty and inclusive, but let's be honest: Organizations often exhibit hidden biases (Buse et al., 2014). To address that situation effectively, grassroots advisory boards provide a voice for those on the front lines facing obstacles to full participation; they help shape policies so everyone has equal chances. But talking isn't enough—we must also act accordingly! That means implementing the expertise of marginalized colleagues and creating an ethical governance system while being responsive to the ever-evolving challenges of equitable access. Auditing, revising, and reassessing our policies becomes an ongoing learning cycle, with those we serve leading us forward.

Here's where things get exciting: This grassroots advisory board model doesn't stay where it started—no, no! Instead, it spreads quickly throughout an organization, cutting across departments, harnessing the power of diversity for inclusion purposes, and embedding that sense of inclusivity throughout the organization's policies and practices. For instance, at a large, prominent investment firm with thousands of financial advisors nationwide, what began as a small diversity task force in HR soon evolved into a network of advisory boards across different divisions. The advisor recruitment team's board identified and addressed biases in their hiring practices, leading to a 30% increase in diverse candidates. Inspired by this success, the client services department formed its own board, which revamped its approach to be more inclusive and culturally sensitive, resulting in improved client satisfaction scores across diverse demographics. Soon, even the executive committee had its own advisory board, ensuring diversity and inclusion were prioritized in high-level strategic decisions. These grassroots advisory boards are game-changers. They bring in fresh perspectives, address biases head-on, and ensure that everyone has an equal voice at the table—not to mention making for great superhero tales!

CQ and Remote Work Trends

As we navigate the digital age, the intersection of CQ with emerging technologies and remote work trends has become increasingly significant. The rise of digital tools has created new avenues for cross-cultural interaction, but also new challenges. Leaders with high CQ are better equipped to leverage these technologies in ways that respect and accommodate cultural differences.

The shift towards remote work has amplified the importance of CQ. Virtual teams often span multiple time zones, cultures, and work styles. Leaders must navigate these differences to foster collaboration and maintain team cohesion.

For example, a culturally intelligent leader might recognize that team members from high-context cultures may struggle with the lack of nonverbal cues in text-based communication and therefore prioritize video calls. They might also be aware that team members from cultures with different attitudes toward hierarchy can have varying comfort levels with speaking up in virtual meetings, so they implement strategies to ensure all voices are heard.

Culturally intelligent leaders understand the need to adapt digital tools to suit different cultural contexts. This might involve considering how various cultures perceive and interact with technology, taking into account factors like trust in digital systems, privacy concerns, and attitudes toward information sharing.

As digital collaboration tools continue to evolve, culturally intelligent leaders must stay attuned to how these technologies influence cross-cultural communication and teamwork. They must be adept at selecting and implementing tools that facilitate inclusive collaboration while considering their team members' diverse needs and preferences. Leaders who can marry technological savvy with CQ will be best positioned to lead diverse, distributed teams and drive innovation in a global context.

Measuring CQ Gains

Expanding CQ is about gauging progress and figuring out what works to unleash employee potential. But launching initiatives blindly? Nope, that's not the way to go. Instead, experts recommend setting up feedback systems with surveys, analytics, and reporting dashboards—those are far more enlightening than just surface-level observations (Guillaume et al., 2017).

By consistently measuring our efforts, we can ensure that all the time, money, and political capital that we invest in inclusion pay off rather than go down the drain. And let me tell you, transformative leaders take this stuff seriously. This is not just some optional principle or a box-ticking exercise; it's a strategic priority. It's all about determining whether marginalized groups feel the fairness and empowerment vibes. That's what we're aiming for!

Organizations should consider implementing a multipronged approach to make the measurement of CQ gains more robust. This could include conducting regular assessments using validated CQ instruments that provide valuable insights into the cognitive, emotional, and physical dimensions of an individual's CQ. These assessments help individuals understand their strengths and areas for improvement in navigating cross-cultural interactions.

In addition to administering individual assessments, organizations should also track diversity and inclusion metrics at the organizational level. This can include monitoring representation, retention, and advancement rates across different demographic groups and measuring employee engagement and satisfaction through surveys and focus groups. By combining individual- and organizational-level data, leaders can gain a comprehensive understanding of their organization's CQ progress and identify areas for improvement.

Surveying Psychological Safety

Several practical tools are available for surveying psychological safety. One such instrument is the pre–post cultural survey, which can give us invaluable insight into how people perceive shifts in belonging, trust, opportunity access, and leadership support after interventions (Boekhorst, 2015). By looking at the results of these surveys, we can see whether our messaging is making a difference for marginalized groups.

Quantitative participation rates give us an idea of how willing people are to provide input. Qualitative narrative shares provide additional depth by helping to capture any nuanced obstacles that the quantitative measures may have overlooked, enabling us to identify details that result in a more comprehensive understanding of the situation.

Assessments must take place at various points throughout the implementation process so that we can properly evaluate our initiatives. Specifically, some of the important moments for identifying trends and maintaining continuity in our data are before launch, six months post-launch, and annually after that.

Let's now discuss what exactly we should be monitoring. We must consider key dimensions such as perceptions of equity in our policies, safe reporting procedures, openness to diverse leadership styles, and value alignment. By disaggregating our data according to demographic attributes, we can illuminate which groups have unique unmet needs.

So let's say, for instance, that our aggregate scores show an improvement in satisfaction among our racial minority staff—that sounds good, right? However, when we break it down further by race and gender, we may discover that, for instance, Black women still report being excluded from informal networking opportunities and lacking senior role models at double the rate of Asian women or Black men. This analysis shows where progress has been made or still needs to be made. Tracking sentiment across various attributes can ensure that our data summaries don't obscure pockets of employees who may still need our support.

Using Analytics to Identify Barriers to Advancement

HR analytics offer valuable insight into the behavior and trends of different groups of employees (Brimhall et al., 2014). Hitting diversity targets is essential when recruiting. However, beyond that point, hidden barriers can prevent career development or progression—and we can identify those barriers by analyzing applicants, new hires, promotions, and attrition rates over multiple years.

Gender diversity is such an intriguing topic. Yes, we can set those hiring targets and pat ourselves on the back, but let's dig deeper, folks. Are women genuinely getting the fair shot they deserve at those higher positions? Are there any sneaky problems, like biased performance assessments or some less-than-stellar managers who are causing burnout and messing with retention? Let's roll up our sleeves and dive into the data. We can find specific patterns and areas in need of improvement by thoroughly exploring and segmenting the data at various levels and in various departments.

Now let's address privacy concerns. Analytics teams realize the significance of safeguarding employee data and anonymizing demographic data from performance records to gain valuable insights without jeopardizing individual privacy. It's all about balancing the discovery of exclusion patterns with maintaining confidentiality.

By examining the career trajectories of different generations and groups, we can identify any disparities in hiring, mobility, and attrition rates attributed to race, gender, or age. With the resulting insight, we can spot and address any impediments to equal access or opportunities. Applying dedicated focus in these areas enables us to make meaningful changes that foster an inclusive workplace.

Integrating Dashboards and Synthesizing Insights

Have you heard about inclusion dashboards? They're powerful tools that combine subjective survey results, objective HR indicators, quotes from staff focus groups, and other inputs into one comprehensive picture of how effective your efforts to build CQ in the workplace are. Understanding which strategies are working and which may require additional consideration can show which ones you need to focus on most intensively.

Dashboards do more than provide reports. They're your reliable companions in identifying patterns as you navigate the vast data landscape (Guillaume et al., 2017). Think of them as GPS for strategy adaptations, with shared accountability, based on real experiences from your colleagues—not simply theoretical ideals. Not only that, it's like having a traffic light system for diversity and inclusion efforts: These dashboards make it easy to quickly assess what's working well (green light!), what may need more focus (yellow light!), and any potential threats (red light!). Dashboards also help executives gain clarity as they respond to feedback, refine the support services they offer, and meet their commitments—they're undoubtedly a transformative feature.

When it comes to fostering a positive work environment, cultural audits, inclusive policies, and multifaceted metrics are vital players. These components form a robust framework for boosting CQ in the workplace. By using the valuable insights these tools provide to assess the current climate, incorporate feedback from marginalized communities, and keep track of progress, leaders can make significant strides in promoting belonging, trust, innovation, and collective achievement. It's like turning diversity from an abstract concept into a collaborative accelerator that unlocks incredible potential. It's all about embracing our shared humanity—quirks and all—to reach new heights, together. Our organizations are like mini versions of the world we aspire to see: a place uplifted by compassion and fueled by equity.

Case Study: Navigating Cultural Expectations and Inclusion at the BioGenesis Institute

Julieta, a talented research associate, had recently joined the BioGenesis Institute, a renowned bioscience research organization. As the newest member of her team, Julieta was eager to contribute her expertise and collaborate with her colleagues. However, she soon faced an unexpected challenge when Cinco de Mayo celebrations were being organized at the institute.

As the holiday approached, Julieta's colleagues enthusiastically planned potlucks and after-work activities to commemorate Cinco de Mayo. They decorated the office with colorful papel picado and stocked the break room with tortilla chips, salsa, and horchata. Everyone seemed excited about the upcoming festivities, but Julieta politely declined to participate whenever she was invited.

Unaware of her reservations, Julieta's teammates began to perceive her as antisocial and uninterested in bonding with the group. They whispered among themselves, speculating over why she consistently turned down their invitations. "I don't understand why she doesn't want to join us," remarked one colleague. "Is she too good for our little fiesta?"

Tensions grew between Julieta and her colleagues, which affected their daily interactions and collaboration on projects. Julieta felt increasingly isolated and misunderstood, while her teammates grew frustrated with what they perceived as her lack of engagement.

Travis, the newly appointed director of Julieta's department, noticed friction within the team. He observed strained conversations and awkward silences whenever Cinco de Mayo plans were discussed. Concerned about the impact on team dynamics and productivity, Travis knew he needed to address the situation before it escalated further.

Case Study Questions

1. What cultural assumptions might contribute to the misunderstanding between Julieta and her colleagues?

2. How can Travis approach the situation in a culturally intelligent manner to foster understanding and inclusion among the team members?

3. What steps can the BioGenesis Institute take to create a more inclusive environment that respects and celebrates the diverse backgrounds of its employees?

4. How might open communication and cultural education help bridge the gap between Julieta and her teammates?

5. How can leadership at the BioGenesis Institute effectively model and encourage the development of cognitive, emotional, and physical CQ among employees to create a more inclusive and adaptable workforce?

Case Study Resolution

Recognizing the need for cultural intelligence and inclusion, Travis scheduled a meeting with Julieta to discuss her experiences and concerns. During their conversation, Julieta explained that while she appreciated her colleagues' intentions, she felt uncomfortable participating in Cinco de Mayo celebrations because the holiday held little cultural significance for her as a Mexican.

Julieta told Travis that Cinco de Mayo is not widely celebrated in Mexico and that Independence Day, which falls on September 16th, is more significant. She expressed uneasiness about the stereotypical decorations and the oversimplification of Mexican culture that often accompany Cinco de Mayo celebrations in the United States.

Travis listened attentively and acknowledged Julieta's perspective, demonstrating emotional CQ. He thanked Julieta for her honesty and openness and recognized the importance of understanding and respecting diverse cultural experiences. Travis assured Julieta that he would address the issue with the team and work toward creating a more inclusive environment.

At the next team meeting, Travis facilitated a discussion about CQ and the significance of understanding and appreciating diverse backgrounds. He shared the insights gained from his conversation with Julieta, explaining the cultural context of Cinco de Mayo and the importance of Mexican Independence Day, which showcased his cognitive CQ.

The team members listened intently, and many expressed surprise at their lack of knowledge about the cultural nuances. They apologized to Julieta for making assumptions and expressed a genuine desire to learn more about her heritage, demonstrating that their emotional CQ was growing.

Travis implemented a series of initiatives to foster a more culturally intelligent workplace. He organized training sessions on cognitive, emotional, and physical CQ for all employees to encourage open dialogue and understanding. The institute also established a cultural intelligence committee, which Julieta and other team members joined, to plan events and activities that celebrated the rich tapestry of cultures represented at BioGenesis—an act that promoted physical CQ.

As a result of these efforts, the team dynamics improved significantly. Julieta felt valued and respected for her cultural identity, and her colleagues gained a deeper appreciation for the importance of CQ. They began approaching their interactions with curiosity, empathy, and adaptability, which led to stronger collaboration and a more harmonious work environment.

The BioGenesis Institute's journey toward CQ was an excellent example of how leadership, open communication, and a willingness to learn can transform an organization. By embracing diversity and fostering understanding through the development of cognitive, emotional, and physical CQ, the institute not only improved employee engagement and satisfaction but also unlocked the full potential of its talented and diverse workforce.

Advancing Your Leadership Journey

Reflection Questions

1. How can you effectively link CQ with your organization's DEI initiatives to create a more comprehensive and transformative approach to fostering an inclusive workplace?

2. How can you leverage your CQ to identify and respond to the unique needs and motivations of your team members—particularly those from underrepresented or marginalized groups?

3. How can you apply the principles of "calling in" and "calling out" with compassion to address sensitive issues related to diversity and inclusion within your team or organization?

4. What steps can you take to ensure that your organization's talent development pathways are equitable and inclusive, providing all employees with equal opportunities for growth and advancement?

5. How can you use community advisory boards and grassroots feedback to continuously refine and improve your organization's CQ and its DEI strategies?

Practical Application Activity

Conduct a cultural audit with your team.

1. Craft a survey assessing staff perceptions of inclusion, belonging, and fairness. Include both quantitative rating scales and qualitative questions that gather open-ended feedback.

2. Analyze your results, segmenting the data by demographic categories to identify any gaps that particular cultural groups may be experiencing.

3. Conduct focus groups so that team members can discuss obstacles and propose ideas.

4. Devise 2–3 policy/program adaptations that will help reduce your identified gaps. Launch one of them as a pilot.

- Include a step where participants create an action plan based on the insights gained from the cultural audit, outlining specific steps to address the identified gaps and foster a more inclusive workplace.

- Encourage participants to share their experiences and lessons learned from the cultural audit with their colleagues, promoting open dialogue and collaboration to create a more culturally intelligent organization.

- Incorporate a follow-up activity where participants reflect on their progress and challenges in implementing their action plans to allow for continuous learning and improvement.

- Conduct another survey within six months to assess whether perceptions and participation rates have improved; then, identify areas for refinement and improvement.

By following this comprehensive cultural audit process, you and your team will gain valuable insights into the current state of inclusion and belonging in your organization. The action planning, sharing of experiences, and follow-up activities will ensure that you identify areas for improvement and take concrete steps to address them. This ongoing assessment, action, and reflection process will help you build a more culturally intelligent and inclusive workplace where all team members can thrive.

Let's take a moment to reflect on the key takeaways from this chapter and how they can guide you in your journey toward becoming a more culturally intelligent leader.

Key Takeaways

1. By linking CQ with DEI initiatives, leaders can create a robust framework for eliminating systemic barriers, promoting psychological safety, and harnessing the untapped potential of their employees' diverse talent.

2. Developing CQ requires a multifaceted approach that includes self-reflection, active listening, identification of underlying needs, reframing of conflicts, and provision of resources to support change.

3. Conducting cultural audits and adapting organizational policies to reduce inclusion gaps are essential actions for fostering workplace CQ and overcoming obstacles to diversity and inclusion.

4. Measuring CQ gains through surveys, analytics, and inclusion dashboards is crucial for ensuring the effectiveness of diversity and inclusion initiatives and driving continuous improvement.

Chapter 10

Sustaining Organizational Commitment to CQ

One significant change we are witnessing as globalization evolves is increased ethnic diversity within countries because of factors like immigration and refugee resettlement. Did you know that by 2045, the U.S. is expected to become a majority-minority nation, with over half its population composed of Hispanic, Black, Asian, and multiracial individuals (Frey, 2018)?

Diversity brings many rich benefits, but it also presents unique challenges. As leaders, we need to hone our intercultural communication skills. Why? Well, because this helps us connect with different cultures, communities, and, of course, our amazing employees, clients, and customers. Livermore (2015) noted that organizations lacking CQ often struggle to recruit top talent; additionally, they miss opportunities to foster innovation within their diverse teams, fail to meet culturally specific product demands on time, and risk declining performance if cross-cultural sensitivity training does not become a part of their daily operations.

Diversity doesn't stop at domestic boundaries. Virtually every country in the world is connected through media outlets, social networks, multinational corporations, and, of course, travel. Friedman (2007) described this phenomenon as the "flat world," where technology facilitates cross-cultural interactions and negotiations across borders and global teams, all of which require cross-cultural competencies.

Culture itself is evolving quickly, particularly among the younger generations. More people than ever identify with multiple nationalities and ethnicities. Vertovec (2007) referred to this trend as "super-diversity," in which complex cultural formations arise within societies; other researchers study individuals who fuse two national identities at once or who embrace multiple worldviews and traditions (Ray & Anderson, 2001). With all this cultural diversity in countries and individuals, we must embrace the multiplicity and adapt accordingly.

As we've noted, once people start building up their CQ, amazing things happen that benefit organizations as much as individuals. Companies prioritizing CQ as a core competence experience remarkable success: Top talent is attracted, teams are coordinated seamlessly across global borders, those teams work cohesively, and local markets are penetrated without much effort. That is the power of CQ at work!

CQ goes beyond just cultural sensitivity and cultural awareness for its own sake; it helps you adapt and thrive amid complexity and diversity, to remain connected in today's globalized landscape. Let's discuss some incredible strategies for making sustainable commitments to CQ for ourselves and our organizations.

The Long Game: Key Factors for Sustaining Organizational Change

Implementing transformation initiatives is a daunting challenge for institutions and leaders, requiring ample resources and unwavering commitment. Success doesn't happen overnight. Beer and Nohria (2000) reported that up to 70% of efforts at changing institutional culture fail over time despite initial achievements.

So how can leaders succeed at the long game? The answer lies in firmly embedding new initiatives in an institution's strategy, measurement systems, capabilities, and norms. Doing this creates a firm foundation that stands the test of time. Huber et al. (1993) noted that significant change initiatives typically take five to seven years before coming to fruition. That's a long journey, my friend!

Structural shifts can happen pretty quickly—within two years. However, cultural evolution takes much longer. Over time, though, organizations can gradually adopt new mindsets and behaviors until they become embedded norms. It's a slow and steady process, one that requires consistency. Leaders must be patient, engage partners, and cultivate a learning culture to ensure that change is sustainable. Think of it as a wise gardener tending plants to ensure they flourish.

Now let's consider an overall framework that can assist in creating lasting change. Buchanan et al. (2005) proposed six factors to ensure sustainable organizational transformation:

1. **Securing support from senior management:** Change initiatives are likely to fizzle out without buy-in from the top. Senior leaders must champion the cause, provide resources, and lead by example to demonstrate their commitment to the transformation.

2. **Developing leadership competencies and talent:** It is crucial to equip leaders at all levels with the skills and knowledge needed to drive change. This includes training in change management, communication, and CQ.

3. **Creating ongoing learning environments:** A continuous learning and improvement culture helps organizations adapt to changing circumstances and maintain the momentum of change initiatives. Encourage experimentation, reflection, and knowledge sharing among employees.

4. **Aligning systems and structures:** Ensure that organizational systems, processes, and structures support the desired change. This may involve revising performance management systems, reward structures, and decision-making processes to reinforce new behaviors and values.

5. **Fostering widespread involvement:** Engage employees at all levels in the change process to promote ownership and commitment. Encourage participation through workshops, focus groups, and cross-functional teams to gather diverse perspectives and ideas.

6. **Communicating stories of success:** To maintain motivation and enthusiasm among employees, share positive examples and outcomes of the change initiative. Celebrate milestones, and recognize individuals and teams that exemplify the desired behaviors and values.

These factors help maintain new organizational capabilities even as specific teams or departments change over time.

Studies by Tett (2005) and Fox (2020) reveal an interesting fact: Change initiatives often fail when marginalized voices are excluded. Inclusion and co-creation are the keys to creating lasting change initiatives. If you want your efforts to have enduring effects, make sure everyone participates!

Sustainable change demands dedication, perseverance, and a well-defined strategy. As noted in the preface, transforming an institution is a gradual process rather than an instantaneous process. Those spearheading the change must maintain unwavering commitment throughout the lengthy journey, navigating the complex landscape with a clear vision and steadfast determination.

Enshrining CQ Through Organizational Charters

Establishing a culturally intelligent workforce presents many obstacles. People may unknowingly bring their cultural assumptions into the mix, further complicating matters. But don't despair! Leaders dedicated to developing organizational CQ can make significant progress by formalizing their commitment with signed charters.

What exactly are Cultural Intelligence Commitment Charters? Simply put, they're formal written agreements signed by organizational leaders—a pledge to increase understanding and effectiveness across cross-cultural environments. Instead of merely listing values or discussing CQ in general terms, these charters serve as road maps that foster cultural intelligence over time (Herrera & De Las Heras-Rosas, 2021).

Charters send a powerful signal of commitment to the organization and its various interested parties while providing direction for a change agenda. They identify weaknesses, future improvement goals, and challenges that must be faced head-on. Frequent customer complaints or expatriate employee turnover could indicate gaps in cultural skills in the organization's leadership and teams that require immediate attention. Charters detail the activities necessary to eliminate cultural gaps, such as adding culture-focused modules to onboarding and training programs, creating cross-cultural mentoring systems, and hiring consultants with relevant expertise. Regular assessments through surveys or focus groups make it possible to monitor the progress made against the objectives set.

These charters demonstrate an organization's leaders' commitment to creating a culturally intelligent workforce. By signing the formal contracts, the leaders confirm that they are mean business and will persevere despite any difficulties that may arise during culture shifts. Furthermore, these charters promote accountability, showing a meaningful commitment from the leaders and offering guidance and assistance to the organization when transformation becomes challenging.

CQ charters can also be powerful tools for long-term cultural education. Their formality and specificity make them practical yet effective tools that catalyze progress while acting as guides, leading everyone through the complexities involved in building culturally intelligent workforces.

Integrating CQ Into Leadership Competency Models

As organizations continue expanding internationally, with diverse workforces, markets, and supply chains, the importance of having culturally intelligent leaders cannot be overemphasized. By including CQ criteria in our core leadership competency models, we're setting the stage for developing successful global leaders and encouraging truly cross-cultural teamwork and initiatives. We should carefully examine our existing models to see how well they incorporate CQ elements, identify gaps, and then reduce those gaps by adding relevant CQ standards and behavioral indicators to the established leadership and behavioral indicators.

Consider, for example, the competency "communicates effectively." To incorporate cultural intelligence, we can expand this competency to include the following behaviors:

- Adapts communication style and messaging to suit different cultural contexts
- Demonstrates understanding of and respect for diverse communication styles and preferences
- Actively seeks and values multicultural perspectives in discussions and decision-making

Similarly, the competency "develops talent" can be enhanced to reflect CQ by adding the following behaviors:

- Serves as a cultural mentor, educating team members about relevant cultural norms, values, and behaviors
- Creates opportunities for team members to develop their CQ through training, exposure, and experience
- Fosters an inclusive environment that values and leverages the di-

verse talents and perspectives of all team members

By explicitly reframing these competencies to include CQ indicators, we emphasize the importance of CQ in leadership and provide clear guidelines for demonstrating these skills in practice.

But we shouldn't stop there: CQ should also be integrated into assessments of leadership potential and development planning processes. Rising leaders who wish to assume global or multicultural roles should receive immersive experiential learning opportunities in specific cultures. Coaching on cognitive CQ and perspective-taking techniques, as well as training in working effectively across cultures, should also be provided.

Formal CQ education should also be integrated into early leadership development pipelines, emerging leader programs, and new leader assimilation processes. Training modules may combine insight into the organization's cultural norms and expected behaviors with research-based best practices for cultivating culturally intelligent approaches to core leadership tasks such as building trust, communicating effectively, and developing strategic perspective coaching for success-inspiring change. Infusing any leadership development curriculum with CQ increases its systemic significance early on.

Developing Cultural Fluency: A Curriculum for CQ Development

CQ development is essential to leaders and employees, both individually and organizationally. CQ is not simply about individual competencies but also about developing effective organizational strategies. By investing in CQ through dedicated curricula, we can equip ourselves and our teams to communicate, lead, and collaborate effectively across diverse viewpoints and experiences, in that way protecting ourselves from major missteps as we prepare for an ever-evolving global workplace.

I suggest creating and implementing a comprehensive 12-month development curriculum with activities to develop CQ in your organization. A detailed description of such a curriculum can be found in the Appendix. The journey begins with understanding one's own and others' worldviews, followed by personal coaching and virtual cultural exchanges in months 2–4. In month 5, the focus is on global literacy training and inclusive leadership, and month 6 introduces a cross-cultural mentorship program and puts CQ into action. In month 7, participants engage in an intercultural communication workshop and begin developing group projects. Months 8–9 involve observation, journaling, planning for adaptations, and launching group projects. Month 10 features a Global Leadership Summit with working sessions and project presentations. The curriculum concludes with interim milestone reviews and impact measurements in month 11, and "paying it forward" along with organizational extensions in the final month. The aim is to provide an integrated curriculum that allows for the necessary self-reflection, teachings from experts, peer exchanges, real-world applications, and milestone accountability over the intensive yearlong journey.

As part of crafting this curriculum, it's crucial to balance self-directed reflection and skill-building workshops while remaining mindful of the benefits of instructor-led coaching. This holistic approach emphasizes imparting knowledge, prompts introspection, and enables learners to hone new cultural skills. Over the 12 months, learners can consolidate their learning through self-discovery, skill practice, workplace application, and consolidation—all of which lead to significant increases in cross-cultural partnership, communication, and leadership capacity on both the individual and the institutional levels.

CQ Assessments: Bringing Marginalized Voices to the Forefront

Organizations increasingly realize the significance of hiring employees who can navigate different cultures with agility and respect. Therefore, to gauge the capacity of employees to effectively navigate cross-cultural complexity and challenges, it is crucial to evaluate their CQ in the workplace. While doing so, it's essential that we prioritize participation from historically underrepresented communities. These inclusive assessments will help us prevent blind spots arising from limited perspectives at the top.

Lee and colleagues (2013) found that leaders who have become fully immersed in an organization's culture may overlook subtle exclusionary practices or communication gaps across cultural lines. Unfortunately, this is true! That is why it is vital to create safe spaces for marginalized staff to provide anonymous feedback through one-on-one interviews, focus groups, or surveys—so that they can provide the kind of candid insights into cross-cultural disconnects or microaggressions that generic company surveys may miss.

Leaders who possess an in-depth knowledge of the existing cultural barriers in their organization are better equipped to tailor training, mentoring initiatives, and codes of conduct to ameliorate the specific concerns raised by underrepresented groups. Lee et al. (2013) found that management teams that prioritize diversity by including cultural competence assessments from day one generates an average 19% increase in revenues over four years. That is quite impressive!

As part of a company's cultural intelligence assessment, diverse insights are paramount. Here are some best practices to implement if you want to uncover these insights.

- Leaders must communicate the value of different vantage points so that underrepresented groups feel safe participating (Mor Barak, 2017).
- Making input options anonymous results in more candid feedback.
- Taking action on the recommendations that have been given—whether that action involves new cultural training programs,

policy amendments, accountability measures, or transparent action plans—shows your commitment to progress.

All of these actions can catalyze real change. Also, we must recognize the significance of open dialogue and various contributions; these tools allow organizations to fully leverage diversity without viewing differences as liabilities. However, if authentic conversations about cross-cultural intersections are to occur, those with nondominant perspectives need to be granted a voice. Assessments of workplace CQ help us better understand how we can support and recognize all talent, regardless of background. When more people get involved and support this cause, we all win—both culture and profits are elevated!

Promoting CQ Through Incentives and Performance Management

As globalization increases, organizations are also increasingly realizing the necessity of cultivating employee CQ. But how can companies do this effectively? I'll tell you: Companies must reinforce CQ as a core element throughout their talent management systems and structures. One area that has an incredible impact is incentives and performance evaluations.

You can start by offering incentives to motivate employees to develop their cross-cultural competencies (Lee et al., 2013). Offering annual bonus percentages tied to 360-degree feedback (a process in which employees receive anonymous feedback from their peers, subordinates, and supervisors) on team cooperation across diversity is one way of incentivizing culturally inclusive collaboration. And remember, organizing public recognition programs in which you go beyond the employees' normal expectations of inclusion—that's proper positive reinforcement!

We also do well to celebrate cultural milestones alongside business successes. It is paramount to demonstrate that cultural diversity and success are top priorities at the company. Demonstrating a commitment to developing critical CQ competencies, for example by covering employee participation costs for international leadership workshops or language classes, is another good way to show this dedication.

But hear this: It isn't all about incentives! To truly prioritize cultural agility (Konanahalli et al., 2014), leaders should work closely with their staff in setting specific, measurable goals tailored to global or multicultural responsibilities—for instance, an international marketing specialist might focus on increasing cultural self-awareness while adapting branding strategies so that those strategies resonate locally, or on building relationships with key international partners. Furthermore, directly tying career advancement and rewards to progress made toward CQ development ensures that everyone stays focused on how important that development is.

Here's the thing: When incentives and evaluation structures emphasize intercultural effectiveness, you will start to see your organization's cultural DNA seep into every corner—be it policies, processes, projects, products, or people. Leaders cannot simply speak about cultural diversity; they need to demonstrate it by showing curiosity, empathy, adaptability, and respect in dealing with different peoples across differences themselves. To truly make their efforts effective, they need to ensure that their own and the organization's training, messaging, and operations consistently uphold the company values of inclusion and global cooperation.

Establish an environment that sends clear signals about the importance of CQ and provides employees at all levels with support, and you're setting yourself up for success. When individuals develop skills, gain confidence, and become more willing to navigate complex cultural situations, they can help their organizations unlock access to diverse talent pools, innovative ideas, and market opportunities, giving organizations that fully embrace cultural agility an edge over competitors.

Measuring the ROI of CQ Initiatives

Although the qualitative benefits of cultural intelligence are clear, leaders often need to justify investments in CQ development with quantitative metrics. Measuring the return on investment (ROI) of CQ initiatives can be challenging, but it's crucial for gaining organizational buy-in and sustaining long-term commitment to CQ development.

One approach is to track key performance indicators (KPIs) before and after CQ training initiatives. These might include:

1. **Financial metrics:** revenue growth in diverse markets, cost savings from reduced turnover, increased profitability of multicultural teams, and improved success rates of international mergers and acquisitions.

2. **Operational metrics:** improved productivity of diverse teams, faster time-to-market for products in new cultural contexts, reduced time to resolve cross-cultural conflicts, and increased efficiency in global supply chain management.

3. **Human capital metrics:** increased retention rates of diverse talent, improved employee engagement scores, faster integration times for international assignees, and higher success rates for expatriate assignments.

4. **Customer-related metrics:** higher customer satisfaction scores in diverse markets, increased market share in new cultural contexts, improved ratings on cultural sensitivity from clients, and increased success in forming and maintaining international partnerships.

5. Innovation metrics: increased number of patents filed by diverse teams, higher ratings for product relevance in diverse markets, and improved ability to adapt products and services for different cultural contexts.

A comprehensive study by Herring (2009) provided robust evidence of the significant financial benefits of diversity in the workplace. Analyzing data from over 500 U.S. businesses, Herring identified a clear relationship between diversity and business performance. Companies with the highest levels of racial or gender diversity reported, on average, nearly 15 times more sales revenue than those with the least diversity. Importantly, this analysis controlled for organizational size and other relevant factors, offering a solid case for a causal relationship between diversity and improved financial outcomes.

A decade later, Gartner, a leading research and advisory firm, supported these findings. Its 2019 study strongly correlated diverse and inclusive decision-making teams and enhanced financial performance. The research suggests that organizations that prioritize diversity and inclusion at the decision-making level are more likely to exceed their financial targets in subsequent years (Gartner, 2019). Together, these studies provide compelling evidence that diversity is not just a matter of social responsibility but a strategic business advantage.

Leaders can also consider conducting CQ audits, using tools like the Cultural Intelligence Scale (CQS) to measure improvements in CQ scores over time. By correlating these scores with business outcomes, organizations can demonstrate the tangible impact of their CQ initiatives.

It is important to note that some CQ benefits, such as enhanced reputation and improved stakeholder relationships, may be harder to quantify, but they are no less valuable. A balanced scorecard approach that incorporates both quantitative and qualitative measures can provide a comprehensive view of the ROI on CQ initiatives.

Qualitative measures might include:

- Case studies of successful cross-cultural negotiations or conflict resolutions
- Feedback from diverse employees on feelings of inclusion and belonging
- Testimonials from international clients or partners on the organization's CQ
- Recognition or awards for diversity and inclusion efforts

To implement ROI measurement for CQ initiatives, organizations can follow these steps:

1. Establish a baseline: Measure relevant KPIs before implementing CQ initiatives.

2. Set clear objectives: Define what success looks like for your CQ program.

3. Implement CQ initiatives: This could include training programs, policy changes, or structural adjustments.

4. Monitor and measure: Regularly track KPIs and gather qualitative data.

5. Analyze and report: Compare post-initiative data with the baseline, calculating ROI where possible.

6. Iterate and improve: Use insights gained to refine and enhance CQ initiatives.

By demonstrating a clear ROI, leaders can make a compelling case for continued investment in CQ development. This not only justifies the financial outlay but also reinforces the strategic importance of CQ in achieving organizational goals.

Case Study: Embracing CQ at Harmony Medical Center

Harmony Medical Center, a leading healthcare institution, recognized the importance of CQ as its patient population grew increasingly diverse and its workforce became more multigenerational and internationally experienced. The hospital's senior leadership team, consisting of physicians, nurses, and administrators, embarked on a mission to integrate CQ into their competency models and leadership development programs.

Dr. Patel, a respected cardiologist and a senior leadership team member, noticed that cultural aspects were only partially represented in the hospital's competency models and job profiles. General statements such as "recognizing diversity" and "communicating empathetically" were present, but specific indicators and actionable guidelines were lacking.

During a team meeting, Dr. Patel shared her concerns. "I believe we need to go beyond these broad statements and provide tangible examples of how our leaders can demonstrate cultural intelligence in their daily work," she said. "It's not enough to simply acknowledge diversity; we must actively cultivate an inclusive environment."

The team members agreed with Dr. Patel's assessment and began working on revising their competency models and job profiles. They added specific CQ indicators that aligned with Harmony Medical Center's values of inclusion. Under "communicates effectively," they emphasized the importance of adapting messaging across cultures and styles and summarizing key takeaways to ensure understanding. Under "decision-making," they included categories such as cultural context and impacts.

Additionally, the team stressed that leaders must serve as cultural mentors by educating team members about relevant norms and values. They recognized that this role was crucial in fostering an inclusive work environment where all employees felt valued and understood.

As the hospital began implementing these changes, several challenges emerged. Some long-time leaders resisted the new expectations, arguing they had succeeded without focusing on CQ. A senior surgeon, Dr. Weiner, expressed his doubts during a leadership meeting. "I don't see why we need to change our approach," he said. "We've always treated all patients and staff the same, regardless of their background."

Others struggled to adapt their communication styles and decision-making processes to account for cultural differences. A nurse manager found himself in a difficult situation when a patient's family insisted on using traditional herbal remedies alongside prescribed medications. "I want to respect their cultural beliefs," he confided to a colleague, "but I'm worried about potential interactions with the treatment plan."

Resistance to change and lack of understanding about the importance of CQ created tension among the staff. Some employees felt the new initiatives were unnecessary and time-consuming, and others were unsure about how to apply CQ principles in their daily work.

Despite these challenges, Dr. Patel and the senior leadership team remained committed to their vision. They knew embracing CQ would be challenging, but they believed in the long-term benefits for patients and staff.

Case Study Questions

1. What arguments might Dr. Weiner and other resistant leaders present against implementing CQ initiatives at Harmony Medical Center?

2. How could the nurse manager's dilemma regarding the patient's family's desire to use traditional herbal remedies alongside prescribed medications be resolved using CQ principles?

3. What strategies could the senior leadership team employ to address the tension and resistance among staff members who view the CQ initiatives as unnecessary or overly time-consuming?

4. How might Dr. Patel and the senior leadership team effectively communicate the long-term benefits of embracing CQ to skeptical staff members?

5. In what ways could resistance to change and lack of understanding about the importance of CQ create tension among the staff at Harmony Medical Center, and how might that tension be alleviated?

Case Study Resolution

Recognizing the challenges faced while implementing their CQ initiatives, Harmony Medical Center's senior leadership team took several steps to alleviate staff resistance and lack of understanding.

First, they organized workshops and training sessions to educate employees about the importance of CQ in healthcare. These sessions focused on real-life scenarios and provided practical tools for applying CQ principles to daily work. The senior leadership team participated in these workshops, demonstrating their commitment to the initiative and leading by example.

To address specific concerns and challenges, the senior leadership team established a Cultural Intelligence Task Force comprising representatives from various departments and levels of seniority. The task force served as a forum for employees to share their experiences, ask questions, and provide feedback on the CQ initiatives. This open dialogue helped to foster a sense of ownership and engagement among staff.

The senior leadership team also recognized the need to celebrate successes and share best practices. They implemented a rewards and recognition program that highlighted employees who demonstrated exceptional CQ in their work. These success stories were shared through internal communication channels, showcasing the positive influence of CQ on patient care and staff satisfaction.

Over time, Harmony Medical Center's culture began to shift. Leaders and employees alike became more attuned to the needs of their diverse patients and colleagues. The hospital's reputation for inclusivity and cultural competence grew, and the facility attracted top talent and earned recognition from industry peers.

The journey to embracing CQ at Harmony Medical Center was challenging. However, the senior leadership team's commitment to the initiative and willingness to face obstacles head-on ultimately led to success. Harmony Medical Center demonstrated the power of CQ for transforming healthcare organizations by embedding CQ in their competency models, providing ongoing training and support, and fostering a culture of continuous learning.

Advancing Your Leadership Journey

Reflection Questions

1. What steps can you take to ensure that CQ initiatives are firmly embedded in your organization's strategy, measurement systems, capabilities, and norms?

2. How can you leverage Cultural Intelligence Commitment Charters to formalize your organization's commitment to developing a culturally intelligent workforce?

3. How can you integrate CQ criteria into your organization's leadership competency models to develop culturally intelligent leaders?

4. How will you design and implement a comprehensive CQ development curriculum that balances self-directed reflection, skill-building workshops, and instructor-led coaching?

5. How can you prioritize participation from historically underrepresented communities in your organization's CQ assessments and ensure their insights are acted upon?

Practical Application Activity

Commit to improving the CQ awareness and skills in your organization through sustained development, evaluation, and reinforcement over time.

- Create a Vision Statement articulating your organization's commitment to cultural intelligence and its value to your workforce, customers, and all involved parties. This statement should be aspirational, inspiring, and aligned with your organization's mission and values.

- Develop a Cultural Intelligence Training Policy that outlines the expectations and requirements for CQ training and development across all levels of your organization. This policy should include guidelines for mandatory and optional training programs, resources, and support available to employees.

- Establish a Global Inclusion Policy regarding your organization's commitment to fostering an inclusive and equitable workplace. This policy should speak to nondiscrimination, equal opportunity, and respect for diversity, and it should provide guidance on creating an inclusive environment.

- Draft a CQ Leadership Commitment Charter outlining the specific actions and behaviors expected of leaders to promote and model cultural intelligence. This charter should include commitments to ongoing CQ development, inclusive leadership practices, and accountability for creating a culturally intelligent organization.

- Implement a comprehensive 12-month CQ development curriculum for your organization that includes self-reflection, skill-building workshops, and instructor-led coaching.

- Conduct regular assessments of your organization's CQ, prioritizing participation from historically underrepresented communities. Use the insights gained from these assessments to inform future CQ initiatives and alleviate any identified gaps or challenges.

- Incorporate CQ objectives into performance evaluations and tie them to career advancement opportunities. Doing this will reinforce the importance of cultural intelligence and encourage employees to prioritize their CQ development.

- Partner with external experts, such as cultural intelligence consultants or diversity and inclusion specialists, to provide ongoing guidance and support for your organization's CQ journey.

The Appendix includes samples of a Vision Statement, Global Inclusion Policy, CQ Leadership Commitment Charter, CQ training policy, and 12-month CQ development curriculum for reference and inspiration. These samples can be adapted to suit your organization's specific needs and challenges.

By implementing these practical application activities, you can demonstrate your organization's commitment to cultural intelligence and create a sustainable framework for ongoing CQ development and growth.

Now that you have completed the practical application activity and have a clear understanding of how to sustain organizational commitment to CQ, let's review the key takeaways from this chapter.

Key Takeaways

1. Sustaining organizational change requires firmly embedding new initiatives in an institution's existing strategy, measurement systems, capabilities, and norms. Leaders must engage partners, cultivate a learning culture, and maintain unwavering commitment throughout the lengthy cultural transformation journey.

2. Cultural Intelligence Commitment Charters are potent tools for formalizing an organization's commitment to developing a culturally intelligent workforce. These charters serve as road maps, detailing current weaknesses, future improvement goals, and activities necessary to reduce cultural gaps.

3. Integrating CQ criteria into leadership competency models is essential for developing culturally intelligent leaders. This involves examining existing models, identifying gaps, and adding relevant CQ standards and behavioral indicators. CQ education should also be integrated into leadership development programs at all levels.

4. Promoting CQ through incentives and performance management is crucial for reinforcing cultural intelligence as a core element throughout an organization's talent management systems and structures. This can involve tying bonuses and career advancement to progress made toward CQ development and celebrating cultural milestones alongside business successes.

Conclusion: Heed the Call

Throughout this book, we have explored the transformative potential of CQ in today's interconnected world. As our journey comes to an end, it is important to reflect on the key lessons we have learned and how we can apply them in our personal and professional lives.

We have discovered that CQ is not just a buzzword, but a critical skill set that enables us to navigate the complexities of diverse cultural environments. Developing cognitive, emotional, and physical CQ skills can enhance cultural awareness and competence, leading to more effective communication, collaboration, and decision-making. Improving our CQ has vast benefits, from boosting innovation and financial performance to retaining talent and building resilient partnerships. By integrating CQ into our processes and policies, we can create culturally agile organizations that thrive in the face of change and uncertainty.

Although the journey toward cultural intelligence may initially seem daunting, it is an exciting opportunity for personal and professional growth. With the right mindset and tools, anyone can develop their CQ skills and become a more effective leader in today's diverse world. The key is to approach the journey with curiosity, openness, and a willingness to learn from others.

We have provided a range of resources in the Appendix to support you on your CQ journey. You will find links to assessments, the Culturally Intelligent Leadership Continuum, the Culturally Intelligent Leader's Mindset, the Culturally Intelligent Strategic Decision Blueprint, a Blind Spot Detector, an

Accountability Tracker, and sample organizational documents that can be adapted to fit your organization.

As you embark on this journey, remember that developing CQ is not a one-time event, but an ongoing process of learning and growth. It requires a commitment to challenging assumptions, seeking diverse perspectives, and making equitable policy changes. We can create lasting change and unlock our collective potential by measuring progress responsibly and managing any resulting backlash with care.

As leaders, we have a unique opportunity and responsibility to champion CQ and ensure that our organizations prioritize it at every level. By implementing strategies such as enshrining CQ through organizational charters and promoting it through incentives and performance management, we can build a culturally intelligent workforce that is equipped to thrive in diverse and ever-evolving environments.

Let this book serve as a call to action, inspiring you to pursue bold efforts toward positive change. Our shared humanity awaits discovery, and we must build bridges of compassion. With open minds and hearts, let us go forward together, embracing the power of cultural intelligence to create a more inclusive, equitable, and prosperous world for all.

Acknowledgments

I will forever be thankful to both of my wonderful parents for providing love, support, motivation, and laughter throughout my life. Even though you are no longer with me physically, you remain dear in my memory and heart.

Brian Hilliard deserves my gratitude and acknowledgment for inspiring and believing in my message throughout the writing of this book. Brian, your encouragement was essential in keeping me motivated.

To my mentor and role model, Barbara Crook, thank you for your sage advice and steadfast support and for empowering me to use my voice over the years. You taught me so much about transformational leadership.

Bishop P. Huitt, I immensely appreciate your humor, prayers, and spontaneous singing, which upheld my spirit when challenges arose, and your reminder that work that serves a greater purpose brings happiness.

Coach Buffy, I appreciate how you pushed me hard during our training sessions at the gym, but also knew when I needed to modify the exercises and go lighter, especially when I was exhausted from writing late into the night. Your ability to motivate me while being attuned to my energy levels and limits helped me make great progress. Thank you for your guidance and understanding.

Thank you to Randy Massengale and my network of supportive colleagues and clients for enriching my life; your contributions make this work worth doing!

Many thanks go out to my fantastic team at Harden Consulting Group and Allyship Publishing, who enabled me to focus on writing without worrying about all the little details of publishing a book! I could not have accomplished this without your incredible commitment and assistance.

Last but certainly not least, to Chrysanthemum and Ms. Berry: Thank you for being the most incredible friends a person could ask for. Your unwavering support, the endless laughter we share, and the way you hold me accountable have been invaluable. The times we spend together are true treasures that I will always cherish. I'm so grateful to have you in my life.

Appendix

Visual Concepts and Frameworks, Assessments, & Practical Tools

Appendix

Visual Concepts and Frameworks

Figure 1: Cultural Concepts: Awareness, Sensitivity, and Competence

Figure 2: Cultural Intelligence (CQ) Triad

Figure 3: Roots of Culture Model

Figure 4: Hofstede's Cultural Dimensions Framework

Figure 5: GLOBE Framework of Cultural Dimensions

Figure 6: Trompenaars' Seven Dimensions of Culture

Figure 7: Lewis Model of Cultural Types

Figure 8: Schwartz Theory of Basic Values

Figure 9: The Culturally Intelligent Leader's Mindset Model

Figure 10: The Cultural Intelligence Leadership Continuum

Figure 11: Ladder of Inference

Figure 12: Kübler-Ross Change Transition Model

Assessments

Cultural Intelligence Quiz (CQS) *(see chapters 3, 4, 8)*

https://hardenconsultinggroup.com/cq-quiz

Intercultural Development Inventory (IDI) *(see chapters 3, 4, 8)*

https://www.idiinventory.com/assessment-and-reports

Intercultural Readiness Check (IRC) *(see chapter 8)*

https://interculturalreadiness.com/

Cultural Orientations Indicator (COI) *(see chapters 3, 4, 8)*

https://www.berlitz.com/business-services/culture-training/cultural-orientations-indicator

Implicit Association Test (IAT) *(see chapter 5)*

https://implicit.harvard.edu/implicit/

Practical Tools

Practical Tools

Sample Vision Statement on Cultural Intelligence

Sample Global Inclusion Policy

Sample CQ Leadership Commitment Charter

Sample Cultural Intelligence Training Policy

Sample 12-Month Curriculum for CQ Development

Culturally Intelligent Strategic Decision Blueprint

Blind Spot Detector

CQ Accountability Tracker

Figure 1: (see discussion in Chapter 1)

Cultural Concepts
Awareness, Sensitivity, and Competence

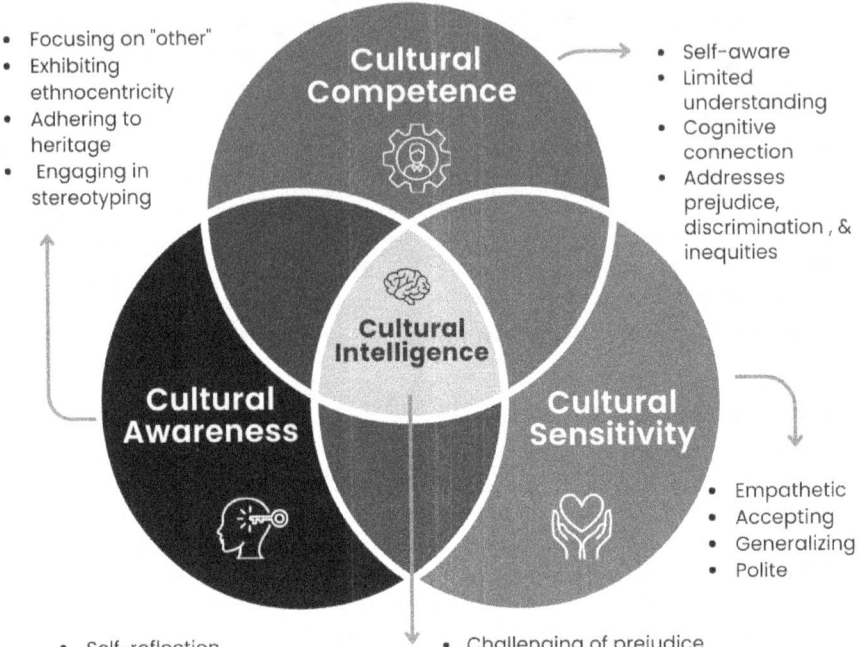

- Focusing on "other"
- Exhibiting ethnocentricity
- Adhering to heritage
- Engaging in stereotyping

Cultural Competence

- Self-aware
- Limited understanding
- Cognitive connection
- Addresses prejudice, discrimination, & inequities

Cultural Intelligence

Cultural Awareness

Cultural Sensitivity

- Empathetic
- Accepting
- Generalizing
- Polite

- Self-reflection
- Consideration of social, political, and historical contexts
- Recognition of historical trauma's impacts and root causes
- Understanding of privilege and systemic bias

- Challenging of prejudice, discrimination, and inequities
- Adaptation to cultural differences
- Emotional and communal connection
- Reduction of power differences between groups

CULTURAL AWARENESS: ACKNOWLEDGES DIFFERENCES

Involves recognizing that people from different cultures may have distinct customs, values, beliefs, and behaviors

CULTURAL COMPETENCE: APPRECIATES DIFFERENCES

Is aware of one's own cultural background and biases and adapts behavior accordingly

CULTURAL SENSITIVITY: RESPECTS CULTURAL DIFFERENCES

Acknowledges and respects differences without necessarily delving deep into understanding or adapting to them

CULTURAL INTELLIGENCE: RESPECTS, APPRECIATES, AND VALIDATES DIFFERENCES

Is capable of functioning effectively in diverse cultural contexts by understanding, adapting to, and leveraging cultural differences

© 2024 Kimberly Harden. All rights reserved.

Figure 2: (see discussion in Chapter 1)

The Cultural Intelligence (CQ) Triad

COGNITIVE CQ

The ability to understand cultural similarities and differences and to acquire and strategize based on cultural knowledge.

Ask Yourself:
What do I need to know to navigate this cultural context effectively?

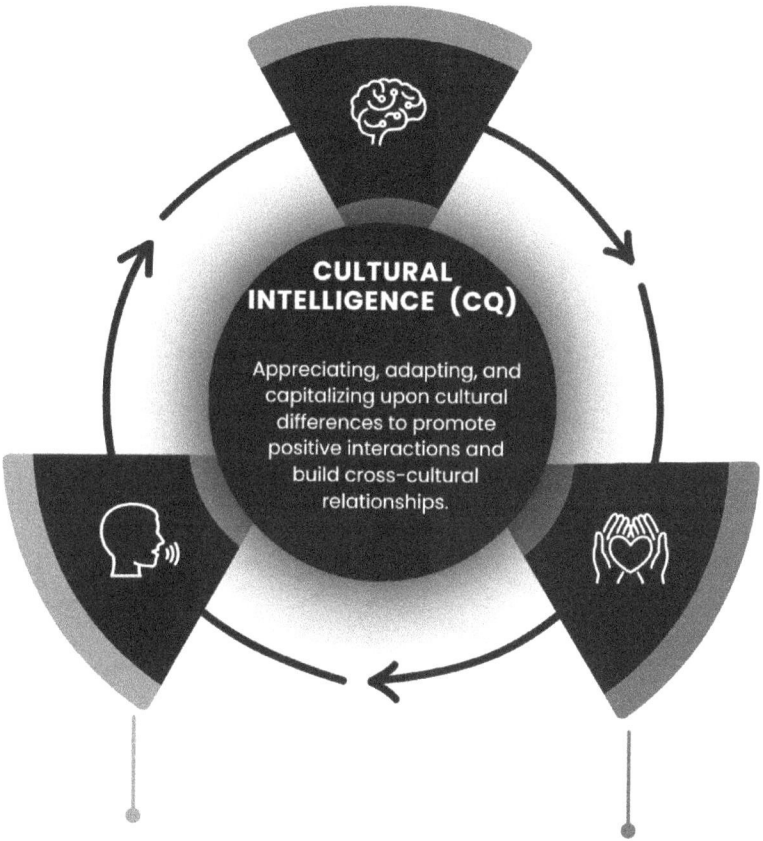

CULTURAL INTELLIGENCE (CQ)

Appreciating, adapting, and capitalizing upon cultural differences to promote positive interactions and build cross-cultural relationships.

PHYSICAL CQ

The capability to adapt verbal and nonverbal behaviors appropriately for different cultural interactions and settings.

Ask Yourself:
Am I flexing my communication style and actions to build rapport and function effectively cross-culturally?

EMOTIONAL CQ

The capacity for cultural empathy and the drive to learn about and adapt to diverse cultural settings.

Ask Yourself:
Am I open to and curious about understanding different cultural perspectives and experiences?

© 2024 Kimberly Harden. All rights reserved.

Figure 3: (see discussion in Chapter 1)

The Roots of Culture Model

Instead of envisioning culture as an iceberg, I liken it to a tree to underscore its organic, interconnected, and living nature. This analogy emphasizes its deep roots while illustrating its capacity to branch out into diverse co-cultures.

BRANCHES:

Extend into co-cultures, branching out to incorporate various dimensions like **age, educational attainment, family status, health status, personal style, skills and talents, ideas, military experience, geographical area, ownership of property, occupation, and socioeconomic status.** These branches showcase the diversity and nuances within the broader cultural context.

LEAVES:

Represent the dynamic and ever-changing aspects of culture. These could include **observable behaviors, symbols, artifacts, expressions, trends, and adaptations of the community.** The leaves reflect the vibrancy and growth within the culture.

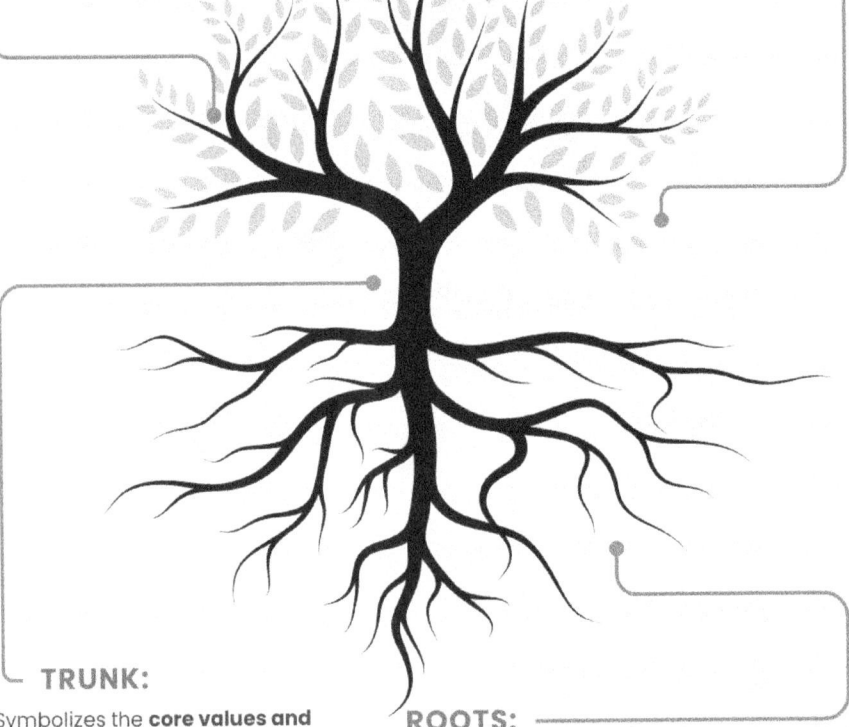

TRUNK:

Symbolizes the **core values and principles that are commonly upheld in the culture.** This includes the fundamental beliefs and ethical guidelines that provide stability and structure to the community.

ROOTS:

Represent the deep, foundational aspects of culture, such as **shared traditions, customs, history, folklore, ethnicity, language, nationality, and religion.** These elements form the cultural bedrock and shape the identity of the immediate community.

© 2024 Kimberly Harden. All rights reserved.

Figure 4: (see discussion in Chapter 2)

Hofstede's Cultural Dimensions

LOW POWER DISTANCE	**POWER DISTANCE** Measures the extent to which less powerful members of a society accept and expect that power is distributed unequally.	HIGH POWER DISTANCE
LOW UNCERTAINTY AVOIDANCE	**UNCERTAINTY AVOIDANCE** Refers to a culture's tolerance of unpredictability and ambiguity.	HIGH UNCERTAINTY AVOIDANCE
INDIVIDUALISTIC	**INDIVIDUALISM VS. COLLECTIVISM** Measures how much cultures emphasize personal choice and recognition versus communal obligations.	COLLECTIVISTIC
MASCULINE	**"MASCULINE" VS. "FEMININE"** is not about gender bias but rather how a culture emphasizes traits traditionally associated with masculinity (e.g., competition, assertiveness) versus femininity (e.g., modesty, work-life balance).	FEMININE
SHORT-TERM ORIENTATION	**LONG-TERM VS. SHORT-TERM ORIENTATION** refers to a culture's focus on the future, ease of adaptation, traditions, and instant gratification.	LONG-TERM ORIENTATION
INDULGENCE	**INDULGENCE VS. RESTRAINT** measures the willingness to enjoy leisure pleasures versus strict self-discipline.	RESTRAINT

Adapted from Hofstede, G. (2003). Cultures and organizations: Software of the mind (3rd ed.). McGraw-Hill.

© 2024 Kimberly Harden. All rights reserved.

Figure 5: (see discussion in Chapter 2)

GLOBE Framework

POWER DISTANCE
Measures the extent to which a society accepts and perpetuates inequalities and hierarchical structures.
To what extent should there be an equal distribution of power in organizations and society?

UNCERTAINTY AVOIDANCE
Assesses a society's tolerance for ambiguity and its capacity to handle unpredictability.
How heavily should people rely on social norms and rules to reduce uncertainty and minimize unpredictability?

INSTITUTIONAL COLLECTIVISM
Evaluates how strongly societal institutions promote collective action and the sharing of resources.
To what degree should leaders promote and reward loyalty to the collective group?

IN-GROUP COLLECTIVISM
Measures the degree of loyalty and commitment individuals have toward their immediate groups or families.
How much pride and loyalty should individuals express toward their family or organizational group?

GENDER EGALITARIANISM
Examines the efforts within a society to reduce gender-based discrimination and enhance equality.
How much effort should be invested in reducing gender discrimination and balancing gender roles?

FUTURE ORIENTATION
Assesses the emphasis a society places on long-term planning and the postponement of immediate gratification.
To what extent should individuals prioritize long-term planning and delay gratification?

PERFORMANCE ORIENTATION
Measures how much a society values achievement, excellence, and continuous improvement.
How much should improvement and excellence be rewarded in society?

HUMANE ORIENTATION
Evaluates the extent to which a society encourages and values kindness, altruism, and generosity.
How much should society promote and reward kindness, fairness, and generosity?

ASSERTIVENESS
Evaluates the prevalence and acceptance of assertive, confrontational, and aggressive behaviors in social interactions within a society.
How assertive and dominant should individuals be in their social interactions?

Adapted from House, R. J., Hanges, P. J., Javidan, M., Dorfman, P. W., & Gupta, V. (2004). *Culture, leadership, and organizations: The GLOBE study of 62 societies.* SAGE.

© 2024 Kimberly Harden. All rights reserved.

Figure 6: (see discussion in Chapter 2)

Trompenaars Cultural Dimension

UNIVERSALISM	To what extent do the same rules apply in all situations, or are they different according to circumstances?	PARTICULARISM
INDIVIDUALISM	Is it more important to be able to act as an individual or to be able to contribute to and stay loyal to the group's goals?	COMMUNITARIANISM
SPECIFIC	Is it important to compartmentalize or to generalize? Is everything linked or is nothing linked?	DIFFUSE
NEUTRAL	Is it better to show emotions or to keep them hidden?	EMOTIONAL
ACHIEVEMENT	Do I gain success from what I do (achieve) or from who I am (ascribed)?	ASCRIPTION
SEQUENTIAL TIME	Is time a finite resource to be closely managed, or can we use it flexibly to juggle lots of different events?	SYNCHRONOUS TIME
INTERNAL DIRECTION	To what extent do we control our environment? Or does our environment control us?	OUTER DIRECTION

Adapted from Trompenaars, F., & Hampden-Turner, C. (1997). Riding the waves of culture: Understanding diversity in global business. McGraw Hill.

© 2024 Kimberly Harden. All rights reserved.

Figure 7: (see discussion in Chapter 2)

The Lewis Model of Cultural Types

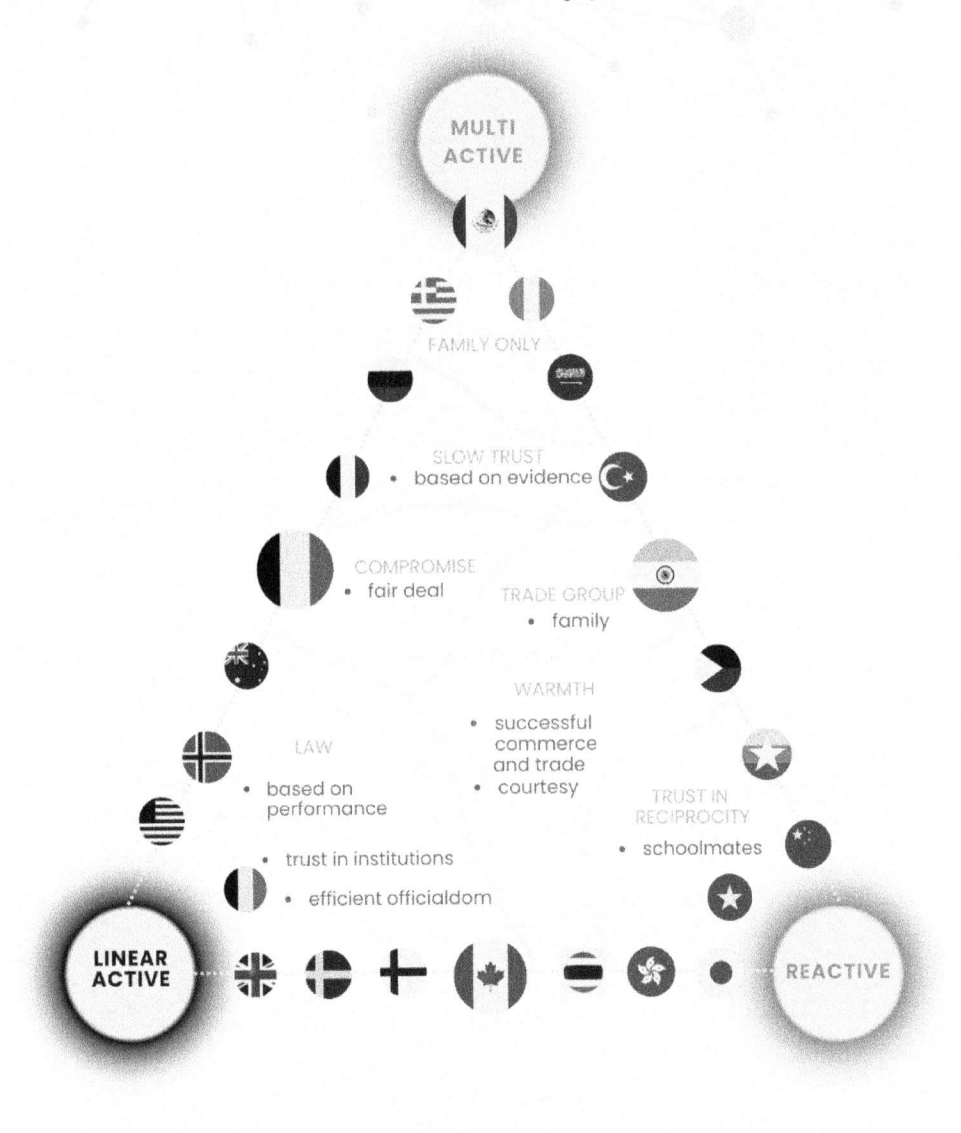

MULTI ACTIVE

FAMILY ONLY

SLOW TRUST
- based on evidence

COMPROMISE
- fair deal

TRADE GROUP
- family

WARMTH
- successful commerce and trade
- courtesy

LAW
- based on performance

TRUST IN RECIPROCITY
- schoolmates

- trust in institutions
- efficient officialdom

LINEAR ACTIVE

REACTIVE

Adapted from Lewis, R. D. (1996). *When cultures collide: Leading across cultures.* Nicholas Brealey International.

© 2024 Kimberly Harden. All rights reserved.

Figure 8: (see discussion in Chapter 2)

Schwartz Theory of Basic Values

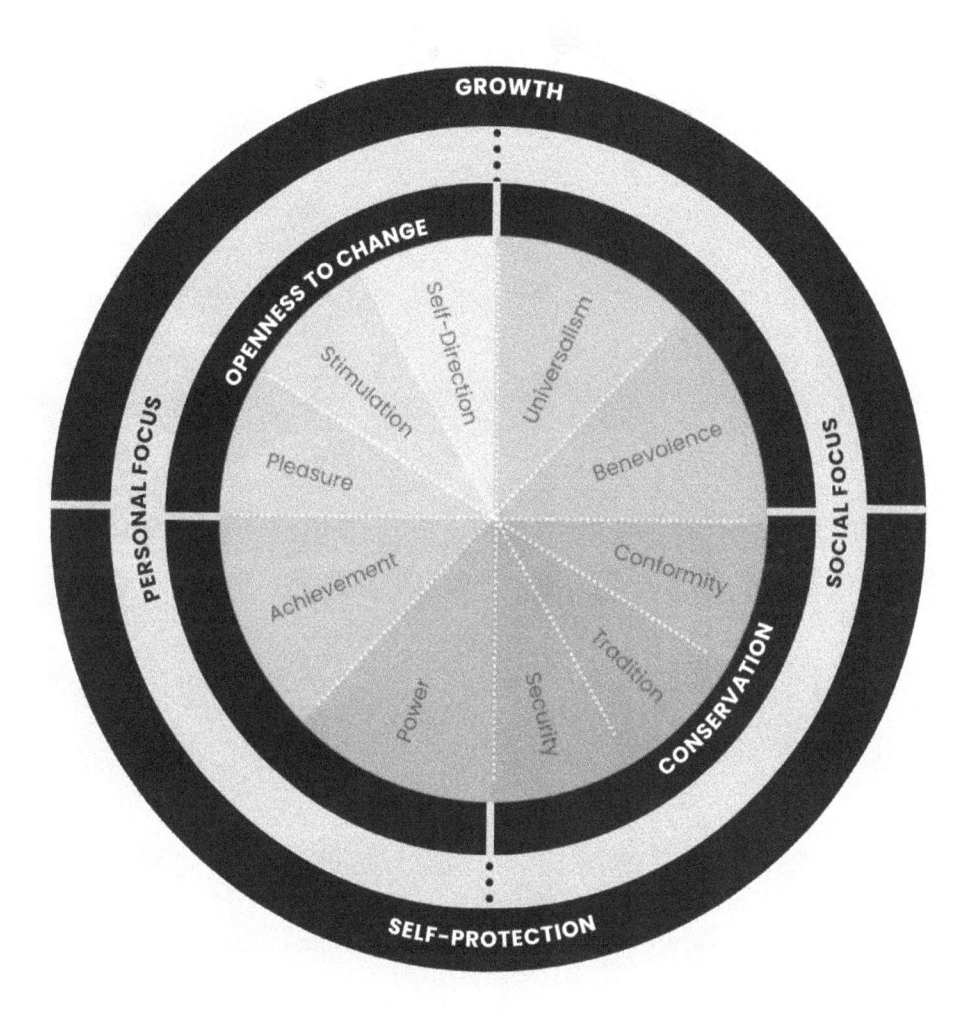

Adapted from Schwartz, S. H. (2012). An overview of the Schwartz theory of basic values. *Online Readings in Psychology and Culture, 2*(1).

© 2024 Kimberly Harden. All rights reserved.

Figure 9: (see discussion in Chapter 4)

The Culturally Intelligent Leader's Mindset

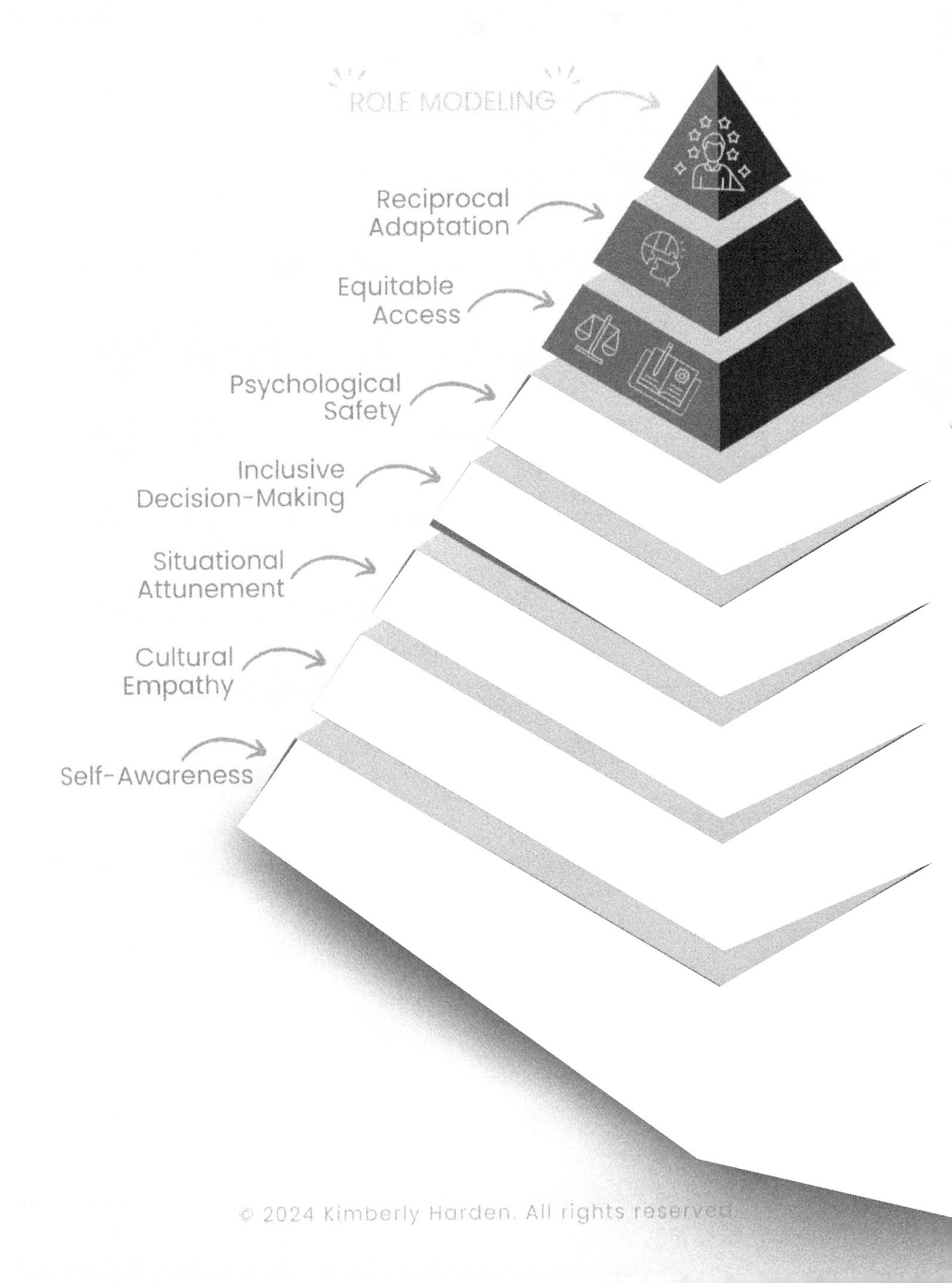

ROLE MODELING

Reciprocal Adaptation

Equitable Access

Psychological Safety

Inclusive Decision-Making

Situational Attunement

Cultural Empathy

Self-Awareness

© 2024 Kimberly Harden. All rights reserved.

Figure 10: (see discussion in Chapter 4)

The Cultural Intelligence
Leadership Continuum

Red Zone:
Culturally Inflexible Leadership

- **Ethnocentric mindset:** Believes that one's cultural values/ways are superior and dismisses differences as irrelevant.
- **Self-awareness deficit:** Holds assumptions about others based on unexplored cultural biases.
- **An uncompromising leadership style:** Imposes one's preferences/style and marginalizes diverse needs.
- **Monocultural decisions:** Takes unilateralist approaches without considering the cultural context.
- **Homogenous teams:** Restricts representation, diminishes diversity value, and limits its representation.

Yellow Zone:
Culturally Emerging Leadership

- **Tolerance stance:** Accepts cultural differences on a surface level but makes little effort to understand deeper meanings or integrate diverse perspectives.
- **Partial self-insight:** Acknowledges the impact of personal culture at an intellectual level but lacks nuance when applied across situations.
- **Inconsistent flexibility:** Sporadically adjusts leadership communication/policies when cultural gaps become apparent, yet falls back into familiar/comfortable behavior patterns.
- **Emerging cultural cues:** Takes account of data trends from across cultures when making decisions; however, implements only if all parties are included.
- **Shallow integration:** Supports diversity numerically on teams without providing psychological safety for nondominant groups to contribute authentically, thus failing to maximize capabilities.

Green Zone:
Culturally Sensitive Leadership

- **Culture-bridging attitude:** Appreciates cultural differences as assets, forms connections across divides, and integrates cultural insights.
- **Self-awareness around blindspots:** Is aware of how one's personal cultural lens impacts what one sees, reflects to identify bias, and works to broaden perspectives.
- **Situationally-skilled flexibility:** Adopts behaviors, language, and policies to foster cross-cultural harmony and belonging.
- **Decision-making that integrates cultural wisdom:** Solicits inputs early and acomprehensively from all groups involved and co-creates solutions that reflect community values.
- **Building psychologically safe and empowering team cultures:** Ensures that all talent feels respected and valued and can freely provide skills and ideas through equitable policies that foster a sense of belongingness.

© 2024 Kimberly Harden. All rights reserved.

Figure 11: (see discussion in Chapter 5)

Ladder of Inference

Minimize Misunderstandings ...

Instead of jumping to CONCLUSIONS, break down the Assumptions, Meanings, Selected Data, and Observations that created them.

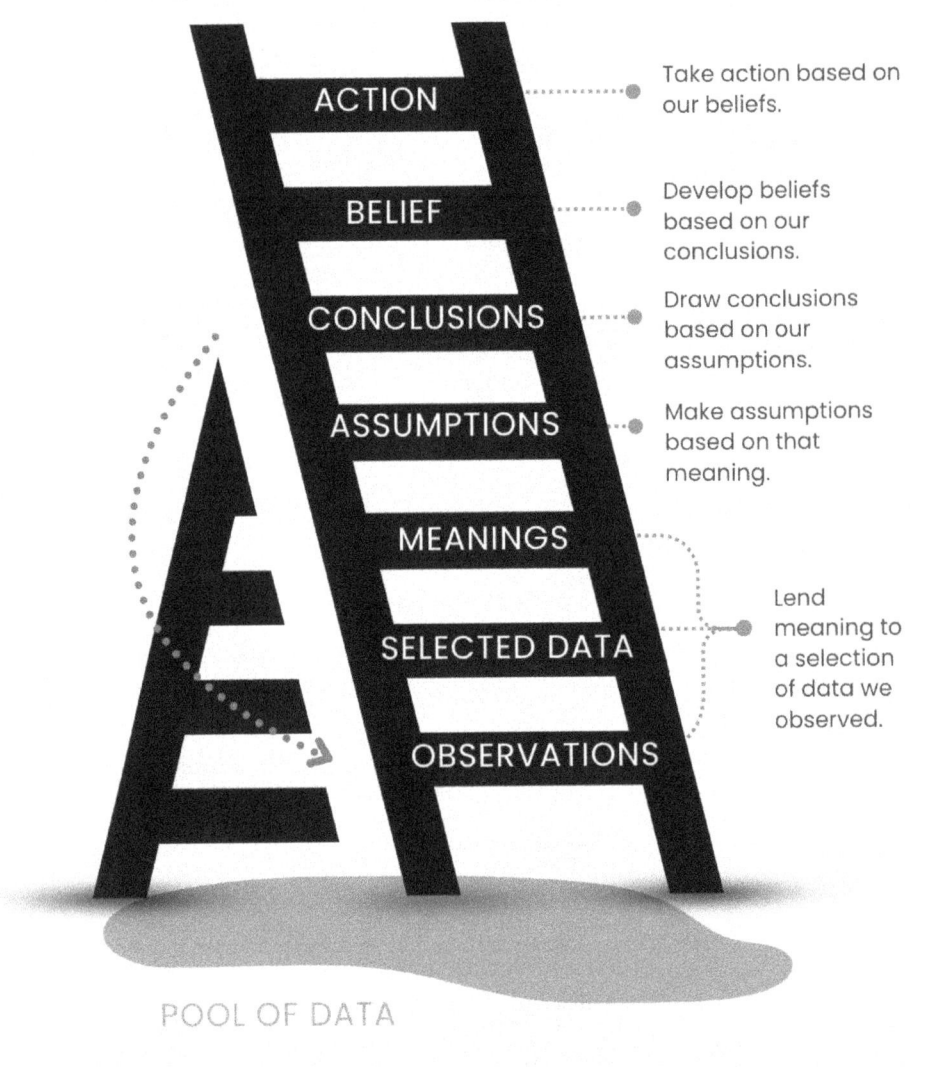

- **ACTION** — Take action based on our beliefs.
- **BELIEF** — Develop beliefs based on our conclusions.
- **CONCLUSIONS** — Draw conclusions based on our assumptions.
- **ASSUMPTIONS** — Make assumptions based on that meaning.
- **MEANINGS**
- **SELECTED DATA** — Lend meaning to a selection of data we observed.
- **OBSERVATIONS**

POOL OF DATA

Adapted from Argyris, C. (1990). *Overcoming organizational defenses: Facilitating organizational learning.* Pearson.

© 2024 Kimberly Harden. All rights reserved.

Figure 12: (see discussion in Chapter 6)

Kübler-Ross Change Transition Model

ACCEPTANCE:

The final stage where individuals come to terms with the change and start to engage constructively with the new reality. They begin to see opportunities in the change and actively work towards implementing it.

DENIAL

The initial stage where individuals refuse to believe that the change is happening or necessary. They may ignore new information or cling to the current way of doing things.

ANGER

As reality sets in, individuals may feel frustrated, anxious, or resentful about the change. They might express this through resistance, criticism, or blame.

DEPRESSION

As the change becomes inevitable, individuals may feel overwhelmed, unmotivated, or uncertain about their ability to adapt. This can lead to decreased productivity or engagement.

BARGAINING

In this stage, individuals try to negotiate or find ways to delay or minimize the impact of the change. They may suggest alternatives or try to maintain some aspects of the old system.

Adapted from Kübler-Ross, E. (1969). *On Death and Dying.* Scribner.

© 2024 Kimberly Harden. All rights reserved.

Sample Vision Statement on Cultural Intelligence

At [Organization Name], we envision a future where cultural intelligence is woven into the fabric of our organization, empowering us to thrive in a diverse, interconnected world. We aspire to be a leader in fostering an environment where every individual's unique perspective is valued and leveraged to drive innovation, enhance customer experiences, and create meaningful connections across global communities. Through our commitment to cultural intelligence, we aim to build bridges of understanding, cultivate empathy, and unlock the full potential of our workforce, ultimately creating sustainable value for our partners and contributing to a more inclusive global society.

Sample Global Inclusion Policy

1. Purpose: [Organization Name] is committed to fostering a diverse, equitable, and inclusive workplace that values and respects individuals from all backgrounds and cultures.

2. Scope: This policy applies to all aspects of employment, including recruitment, hiring, promotion, training, compensation, and termination.

3. Non-Discrimination: We prohibit discrimination based on race, color, religion, gender, sexual orientation, gender identity, national origin, age, disability, or any other protected characteristic.

4. Equal Opportunity: We are committed to providing equal opportunities for all qualified individuals in all employment practices.

5. Inclusive Environment:

a. We encourage open dialogue and the respectful exchange of diverse viewpoints.

b. We promote collaboration across diverse teams and departments.

c. We support employee resource groups and diversity initiatives.

6. Accommodations: We will provide reasonable accommodations for qualified individuals with disabilities or religious beliefs.

7. Reporting and Resolution: We encourage reporting of any perceived violations of this policy and commit to prompt, thorough investigations of all complaints.

8. Training and Education: We will provide ongoing education and training on diversity, equity, and inclusion topics.

9. Accountability: All employees, especially leaders, are responsible for upholding and promoting the principles of this policy.

10. Continuous Improvement: We commit to regularly assessing and improving our inclusive practices and policies.

Sample CQ Leadership Commitment Charter

As leaders at [Organization Name], we commit to:

1. Continual Learning: Engage in ongoing cultural intelligence development and encourage our teams to do the same.

2. Modeling Cultural Humility: Demonstrate openness to learning from others and acknowledging our own cultural biases and limitations.

3. Inclusive Decision-Making: Actively seek out diverse perspectives and consider cultural implications in all decision-making processes.

4. Cultivating Diverse Teams: Prioritize diversity in hiring, development, and promotion practices.

5. Fostering Psychological Safety: Create an environment where team members feel safe to express their authentic selves and diverse viewpoints.

6. Championing CQ Initiatives: Actively support and participate in organizational CQ programs and initiatives.

7. A Global Mindset: Consider global implications and cross-cultural impacts in strategy and operations.

8. Mentoring for CQ: Provide mentorship and guidance to develop cultural intelligence in others.

9. Measuring and Improving: Regularly assess our own CQ and that of our teams, setting goals for continuous improvement.

10. Accountability: Hold ourselves and each other accountable for living up to these commitments and creating a culturally intelligent organization.

By signing this charter, we pledge to embody these commitments and lead [Organization Name] toward becoming a truly culturally intelligent organization.

[Signature lines for leadership team]

Sample Cultural Intelligence Training Policy

1. Purpose: This policy establishes guidelines for cultural intelligence (CQ) training and development across [Organization Name] to enhance our collective ability to work effectively across cultures and leverage diversity for organizational success.

2. Scope: This policy applies to all employees, contractors, and temporary staff at all organizational levels.

3. Mandatory Training:

a. New Employee Orientation: All new hires must complete an introductory CQ awareness course within 30 days.

b. Annual Refresher: All employees must complete an annual CQ refresher course.

c. Leadership Training: Managers and above must complete advanced CQ training annually.

4. Optional Training:

a. Employees are encouraged to participate in additional CQ workshops, seminars, and e-learning modules available through our learning management system (LMS).

b. The organization will support employee-initiated CQ learning opportunities, subject to approval.

5. Resources and Support:

a. We will establish and maintain a dedicated CQ resource library that is accessible to all employees.

b. CQ mentoring programs will be available for interested employees.

c. The HR department will guide and support CQ-related inquiries and development plans.

6. Evaluation and Accountability:

a. Completion of mandatory CQ training will be tracked and incorporated into performance reviews.

b. Managers are responsible for ensuring their team members comply with this policy.

7. Policy Review: This policy will be reviewed annually and updated as necessary to reflect best practices in CQ development.

Sample 12-Month Curriculum for CQ Development

This sample 12-month curriculum provides organizations with a structured road map for developing cultural intelligence and discernment capabilities in their workforce over time. It is designed as a comprehensive, immersive learning journey that combines workshops, coaching, mentorship, experiential learning, and practical application.

The curriculum aims to help employees:

1. Gain self-awareness about their own cultural biases and perspectives.

2. Develop empathy and understanding of diverse cultural viewpoints.

3. Enhance cross-cultural communication and collaboration skills.

4. Adapt leadership styles and decision-making processes to be more culturally inclusive.

5. Drive organizational change towards greater cultural flexibility and global competence.

The curriculum progressively builds cultural intelligence through a mix of individual reflection, group dialogue, skill-building workshops, mentorship, and real-world application. It culminates in participants' "paying it forward" by designing customized curricula for others, ensuring the ongoing dissemination of cultural intelligence throughout the organization.

The curriculum is designed to be adaptable for different levels of employees, including executives, managers, and individual contributors. The content and activities can be tailored to each group's specific needs and responsibilities.

The effectiveness of the curriculum will be measured through a combination of qualitative and quantitative metrics, including:

- Pre- and post-curriculum assessments of employee cultural intelligence.

- Retention and engagement rates of diverse talent.

- Number and quality of global partnerships and market expansion in diverse segments.

- Participant feedback and testimonials on personal and organizational transformation.

- Successful implementation of cultural adaptations in products, policies, and processes.

The estimated costs and resources required to implement the curriculum may include:

- Fees for workshop facilitators and executive coaches (internal or external).

- Travel and accommodations for offsite workshops and summits.

- Materials and assessments for participants.

- Technology for virtual coaching and e-learning components.

- Time investment for participants and mentors.

- Internal resources (e.g., HR, Learning & Development) to support implementation.

- External consultants with expertise in cultural intelligence and global leadership. development

Sample Curriculum

Month 1: Understanding Self and Others' Worldviews Workshop

- Two-day offsite workshop for self-reflection and cross-cultural dialogue

- Implicit bias assessment

- Reflection questions on identity development

- Exploration of personal cultural programming through identity assessments

- Discussion of the concepts of cultural bias and privilege

- Intergroup conversations on navigating cultural differences

Months 2–4: Personal Coaching and Virtual Cultural Exchange

- One-hour individual executive coaching sessions every three weeks

- Leadership values questionnaire

- Short video lessons on cultural value frameworks

- Debriefing on self-assessments to reveal blind spots

- Setting of 3–6-month leadership development goals around empathy building, situational attunement, and decision-making practices

- Introduction to empathetic frameworks: user interviewing, journey mapping, and persona creation to deeply understand user perspectives and needs

- Virtual cultural exchange: Participants engage in asynchronous online discussions or activities with colleagues from different cultural backgrounds to broaden their perspectives and practice cross-cultural communication skills.

Month 5: Global Literacy Training and Inclusive Leadership Module

- Review of cultural dimension analyses by country, covering communication styles, authority concepts, motivational norms

- Cross-cultural case study analysis

- Comparisons of contextual data by country

- Discussion of case studies showcasing cultural collisions abroad

- Discussion of best practices for local adaptation of policies and processes

- Inclusive leadership module: Strategies for creating psychologically safe and culturally responsive team environments

Month 6: Cross-Cultural Mentorship Program and Cultural Intelligence in Action

- Six-month partnership with a mentor in another function/country

- Cultural partnership plan with shared learning goals

- Reflective blog post written by participants describing eye-opening leadership observations from their mentorship experience

- Self-assessment of progress on cultural goal setting

- Leadership shadowing to observe global servant-leadership

- Cultural intelligence in action: Participants share personal stories and examples of how they have applied their learnings to navigate cultural differences effectively in their work or personal lives.

Month 7: Intercultural Communication Workshop and Group Project Development

- Assessment of conflict style, focused on culture

- Video lesson on negotiation protocols

- Two-day experiential workshop on cultural verbal and nonverbal communication

- Role plays practicing feedback, negotiations, and relationship development across cultures

- Core protocols for culturally appropriate correspondence

- Group project development: Teams work on their cultural intelligence initiatives or solutions, applying learnings from the curriculum.

Months 8–9: Observing, Journaling, Planning for Adaptations, and Group Project Launch

- Preparation of a cultural adaptation draft for a specific product/policy

- Creation of an infographic capturing the key workshop takeaways

- Journaling of key learnings and observations from mentorship/workshops

- Creation of a worksheet outlining next-quarter global priorities

- Recording of a cross-cultural customer interview

- Two individual coaching sessions to discuss application to projects

- Consultations on planning communications, policies, and people practices

- Group project launch: Participants form teams to collaborate on developing a cultural intelligence initiative or solution for a real-world business challenge faced by the organization.

Month 10: Global Leadership Summit, Working Session, and Group Project Presentations

- Post-summit ideation presentation

- Readings about designing cultural resonance into offerings

- Keynotes from culturally dexterous leaders across sectors

- Cross-cultural team simulation exercises

- Workshops on design thinking to reimagine decision protocols

- Group project presentations: Teams present their cultural intelligence initiatives or solutions to the organization's leadership and receive feedback.

Month 11: Interim Milestone Reviews and Measuring Cultural Intelligence Impact

- Quantitative survey on program impact

- Written testimony on personal and organizational transformations undergone

- Evaluation of progress against original developmental goals

- Quantification of wins on key performance indicators involving enhanced global partnership, employee retention, and market expansion in diversity segments

- Measuring cultural intelligence impact: Participants learn to track and report on relevant metrics to demonstrate the value of their efforts to key organizational members.

Month 12: Paying It Forward and Organizational Extensions

- Assessment of mentee needs within each participant's department or team

- Design by participants of customized 12-month cultural intelligence curricula for their respective departments or teams based on the specific needs identified in the assessment

- Establishment of mentor-mentee relationships with new or less experienced employees to guide them through the customized curricula

- Prototype testing of a portion of the new 12-month curricula before full rollout within each department or team

- 1:1 coaching sessions between participants and their mentees to share insights and learnings from the original program

- Exploration of organizational extensions and initiatives to enhance cultural flexibility and intelligence long-term, beyond the mentorship program

These extensions could include:

- Designing cultural intelligence training modules for new hires during onboarding.

- Establishing a cultural intelligence resource library or online platform for employees.

- Incorporating cultural intelligence objectives into performance reviews and recognition programs.

Culturally Intelligent Strategic Decision Blueprint

The Culturally Intelligent Strategic Decision Blueprint provides a comprehensive framework to guide leaders in inclusive decision-making across various cultural contexts. This blueprint offers a path for multiplying collective wisdom during strategic development.

The blueprint is valuable for leaders seeking to make inclusive and equitable decisions across diverse cultural contexts. It ties into multiple dimensions of cultural intelligence (CQ):

Cognitive CQ: By gathering insights from marginalized communities, analyzing potential cultural impacts, and constructing scenarios reflecting cultural friction points, leaders expand their knowledge and understanding of different cultural perspectives, values, and priorities.

Emotional CQ: Proactively engaging with diverse communities and hosting open forums for collaborative solution development helps leaders build empathy, sensitivity, and emotional intelligence. They learn to recognize and respond appropriately to the emotions and concerns of various cultural groups.

Physical CQ: Practicing cultural agility through continuous monitoring and feedback channels enables leaders to adapt their behavior and communication style to resonate with different cultural norms and expectations, demonstrating high physical CQ.

Implementing the Culturally Intelligent Strategic Decision Blueprint will improve workplace culture and team dynamics by promoting inclusive decision-making, enhancing trust and collaboration, reducing cultural friction, and improving cultural competence among teams.

The blueprint consists of ten key components:

1. Inclusive Insight Gathering

Proactively gather data, perspectives, and insights from marginalized communities affected by the decision(s) being made.

2. Modeling Predicted Cultural Impacts

Analyze how the decision could affect opportunities, resource allocation, and harms/benefits for various cultural groups.

3. Resonance Stress Testing

Construct scenarios that reflect potential cultural friction points and community reactions.

4. Co-Designing Solutions

Host open forums, accessible and welcoming to employees from all cultural backgrounds, for developing collaborative solutions that respond to cultural priorities.

5. Practicing Cultural Agility

Develop feedback channels to continuously monitor cultural resonance and impacts by subgroup.

6. Training and Resources

Provide workshops on cultural sensitivity and scenario planning to support leaders in effectively implementing the blueprint.

7. Accessible Open Forums

Ensure that co-design solution teams consider factors like language, timing, and format to include employees from all cultural backgrounds.

8. Celebration of Success

Showcase successful examples of culturally intelligent decision-making to reinforce the importance and benefits of this approach.

9. Continuous Improvement

Regularly review and update the blueprint based on employee feedback and changing cultural dynamics to ensure it remains relevant and effective.

10. Accountability and Metrics

Establish clear accountability measures and metrics to track progress and ensure leaders consistently apply the blueprint in their decision-making processes.

By incorporating the Culturally Intelligent Strategic Decision Blueprint into their leadership practices, organizations can foster a more inclusive, equitable, and culturally competent workplace culture that leverages the strengths of diversity for improved decision-making and team performance.

Blind Spot Detector

Becoming a culturally intelligent leader involves identifying and addressing blind spots that can perpetuate bias and exclusion. Doing this requires self-reflecting courageously, actively seeking input from marginalized voices, and continuously refining organizational systems and policies through an ethical lens.

The Blind Spot Detector is a valuable tool for developing cultural intelligence because it helps leaders identify and address personal, interpersonal, and organizational biases that can perpetuate exclusion and hinder the creation of an inclusive environment. By providing practical strategies and reflective exercises, this tool enables leaders to enhance their self-awareness, empathy, and critical thinking skills, which are essential components of cultural intelligence.

A. Personal Blind Spots

Implicit Bias Assessments

Taking implicit association tests helps us uncover any reflexive prejudices and subconscious tendencies toward stereotyping that we may hold. Recognizing these split-second reactions through intentional self-awareness and perspective-taking is essential to countering our biases.

Privilege Audits

Examining the unearned advantages that we experience related to facets of our identity helps us recognize our complicity (even if unwitting) in perpetuating systemic imbalances. Checking our privileges—such as social access, career mobility, and freedom from discrimination—grounds us in humility as leaders.

Cultural Milestone Timeline

Revisiting the key personal and cultural milestones that have shaped our values, perspectives, and biases throughout our lives enhances our self-understanding. Reflecting on our moments of hardship and ease can allow us, as leaders, to question notions of meritocracy.

Introspective Assumption Journaling

Journaling while we visualize life experiences from minority viewpoints can surface our hidden assumptions about certain groups. Write down the perceptions that arise when you imagine walking in another's shoes. Discuss your discoveries with a trusted friend or peer to further uncover your personal blind spots.

Contrary Opinions

Our confirmation bias leads us to seek out and recall information that reinforces our existing assumptions and to interpret old and new information in a way that further reinforces them. As leaders, we should proactively fact-check the information we receive and seek out dissenting views that challenge our convenient cultural assumptions. This stretches our critical thinking.

B. Interpersonal Blind Spots

Community Advisory Councils

Establishing councils of employees from historically marginalized groups provides us and our organizations with invaluable perspectives on our existing policies and practices. This helps us recognize exclusion risks and microaggressions that most teams will otherwise miss.

Power Dynamic Reflection

Reflecting on cultural norms, communication patterns, and power differentials before the beginning of a meeting helps create an environment in which everyone feels psychologically safe participating. Seek to elevate voices that have often been inadvertently silenced.

Delayed Judgment

When interpersonal tensions arise, resist immediate judgment. Probe first to understand the different motivations and values that are influencing the behaviors of the various participants within their cultural contexts. This thoughtfulness will help you to avoid misattributing intent or placing undue blame without considering alternative cultural perspectives.

C. Organizational Blind Spots

Journey Mapping

Intersectional employee journey maps reveal some pain points and exclusion experiences that quantitative data may hide. Understanding the unique challenges that various employees face across race, gender, age, etc., can help you focus your efforts on supporting all your team members.

Equity Analysis

Conduct equity analyses on talent advancement and outcomes in your organization, assessing for implicit systemic biases that may be consciously or unconsciously advantaging majority groups. In conducting these analyses, partnering with historically marginalized groups will enable you to identify and remove such barriers.

Establish Community Advisory Councils

Marginalized employee voices on advisory councils can provide "outsider within" viewpoints on your institution's policies, proposals, and organizational culture. This input sharpens our understanding of the risks and harms of exclusion.

Assess Meetings for Biased Patterns

Individually and collectively, reflect on the group dynamics during meetings to identify biased patterns. Are some cultural styles favored whereas others feel restricted or dismissed? How could you change the facilitation of your meetings or your organization's policies to become more inclusive?

Participatory Budgeting

Participatory budgeting allows community members to directly allocate public resource investments through an inclusive proposal development process and democratic voting, thereby embedding the community's priorities.

Probe First Before Adapting Response

When confronted with unfamiliar behaviors or motivations, pause before responding. First, probe to understand the cultural context; then, consider how to adapt your leadership response. Suspend your assumptions, show empathy, and find common ground with the people you interact with.

Addressing blind spots is an ongoing process. Make a specific action plan with measurable goals to track your progress in these areas over time. Seek additional training, mentors, and resources to deepen cultural intelligence.

The benefits are substantial—improved decision-making, innovation, employee engagement, and retention. Most importantly, you'll be creating a workplace of true belonging. Cultural intelligence is key to your evolution as a leader and an organization.

CQ Accountability Tracker

Building cultural intelligence is an ongoing process that requires consistent effort and self-reflection. This Accountability Tracker is designed to help you stay committed to your goals, monitor your progress, and improve your CQ over time.

By regularly filling out this tracker, you'll be able to:

1. Set specific, actionable goals related to building CQ.

2. Hold yourself accountable for taking consistent action towards your goals.

3. Reflect on your experiences and learn from them.

4. Visualize your progress and stay motivated.

How to use this tracker:

1. Set a specific, measurable goal for building CQ (e.g., "Learn about the business etiquette of three different cultures").

2. Break your goal into smaller, actionable steps and write them in the "Action Steps" column.

3. Each week, fill in the days of the week at the top of the tracker.

4. As you complete each action step, mark it off in the corresponding box.

5. At the end of the week, reflect on your progress and write down any insights or lessons learned in the "Weekly Reflection" space.

6. Repeat the process for the following weeks, adjusting your action steps as needed based on your reflections and progress.

Remember, building CQ is a lifelong journey. Celebrate your progress, learn from your experiences, and keep pushing yourself to grow and develop in this critical skill area.

Accountability Tracker

GOALS:

WEEK OF

ACTION STEPS

	MON	TUE	WED	THU	FRI	SAT	SUN
	○	○	○	○	○	○	○
	MON	TUE	WED	THU	FRI	SAT	SUN
	○	○	○	○	○	○	○
	MON	TUE	WED	THU	FRI	SAT	SUN
	○	○	○	○	○	○	○

Weekly Reflection

Next Week's Focus

© 2024 Kimberly Harden. All rights reserved.

References

A

Ahmad, S., & Azad, S. K. (2019). Cultural intelligence and leadership effectiveness in global workplaces. *International Journal on Leadership, 7*(1), 1–7.

Aldrich, H. E. (2014). *The democratization of entrepreneurship? Hackers, makerspaces, and crowdfunding*. Presentation at the Academy of Management, Philadelphia, PA, August 2014. https://doi.org/10.5465/ambpp.2014.10622symposium

Allen, R. (2017, July 24). Gilbert on controversial downtown sign: 'We screwed up badly'. *Detroit Free Press.* https://www.freep.com/story/news/local/michigan/detroit/2017/07/24/gilbert-downtown-detroit-sign/503929001/

Anand, R., & Winters, M. F. (2008). A retrospective view of corporate diversity training from 1964 to the present. *Academy of Management Learning & Education, 7*(3), 356–372. https://doi.org/10.5465/amle.2008.34251673

Ang, S., & Van Dyne, L. (2008). *Handbook of cultural intelligence: Theory, measurement and applications*. Routledge.

Ang, S., Van Dyne, L., Koh, C., Ng, K. Y., Templer, K. J., Tay, C., & Chandrasekar, N. A. (2007). Cultural intelligence: Its measurement and effects on cultural judgment and decision making, cultural adaptation and task performance. *Management and Organization Review, 3*(3), 335–371. https://doi.org/10.1111/j.1740-8784.2007.00082.x

Aoun, R. (2022). *The AI-first company: How to compete and win with artificial intelligence*. Portfolio.

Aramo-Immonen, H., Jussila, J., & Huhtamäki, J. (2016). Exploring co-learning behavior of conference participants with visual network analysis of Twitter data. *Computers in Human Behavior, 55*, 1154–1162. https://doi.org/10.1016/j.chb.2015.02.033

Ardichvili, A., Natt och Dag, K., & Manderscheid, S. (2014). Leadership development: Current and emerging models and practices. *Advances in Developing Human Resources, 16*(3), 275–285. https://doi.org/10.1177/1523 422316645506

Argyris, C. (1990). *Overcoming organizational defenses: Facilitating organizational learning*. Pearson.

Armstrong, M. B., & Landers, R. N. (2018). An evaluation of gamified training: Using narrative to improve reactions and learning. *Simulation & Gaming, 49*(6), 513–538. https://doi.org/10.1177/1046878117703749

Atewologun, D. 2018. *Intersectionality theory and practice*. Oxford Research Encyclopedia of Business and Management. https://doi.org/10.1093/acrefore/9780190224851.013.48

B

Balliet, D., Wu, J., & De Dreu, C. K. (2014). Ingroup favoritism in cooperation: A meta-analysis. *Psychological Bulletin, 140*(6), 1556–1581. https://doi.org/10.1037/a0037737

Bandura, A. (1977). Self-efficacy: toward a unifying theory of behavioral change. *Psychological Review, 84*(2), 191–215. https://doi.org/10.1037/0033-295X.84.2.191

Beer, M., & Nohria, N. (2000). Cracking the code of change. *Harvard Business Review, 78*(3), 133–141.

Bennett, M. J. (2004). Becoming interculturally competent. In J.S. Wurzel (Ed.) *Toward multiculturalism: A reader in multicultural education* (pp.62-77). Intercultural Resource Corporation.

Bird, A., Mendenhall, M., Stevens, M. J., & Oddou, G. (2010). Defining the content domain of intercultural competence for global leaders. *Journal of Managerial Psychology, 25*(8), 810–828. https://doi.org/10.1108/02683941011089107

Blake-Beard, S., Bayne, M. L., Crosby, F. J., & Muller, C. B. (2011). Matching by race and gender in mentoring relationships: Keeping our eyes on the prize. *Journal of Social Issues, 67*(3), 622–643. https://doi.org/10.1111/j.1540-4560.2011.01717.x

Boekhorst, J. A. (2015). The role of authentic leadership in fostering workplace inclusion: A social information processing perspective. *Human Resource Management, 54*(2), 241–264. https://doi.org/10.1002/hrm.21669

Bourke, J., & Dillon, B. (2016a). The diversity and inclusion revolution: Eight powerful truths. *Deloitte Review*, (22), 82–95.

Bourke, J., & Dillon, B. (2016b). The six signature traits of inclusive leadership. *Deloitte Insights.* https://www2.deloitte.com/us/en/insights/topics/talent/six-signature-traits-of-inclusive-leadership.html

Bourke, J., Garr, S., van Berkel, A., & Wong, J. (2017). *Diversity and inclusion: The reality gap.* Global Human Capital Trends. Deloitte University Press. https://www2.deloitte.com/xe/en/insights/focus/human-capital-trends/2017/diversity-and-inclusion-at-the-workplace.html

Boyatzis, R. E., Brizz, T., & Godwin, L. (2011). The effect of religious leaders' emotional and social competencies on improving parish vibrancy. *Journal of*

Leadership & Organizational Studies, 18(2), 192–206. https://doi.org/10.1177/1548051810369676

Bridges, W. (1991). *Managing transitions: Making the most of change*. Da Capo Lifelong Books.

Brimhall, K. C., Lizano, E. L., & Barak, M. E. M. (2014). The mediating role of inclusion: A longitudinal study of the effects of leader-member exchange and diversity climate on job satisfaction and intention to leave among child welfare workers. *Children and Youth Services Review, 40*, 79–88. https://doi.org/10.1016/j.childyouth.2014.03.003

Brislin, R., Worthley, R., & MacNab, B. (2006). Cultural intelligence: Understanding behaviors that serve people's goals. *Group & Organization Management, 31*(1), 40–55. https://doi.org/10.1177/1059601105275262

Brown, B. (2018). *Dare to lead: Daring greatly and rising strong at work*. Penguin Books.

Brown, M. E., & Treviño, L. K. (2014). Do role models matter? An investigation of role modeling as an antecedent of perceived ethical leadership. *Journal of Business Ethics, 122*(4), 587–598. https://doi.org/10.1007/s10551-013-1769-0

Bruneau, E. G., & Saxe, R. (2012). The power of being heard: The benefits of 'perspective-giving' in the context of intergroup conflict. *Journal of Experimental Social Psychology, 48*(4), 855–866. https://doi.org/10.1016/j.jesp.2012.02.017

Bücker, J. J., Furrer, O., & Lin, Y. (2014). Measuring cultural intelligence (CQ): A new test of the CQ scale. *International Journal of Cross Cultural Management, 15*(3), 259–284. https://doi.org/10.1177/1470595815606741

Bücker, J. J., Furrer, O., Poutsma, E., & Buyens, D. (2014). The impact of cultural intelligence on communication effectiveness, job satisfaction and anxiety for Chinese host country managers working for foreign multinationals.

The International Journal of Human Resource Management, 25(14), 2068–2087. https://doi.org/10.1080/09585192.2013.870293

Buchanan, D., Fitzgerald, L., Ketley, D., Gollop, R., Jones, J. L., Lamont, S. S., Neath, A., & Whitby, E. (2005). No going back: A review of the literature on sustaining organizational change. *International Journal of Management Reviews, 7*(3), 189–205. https://doi.org/10.1111/j.1468-2370.2005.00111.x

Burnes, B. (2004). Kurt Lewin and the planned approach to change: A re-appraisal. *Journal of Management Studies, 41*(6), 977–1002. https://doi.org/10.1111/j.1467-6486.2004.00463.x

Buse, K. R., Bernstein, R. S., & Bilimoria, D. (2014). The influence of board diversity, board diversity policies and practices, and board inclusion behaviors on nonprofit governance practices. *Journal of Business Ethics, 133*(1), 179–191. https://doi.org/10.1007/s10551-014-2352-z

C

Caligiuri, P., & Tarique, I. (2012). Dynamic cross-cultural competencies and global leadership effectiveness. *Journal of World Business, 47*(4), 61–-622. https://doi.org/10.1016/j.jwb.2012.01.014

Caprar, D. V., Devinney, T. M., Kirkman, B. L., & Caligiuri, P. (2015). Conceptualizing and measuring culture in international business and management: From challenges to potential solutions. *Journal of International Business Studies, 46*(9), 1011–1027. https://doi.org/10.1057/jibs.2015.33

Carper, W. B. (2014). Global business: A cultural perspective. *Journal of Applied Business and Economics, 16*(6), 109–118.

Carter, P. L. (2013). Student and school cultures and the opportunity gap. In P. L. Carter & K. G. Welner (Eds.), *Closing the opportunity gap: What America must do to give every child an even chance* (pp. 143–155). Oxford University Press.

Castilla, E. J. (2008). Gender, race, and meritocracy in organizational careers. *American Journal of Sociology, 113*(6), 1479–1526.

Castilla, E. J. (2011). Bringing managers back in: Managerial influences on workplace inequality. *American Sociological Review, 76*(5), 667–694. https://doi.org/10.1177/0003122411420814

Chao, M. M., Takeuchi, R., & Farh, J. L. (2017). Enhancing cultural intelligence: The roles of implicit culture beliefs and adjustment. *Personnel Psychology, 70*(1), 257–292. https://doi.org/10.1111/peps.12142

Chen, G., Kirkman, B. L., Kim, K., Farh, C. I., & Tangirala, S. (2010). When does cross-cultural motivation enhance expatriate effectiveness? A multilevel investigation of the moderating roles of subsidiary support and cultural distance. *Academy of Management Journal, 53*(5), 1110–1130. https://doi.org/10.5465/amj.2010.54533217

Chen, M. L., & Lin, C. P. (2013). Assessing the effects of cultural intelligence on team knowledge sharing from a socio-cognitive perspective. *Human Resource Management, 52*(5), 675–695. https://doi.org/10.1002/hrm.21558

Chin, J. L. (2013). Diversity leadership: Influence of ethnicity, gender, and minority status. *Open Journal of Leadership, 2*(1), 1–10. http://dx.doi.org/10.4236/ojl.2013.21001

Cialdini, R. B., & Goldstein, N. J. (2004). Social influence: Compliance and conformity. *Annual Review of Psychology, 55*, 591–621. https://doi.org/10.1146/annurev.psych.55.090902.142015

City of Seattle. (2012). *Racial equity toolkit: To assess policies, initiatives, programs, and budget issues*. https://www.seattle.gov/Documents/Departments/RSJI/RacialEquityToolkit_FINAL_August2012.pdf

Clark, T. R. (2020). *The 4 Stages of psychological safety: Defining the path to inclusion and innovation*. Berrett-Koehler.

Connor, K. M., & Davidson, J. R. T. (2003). Development of a new resilience scale: The Connor Davidson resilience scale (CD-RISC). *Depression and Anxiety, 18*, 76–82. https://doi.org/10.1002/da.10113

Cook, A., & Glass, C. (2013). Glass cliffs and organizational saviors: Barriers to minority leadership in work organizations. *Social Problems, 60*(2), 168–187. https://doi.org/10.1525/sp.2013.60.2.168

Crenshaw, K. W. (2017). *On intersectionality: Essential writings*. The New Press.

Cross, T. L. (1989). *Towards a culturally competent system of care: A monograph on effective services for minority children who are severely emotionally disturbed*. https://eric.ed.gov/?id=ED330171

D

Daly, K. (2017). Restorative justice: The real story. In D. Roche (Ed.), *Restorative justice* (pp. 85–109). Routledge.

de la Garza Carranza, M. T., & Egri, C. P. (2010). Managerial cultural intelligence and small business in Canada. *Management Revue*, 353–371. https://www.jstor.org/stable/41783658

Deloitte. (2023). *2023 Gen Z and millennial survey: Waves of change: Acknowledging progress, confronting setback*. Retrieved August 20, 2024, from https://www.deloitte.com/global/en/issues/work/content/genzmillennialsurvey.html

Devine, P. G., Forscher, P. S., Austin, A. J., & Cox, W. T. (2012). Long-term reduction in implicit race bias: A prejudice habit-breaking intervention. *Journal of Experimental Social Psychology, 48*(6), 1267–1278. https://doi.org/10.1016/j

Diamond, M. C. (1988). *Enriching heredity: The impact of the environment on the anatomy of the brain*. Free Press.

Dobbin, F., & Kalev, A. (2016). Why diversity programs fail. *Harvard Business Review, 94*(7), 14.

Duhigg, C. (2016). What Google learned from its quest to build the perfect team. *New York Times Magazine,* 26. https://www.nytimes.com/2016/02/28/magazine/what-google-learned-from-its-quest-to-build-the-perfect-team.html

Dweck, C. S. (2008). *Mindset: The new psychology of success.* Random House Digital.

E

Eagan, K., Stolzenberg, E. B., Ramirez, J. J., Aragon, M. C., Suchard, M. R., & Hurtado, S. (2014). *The American freshman: National norms Fall 2014.* Higher Education Research Institute, UCLA.

Earley, P. C., & Ang, S. (2003). *Cultural intelligence: Individual interactions across cultures.* Stanford University Press.

Earley, P. C., & Mosakowski, E. (2004). Cultural intelligence. *Harvard Business Review, 82*(10), 139–158. Retrieved August 20, 2024, from https://hbr.org/2004/10/cultural-intelligence

Earley, P. C., & Peterson, R. S. (2004). The elusive cultural chameleon: Cultural intelligence as a new approach to intercultural training for the global manager. *Academy of Management Learning & Education, 3*(1), 100–115. https://doi.org/10.5465/amle.2004.12436826

Edmondson, A. (2019). *The fearless organization: Creating psychological safety in the workplace for learning, innovation, and growth.* John Wiley & Sons.

Eisenberg, J., Lee, H. J., Brück, F., Brenner, B., Claes, M. T., Mironski, J., & Bell, R. (2013). Can business schools make students culturally competent? Effects of cross-cultural management courses on cultural intelligence. *Academy of Management Learning & Education, 12*(4), 603–621.

Ely, R. J., & Thomas, D. A. (2020). Getting serious about diversity: Enough already with the business case. *Harvard Business Review, 98*(6), 54–65.

F

Ferdman, B. M. (2017). Paradoxes of inclusion: Understanding and managing the tensions of diversity and multiculturalism. *The Journal of Applied Behavioral Science, 53*(2), 235–263. https://doi.org/10.1177/0021886317702608

Fox, J. (2020). Contested terrain: International development projects and countervailing power for the excluded. *World Development, 133*, 104978. https://doi.org/10.1016/j.worlddev.2020.104978

Frazier, M. L., Fainshmidt, S., Klinger, R. L., Pezeshkan, A., & Vracheva, V. (2017). Psychological safety: A meta-analytic review and extension. *Personnel Psychology, 70*(1), 113–165. https://doi.org/10.1111/peps.12183

Frey, W. H. (2018, March 14). *The US will become 'minority white' in 2045, Census projects: Youthful minorities are the engine of future growth*. Brookings. Retrieved August 24, 2024, from https://www.brookings.edu/blog/the-avenue/2018/03/14/the-us-will-become-minority-white-in-2045-census-projects/

Friedman, T. L. (2007). *The world is flat 3.0: A brief history of the twenty-first century*. Picador.

Fuller, P., Murphy, M., & Chow, A. (2020). *The leader's guide to unconscious bias: How to reframe bias, cultivate connection, and create high-performing teams*. Simon & Schuster.

G

Gagné, M., & Deci, E. L. (2005). Self-determination theory and work motivation. *Journal of Organizational Behavior, 26*(4), 331–362. https://doi.org/10.1002/job.322

Gallup. (2023). *State of the global workplace 2023 report: The voice of the world's employees.* https://www.gallup.com/workplace/349484/state-of-the-global-workplace.aspx

Ganesh, S., & McAllum, K. (2012). Volunteering and professionalization: Trends in tension? *Management Communication Quarterly, 26*(1), 152–158. https://doi.org/10.1177/0893318911423762

Gartner. (2019). *Diversity and inclusion build high-performance teams.* Retrieved August 24, 2024, from https://www.gartner.com/smarterwithgartner/diversity-and-inclusion-build-high-performance-teams

Geertz, C. (1973). *The interpretation of cultures.* Basic Books.

Gelfand, M. J., Nishii, L. H., & Raver, J. L. (2006). On the nature and importance of cultural tightness-looseness. *Journal of Applied Psychology, 91*(6), 1225–1244. https://doi.org/10.1037/0021-9010.91.6.1225

Gelfand, M. J., Nishii, L. H., Raver, J. L., & Schneider, B. (2004). Discrimination in organizations: An organizational-level systems perspective. In R. L. Dipboye & A. Colella (Eds.). *Discrimination at work: The psychological and organizational bases* (pp. 89–116). Psychology Press. https://doi.org/10.4324/9781410611567

Greenwald, A. G., McGhee, D. E., & Schwartz, J. L. (1998). Measuring individual differences in implicit cognition: The implicit association test. *Journal of Personality and Social Psychology, 74*(6), 1464–1480. https://doi.org/10.1037/0022-3514.74.6.1464

Groves, K. S., & Feyerherm, A. E. (2011). Leader cultural intelligence in context: Testing the moderating effects of team cultural diversity on leader and team performance. *Group & Organization Management, 36*(5), 535–566. https://doi.org/10.1177/1059601111415664

Groysberg, B., & Slind, M. (2012). Leadership is a conversation. *Harvard Business Review, 90*(6), 76–84. Retrieved July 31, 2024, from https://hbr.org/2012/06/leadership-is-a-conversation

Gudykunst, W. B. (1998). Applying anxiety uncertainty management (AUM) theory to intercultural adjustment training. *International Journal of Intercultural Relations, 22*(2), 227–250. https://doi.org/10.1016/S0147-1767(98)00005-4

Gudykunst, W. B., & Kim, Y. Y. (1984). *Communicating with strangers: An approach to intercultural communication*. Random House.

Guillaume, Y. R., Dawson, J. F., Otaye-Ebede, L., Woods, S. A., & West, M. A. (2017). Harnessing demographic differences in organizations: What moderates the effects of workplace diversity? *Journal of Organizational Behavior, 38*(2), 276–303. https://doi.org/10.1002/job.2040

H

Hajro, A., Gibson, C.B. & Pudelko, M. (2017). Knowledge exchange processes in multicultural teams: Linking organizational diversity climates to teams' effectiveness. *Academy of Management Journal, 60*(1), 345–372. https://doi.org/10.5465/amj.2014.0442

Halverson, S. K., Holladay, C. L., Kazama, S. M., & Quinones, M. A. (2004). Self-sacrificial behavior in crisis situations: The competing roles of behavioral and situational factors. *The Leadership Quarterly, 15*(2), 263–275. https://doi.org/10.1016/j.leaqua.2004.02.001

Hammer, M. R. (2011). Additional cross-cultural validity testing of the Intercultural Development Inventory. *International Journal of Intercultural Relations, 35*(4), 474–487. https://psycnet.apa.org/doi/10.1016/j.ijintrel.2011.02.014

Hampden-Turner, C., & Trompenaars, F. (2006). Cultural intelligence: Is such a capacity credible? *Group & Organization Management, 31*(1), 56-63. https://doi.org/10.1177/1059601105276942

Harden, K. (2021). *The allyship challenge: How to move beyond performative allyship and become a genuine accomplice.* Allyship.

Hardy, A. (2018, July 8). H&M dressed a Black child in a monkey sweatshirt on its website and people are outraged. *Teen Vogue.* Retrieved May 17, 2024, from https://www.teenvogue.com/story/handm-dressed-a-black-child-model-in-a-monkey-hoodie-and-people-are-outraged

Herrera, J., & De Las Heras-Rosas, C. (2021). The organizational commitment in the company and its relationship with the psychological contract. *Frontiers in Psychology, 11,* 609211. https://doi.org/10.3389/fpsyg.2020.609211Herring, C. (2009). Does diversity pay?: Race, gender, and the business case for diversity. *American Sociological Review, 74*(2), 208-224. https://doi.org/10.1177/000312240907400203

Hewlett, S. A., Marshall, M., & Sherbin, L. (2013). How diversity can drive innovation. *Harvard Business Review, 91*(12).

Hewlett, S. A., Peraino, K., Sherbin, L., & Sumberg, K. (2010). *The sponsor effect: Breaking through the last glass ceiling.* Harvard Business Review.

Hirak, R., Peng, A. C., Carmeli, A., & Schaubroeck, J. M. (2012). Linking leader inclusiveness to work unit performance: The importance of psychological safety and learning from failures. *The Leadership Quarterly, 23*(1), 107–117. https://doi.org/10.1016/j.leaqua.2011.11.009

Hofhuis, J., van der Zee, K. I., & Otten, S. (2020). Dealing with differences: The impact of perceived diversity outcomes on selection and assessment of minority candidates. *International Journal of Human Resource Management, 31*(14), 1773–1797. https://doi.org/10.1080/09585192.2015.1072100

Hofstede, G. (1993). Cultural constraints in management theories. *Academy of Management Perspectives, 7*(1), 81–94. https://doi.org/10.5465/ame.1993.9409142061

Hofstede, G. (2001). *Culture's consequences: Comparing values, behaviors, institutions and organizations across nations.* SAGE.

Hofstede, G. (2003). *Cultures and organizations: Software of the mind* (3rd ed.). Profile Books.

Hofstede, G. (2015). Culture's causes: The next challenge. *Cross Cultural Management, 22*(4), 545–569. https://doi.org/10.1108/CCM-03-2015-0040

Holladay, C. L., & Quiñones, M. A. (2008). The influence of training focus and trainer characteristics on diversity training effectiveness. *Academy of Management Learning & Education, 7*(3), 343–352. https://doi.org/10.5465/AMLE.2008.34251672

House, R. J., Hanges, P. J., Javidan, M., Dorfman, P. W., & Gupta, V. (2004). *Culture, leadership, and organizations: The GLOBE study of 62 societies.* SAGE.

Huber, G. P., Sutcliffe, K. M., Miller, C. C., & Glick, W. H. (1993). Understanding and predicting organizational change. In G. P. Huber & W. H. Glick (Eds.), *Organizational change and redesign: Ideas and insights for improving performance* (pp. 215–265). Oxford University Press.

Hunt, V., Yee, L., Prince, S., & Dixon-Fyle, S. (2018, January 18). *Delivering through diversity.* https://www.mckinsey.com/~/media/mckinsey/business%20functions/peo

ple%20and%20organizational%20performance/our%20insights/delivering%20through%20diversity/delivering-through-diversity_full-report.pdf

Hurn, B. J. (2011). Simulation training methods to develop cultural awareness. *Industrial and Commercial Training, 43*(4), 199–205. https://doi.org/10.1108/00197851111137816

I

Illeris, K. (2014). Transformative learning and identity. *Journal of Transformative Education, 12*(2), 148–163. https://doi.org/10.1177/1541344614548423

J

Jack, G., & Westwood, R. (2009). *International and cross-cultural management studies: A postcolonial reading.* Palgrave Macmillan.

Jaiswal, A., & Dyaram, L. (2020). Perceived diversity and employee well-being: Mediating role of inclusion. *Personnel Review, 49*(5), 1121–1139. https://doi.org/10.1108/PR-12-2018-0511

Janssens, M., & Zanoni, P. (2014). Alternative diversity management: Organizational practices fostering ethnic equality at work. *Scandinavian Journal of Management, 30*(3), 317–331. https://doi.org/10.1016/j.scaman.2013.12.006

Jefferson, H. (2023). The politics of respectability and Black Americans' punitive attitudes. *American Political Science Review, 117*(4), 1448–1464. https://doi.org/10.1017/S0003055422001289

Jirwe, M., Gerrish, K., Emami, A., & Latifi, S. A. (2009). The theoretical framework of cultural competence. *The Journal of Multicultural Nursing & Health, 15*(2), 6–16.

Johnson, J. P., Lenartowicz, T., & Apud, S. (2006). Cross-cultural competence in international business: Toward a definition and a model. *Journal of International Business Studies, 37*(4), 525–543. https://doi.org/10.1057/palgrave.jibs.8400205

Johnson, R. B., & Onwuegbuzie, A. J. (2004). Mixed methods research: A research paradigm whose time has come. *Educational Researcher, 33*(7), 14–26. https://doi.org/10.3102/0013189X033007014

Jordan, A. T. (2012). *Business anthropology* (2nd ed.). Waveland Press.

K

Kankanhalli, A., Charalabidis, Y., & Mellouli, S. (2019). IoT and AI for smart government: A research agenda. *Government Information Quarterly, 36*(2), 304–309. https://doi.org/10.1016/j.giq.2019.02.003

Kankanhalli, A., Hahn, J., Tan, S., & Gao, G. (2016). Big data and analytics in healthcare: Introduction to the special section. *Information Systems Frontiers, 18*, 233–235. https://doi.org/10.1007/s10796-016-9641-2

Keung, E. K., & Rockinson-Szapkiw, A. J. (2013). The relationship between transformational leadership and cultural intelligence. *Journal of Educational Administration, 51*(6), 836–854. https://doi.org/10.1108/JEA-04-2012-0049

Klein, G. A., & Hoffman, R. R. (1992). Seeing the invisible: Perceptual-cognitive aspects of expertise. In M. Rabinowitz (Ed.), *Cognitive science foundations of instruction* (pp. 203–226). Lawrence Erlbaum.

Konanahalli, A., Oyedele, L. O., Spillane, J., Coates, R., Von Meding, J., & Ebohon, J. (2014). Cross-cultural intelligence (CQ): It's impact on British expatriate adjustment on international construction projects. *International Journal of Managing Projects in Business, 7*(3), 423–448. https://doi.org/10.1108/IJMPB-10-2012-0062

Kübler-Ross, E. (1969). *On death and dying*. Scribner.

Kulik, C. T. (2014). Working below and above the line: The research-practice gap in diversity management. *Human Resource Management Journal, 24*(2), 129–144. https://doi.org/10.1111/1748-8583.12038

L

Lanvin, B., & Evans, P. (Eds.). (2018). *Global talent competitiveness index*. Adecco Group.

LeBaron, M. (2003). Culture and conflict. In G. Burgess & H. Burgess (Eds.). *Culture and conflict*. Conflict Information Consortium, University of Colorado, Boulder. http://www.beyondintractability.org/essay/culture-conflict

Lee, L. Y., Veasna, S., & Wu, W. Y. (2013). The effects of social support and transformational leadership on expatriate adjustment and performance: The moderating roles of socialization experience and cultural intelligence. *Career Development International, 18*(4), 377–415. https://doi.org/10.1108/CDI-06-2012-0062

Leininger, M. (1994). Quality of life from a transcultural nursing perspective. *Nursing Science Quarterly, 7*(1), 22–28. https://doi.org/10.1177/089431849400700109

Leonardo, Z., & Porter, R. K. (2010). Pedagogy of fear: Toward a Fanonian theory of 'safety' in race dialogue. *Race Ethnicity and Education, 13*(2), 139–157. https://doi.org/10.1080/13613324.2010.482898

Leslie, L. M. (2019). Diversity initiative effectiveness: A typological theory of unintended consequences. *Academy of Management Review, 44*(3), 538–563. https://doi.org/10.5465/amr.2017.0087

Leung, K., Ang, S., & Tan, M. L. (2014). Intercultural competence. *Annual Review of Organizational Psychology and Organizational Behavior, 1*(1), 489–519. https://doi.org/10.1146/annurev-orgpsych-031413-091229

Leung, A. K., & Chiu, C. (2008). Interactive effects of multicultural experiences and openness to experience on creative potential. *Creativity Research Journal, 20*(4), 376–382. https://doi.org/10.1080/10400410802391371

Leung, A. K., & Chiu, C. (2010). Multicultural experience, idea receptiveness, and creativity. *Journal of Cross-Cultural Psychology, 41*(5–6), 723–741. https://doi.org/10.1177/0022022110361707

Lewis, R. D. (1996). *When cultures collide: Leading across cultures*. Nicholas Brealey International.

Lindgren, M., & Bandhold, H. (2009). *Scenario planning: The link between future and strategy*. Palgrave Macmillan.

Lindsey, A., King, E., Membere, A., & Lee, A. (2017, July 28). Two types of diversity training that really work. *Harvard Business Review, 28*. Retrieved August 20, 2024, from https://hbr.org/2017/07/two-types-of-diversity-training-that-really-work

Livermore, D. A. (2015). *Leading with cultural intelligence: The real secret to success*. AMACOM.

Lorenzo, R., Voigt, N., Tsusaka, M., Krentz, M., & Abouzahr, K. (2018). How diverse leadership teams boost innovation. *Boston Consulting Group, 23*, 112–134. Retrieved May 17, 2024, from https://www.bcg.com/publications/2018/how-diverse-leadership-teams-boost-innovation

Lutz, D. W. (2009). African Ubuntu philosophy and global management. *Journal of Business Ethics, 84*, 313–328. https://doi.org/10.1007/s10551-009-0204-z

M

MacNab, B. R., & Worthley, R. (2012). Individual characteristics as predictors of cultural intelligence development: The relevance of self-efficacy. *International Journal of Intercultural Relations, 36*(1), 62-71. https://doi.org/10.1016/j.ijintrel.2010.12.001

Maslow, A. H. (1943). A theory of human motivation. Psychological Review, 50(4), 370–396.

Mavletova, A. (2013). Data quality in PC and mobile web surveys. *Social Science Computer Review, 31*(4), 417–439. 01

Mayer, D. M., Aquino, K., Greenbaum, R. L., & Kuenzi, M. (2012). Who displays ethical leadership, and why does it matter? An examination of antecedents and consequences of ethical leadership. *Academy of Management Journal, 55*(1), 151–171. https://doi.org/10.5465/amj.2008.0276

McDonald, S., Lin, N., & Ao, D. (2009). Networks of opportunity: Gender, race, and job leads. *Social Problems, 56*(3), 385–402. https://doi.org/10.1525/sp.2009.56.3.385

McIntosh, P. (1989). White privilege: Unpacking the invisible knapsack. *Peace and Freedom Magazine*, 10–12.

McKinsey & Company. (2020). *Diversity wins: How inclusion matters.* https://www.mckinsey.com/featured-insights/diversity-and-inclusion/diversity-wins-how-inclusion-matters

McKinsey & Company. (2022). *Women in the workplace 2022.* Lean in & McKinsey & Company.

Mendenhall, M. E., Stevens, M. J., Bird, A., & Oddou, G. R. (2008). Specification of the content domain of the Global Competencies Inventory (GCI). *The Kozai Monograph Series, 1*(1), 1–43.

Mitchell, R., Boyle, B., Parker, V., Giles, M., Joyce, P., & Chiang, V. (2014). Transformation through tension: The moderating impact of negative affect on transformational leadership in teams. *Human Relations, 67*(9), 1095–1121. https://doi.org/10.1177/0018726714521645

Molinsky, A. (2013). The psychological processes of cultural retooling. *Academy of Management Journal, 56*(3), 683–710. https://doi.org/10.5465/amj.2010.0492]

Moon, T. (2013). The effects of cultural intelligence on performance in multicultural teams. *Journal of Applied Social Psychology, 43*(12), 2414–2425. https://doi.org/10.1111/jasp.12189

Mor Barak, M. (2017). *Managing diversity: Toward a globally inclusive workplace* (4th ed.). SAGE.

Moua, M. (2010). *Culturally intelligent leadership: Essential concepts to leading and managing intercultural interactions.* Business Expert Press.

N

Ng, K.-Y., Van Dyne, L., & Ang, S. (2012). Cultural intelligence: A review, reflections, and recommendations for future research. In A. M. Ryan, F. T. L. Leong, & F. L. Oswald (Eds.), *Conducting multinational research: Applying organizational psychology in the workplace* (pp. 29–58). American Psychological Association. https://doi.org/10.1037/13743-002

Nickerson, R. S. (1998). Confirmation bias: A ubiquitous phenomenon in many guises. *Review of General Psychology, 2*(2), 175–220. https://doi.org/10.1037/1089-2680.2.2.175

Nisbett, R. E., & Miyamoto, Y. (2005). The influence of culture: Holistic versus analytic perception. *Trends in Cognitive Sciences, 9*(10), 467–473. https://doi.org.10.1016/j.tics,2005.08.004

Nishii, L. H., & Mayer, D. M. (2009). Do inclusive leaders help to reduce turnover in diverse groups? The moderating role of leader-member exchange in the diversity to turnover relationship. *Journal of Applied Psychology, 94*(6), 1412. https://doi.org/10.1037/a0017190

Nkomo, S., & Hoobler, J. M. (2014). A historical perspective on diversity ideologies in the United States: Reflections on human resource management research and practice. *Human Resource Management Review, 24*(3), 245–257. https://doi.org/10.1016/j.hrmr.2014.03.006

Noon, M. (2018). Pointless diversity training: Unconscious bias, new racism and agency. *Work, Employment and Society, 32*(1), 198–209. https://doi.org/10.1177/0950017017719841

Nosratabadi, S., Bahrami, P., Palouzian, K., & Mosavi, A. (2020). Leader cultural intelligence and organizational performance. *Cogent Business & Management, 7*(1), 1809310. https://doi.org/10.1080/23311975.2020.1809310

O

Okoro, E. A., & Washington, M. C. (2012). Workforce diversity and organizational communication: Analysis of human capital performance and productivity. *Journal of Diversity Management, 7*(1), 57–62. https://doi.org/10.19030/jdm.v7i1.6936

Oliver, B. (2019). *Making microcredentials work for learners, employers and providers*. Deakin University. http://hdl.voced.edu.au/10707/515939

Ott, D. L., & Michailova, S. (2018). Cultural intelligence: A review and new research avenues. *International Journal of Management Reviews, 20*(1), 99–119. https://doi.org/10.1111/ijmr.12118

P

Paige, R. M. (Ed.). (1993). *Education for the intercultural experience*. Intercultural Press.

Paige, R. M., Jacobs-Cassuto, M., Yershova, Y. A., & DeJaeghere, J. (2003). Assessing intercultural sensitivity: An empirical analysis of the Hammer and Bennett Intercultural Development Inventory. *International Journal of Intercultural Relations, 27*(4), 467–486. https://doi.org/10.1016/S0147-1767(03)00034-8

Palmer, A. (2006). CEO Briefing: Corporate priorities for 2006 and beyond. *The Economist*. http://graphics.eiu.com/files/ad_pdfs/ceo_Briefing_UKTI_wp.pdf

Patterson, P. G., Cowley, E., & Prasongsukarn, K. (2006). Service failure recovery: The moderating impact of individual-level cultural value orientation on perceptions of justice. *International Journal of Research in Marketing, 23*(3), 263–277. https://doi.org/10.1016/j.ijresmar.2006.02.004

Phillips, K. W., Mannix, E. A., Neale, M. A., & Gruenfeld, D. H. (2004). Diverse groups and information sharing: The effects of congruent ties. *Journal of Experimental Social Psychology, 40*(4), 497–510. https://doi.org/10.1016/j.jesp.2003.10.003

Pless, N. M., & Maak, T. (2004). Building an inclusive diversity culture: Principles, processes and practice. *Journal of Business Ethics, 54*(2), 129–147. https://doi.org/10.1007/s10551-004-9465-8

R

Rankin, J. (2014, December 22). Kingfisher sells B&Q China stake as DIY fails to take off. *The Guardian*. Retrieved August 21, 2024, from https://www.theguardian.com/business/2014/dec/22/kingfisher-china-diy-bq

Ray, P. H., & Anderson, S. R. (2001). *The cultural creatives: How 50 million people are changing the world*. Crown.

Rew, L., Becker, H., Cookston, J., Khosropour, S., & Martinez, S. (2003). Measuring cultural awareness in nursing students. *Journal of Nursing Education, 42*(6), 249–257. https://doi.org/10.3928/01484834-20030515-07

Robbins, S. P. (2003). *Organizational behavior* (10th ed.). Prentice Hall.

Roberto, M. A. (2005). *Why great leaders don't take yes for an answer: Managing for conflict and consensus*. FT Press.

Roberson, Q. M. (2006). Disentangling the meanings of diversity and inclusion in organizations. *Group & Organization Management, 31*(2), 212–236. https://doi.org/10.1177/1059601104273064

Roberson, Q. M., Ryan, A. M., & Ragins, B. R. (2017). The evolution and future of diversity at work. *Journal of Applied Psychology, 102*(3), 483–499. http://dx.doi.org/10.1037/apl0000161

Rockstuhl, T., Seiler, S., Ang, S., Van Dyne, L., & Annen, H. (2011). Beyond general intelligence (IQ) and emotional intelligence (EQ): The role of cultural intelligence (CQ) on cross-border leadership effectiveness in a globalized world. *Journal of Social Issues, 67*(4), 825–840. https://doi.org/10.1111/j.1o540-4560.2011.01730.x

Rosenberg, M. B. (2015). *Nonviolent communication: A language of life*. PuddleDancer Press.

Rozin, P., & Royzman, E. B. (2001). Negativity bias, negativity dominance, and contagion. *Personality and Social Psychology Review, 5*(4), 296–320. https://doi.org/10.1207/S15327957PSPR0504_2

S

Sabharwal, M. (2014). Is diversity management sufficient? Organizational inclusion to further performance. *Public Personnel Management, 43*(2), 197–217. https://doi.org/10.1177/0091026014522202

Salovey, P., & Mayer, J. D. (1990). Emotional intelligence. *Imagination, Cognition and Personality, 9*(3), 185–211.

Schaetti, B. F., Ramsey, S. J., & Watanabe, G. C. (2008). *Personal leadership: Making a world of difference.* Intercultural Press.

Schilke, O., Reimann, M., & Thomas, J. S. (2009). When does international marketing standardization matter to firm performance? *Journal of International Marketing, 17*(4), 24–46. https://doi.org/10.1509/jimk.17.4.24

Schwartz, S. H. (1999). A theory of cultural values and some implications for work. *Applied Psychology: An International Review, 48*(1), 23–47. https://doi.org/10.1111/j.1464-0597.1999.tb00047.x

Schwartz, S. H. (2012). An overview of the Schwartz theory of basic values. *Online Readings in Psychology and Culture, 2*(1). https://doi.org/10.9707/2307-0919.1116

Sharma, R. (2008). *The greatness guide: Realize your genius and optimize your life.* Jaico.

Shenkar, O., Luo, Y., & Yeheskel, O. (2008). From "distance" to "friction": Substituting metaphors and redirecting intercultural research. *Academy of*

Management Review, 33(4), 905–923. https://doi.org/10.5465/amr.2008.34421999

Shore, L. M., Cleveland, J. N., & Sanchez, D. (2018). Inclusive workplaces: A review and model. *Human Resource Management Review, 28*(2), 176-189. https://doi.org/10.1016/j.hrmr.2017.07.003

Shore, L. M., Randel, A. E., Chung, B. G., Dean, M. A., Holcombe Ehrhart, K., & Singh, G. (2011). Inclusion and diversity in work groups: A review and model for future research. *Journal of Management, 37*(4), 1262-1289. https://doi.org/10.1177/0149206310385943

Showunmi, V., Atewologun, D., & Bebbington, D. (2016). Ethnic, gender and class intersections in British women's leadership experiences. *Educational Management Administration & Leadership, 44*(6), 917-935. https://doi.org/10.1177/1741143215587308

Silzer, R., & Dowell, B. E. (Eds.). (2009). *Strategy-driven talent management: A leadership imperative* (Vol. 28). John Wiley & Sons, Inc.

Sims, R. H., & Schraeder, M. (2004). An examination of salient factors affecting expatriate culture shock. *Journal of Business & Management, 10*(1), 73-87.

Singh, B., Winkel, D. E., & Selvarajan, T. T. (2013). Managing diversity at work: Does psychological safety hold the key to racial differences in employee performance? *Journal of Occupational and Organizational Psychology, 86*(2), 242-263. https://doi.org/10.1111/joop.12015

Sue, D.W. (2016). *Race talk and the conspiracy of silence: Understanding and facilitating difficult dialogues on race.* John Wiley & Sons, Inc.

Sue, D. W., Alsaidi, S., Awad, M. N., Glaeser, E., Calle, C. Z., & Mendez, N. (2019). Disarming racial microaggressions: Microintervention strategies for targets, White allies, and bystanders. *American Psychologist, 74*(1), 128-142. https://doi.org/10.1037/amp0000296

Sue, D. W., Capodilupo, C. M., Torino, G. C., Bucceri, J. M., Holder, A., Nadal, K. L., & Esquilin, M. (2007). Racial microaggressions in everyday life: implications for clinical practice. *American Psychologist, 62*(4), 271. https://doi.org/10.1037/0003-066X.62.4.271

T

Tadmor, C. T., Tetlock, P. E., & Peng, K. (2009). Acculturation strategies and integrative complexity: The cognitive implications of biculturalism. *Journal of Cross-Cultural Psychology, 40*(1), 105–139. https://doi.org/10.1177/0022022108326279

Taras, V., Rowney, J., & Steel, P. (2013). Work-related acculturation: Change in individual work-related cultural values following immigration. *The International Journal of Human Resource Management, 24*(1), 130–151. https://doi.org/10.1080/09585192.2012.672446

Tett, L. (2005) Partnerships, community groups and social inclusion. *Studies in Continuing Education, 27*(1), 1–15. https://doi.org/10.1080/01580370500056364

Ting-Toomey, S., & Oetzel, J. G. (2001). *Managing intercultural conflict effectively*. SAGE.

Trompenaars, F., & Hampden-Turner, C. (1997). *Riding the waves of culture: Understanding diversity in global business*. McGraw Hill.

V

Van Dyne, L., Ang, S., & Koh, C. (2008). Development and validation of the CQS: The cultural intelligence scale. In S. Ang & L. Van Dyne (Eds.), *Handbook of cultural intelligence: Theory, measurement and applications* (pp. 16–38). Routledge.

Van Dyne, L., Ang, S., Ng, K. Y., Rockstuhl, T., Tan, M. L. & Koh, C. (2012). Sub-dimensions of the four factor model of cultural intelligence: Expanding the conceptualization and measurement of cultural intelligence. *Social and Personality Psychology Compass, 6*(4), 295–313. https://doi.org/10.1111/j.1751-9004.2012.00429.x

Vertovec, S. (2007). Super-diversity and its implications. *Ethnic and Racial Studies, 30*(6), 1024–1054. https://doi.org/10.1080/01419870701599465

W

Wang, Y. W., Davidson, M. M., Yakushko, O. F., Savoy, H. B., Tan, J. A., & Bleier, J. K. (2003). The scale of ethnocultural empathy: Development, validation, and reliability. *Journal of Counseling Psychology, 50*(2), 221–234. https://doi.org/10.1037/0022-0167.50.2.221

Wasserman, I. C., Gallegos, P. V., & Ferdman, B. M. (2008). Dancing with resistance: Leadership challenges in fostering a culture of inclusion. In K. M. Thomas (Ed.), *Diversity resistance in organizations*, (pp. 175-200). Lawrence Erlbaum Associates Publishers.

Weick, K. E., & Sutcliffe, K. M. (2015). *Managing the unexpected: Sustained performance in a complex world* (3rd ed.). John Wiley & Sons, Inc.

Williams, D. A., & Wade-Golden, K. C. (2023). *The chief diversity officer: Strategy structure, and change management*. Taylor & Francis.

Wilson, H. J., & Daugherty, P. R. (2018). Collaborative intelligence: humans and AI are joining forces. *Harvard Business Review, 96*(4), 114-123.

Winowiecki, E. (2017, July 24). Mostly-white "See Detroit Like We Do" ad draws backlash and apologies. *Michigan Public NPR*. https://www.michiganpublic.org/news/2017-07-24/mostly-white-see-detroit-like-we-do-ad-draws-backlash-and-apologies

Y

Yan, A., & Luo, Y. (2001). *International joint ventures: Theory and practice* (1st ed.). Routledge.

About the Author

Dr. Kimberly Harden, president and CEO of Harden Consulting Group, is a highly regarded Leadership and Culture consultant specializing in Cultural Intelligence (CQ) solutions. Widely recognized for her contributions to leadership development and workplace transformation, Dr. Harden partners with organizations to build cohesive, high-performing, WE-Centric teams. With a doctorate in Transformational Leadership, she equips leaders with tools to improve interpersonal communication, navigate complex cultural dynamics, and address workplace challenges while fostering strategic talent management.

A sought-after consultant and keynote speaker, Dr. Harden draws on more than a decade of experience teaching communication studies. Her award-winning DEBIT Training™ framework transforms workplace culture by integrating cultural intelligence, belonging, effective communication, and innovative practices into organizational systems. Grounded in the belief that educating the mind without educating the heart is no education at all, Dr. Harden's work inspires meaningful connections and empowers organizations to unlock their full potential. Ready to transform your workplace culture? Visit www.hardenconsultinggroup.com to begin your journey.